Meeting Point 1re

TOUTES SÉRIES

Josette STARCK
Lycée Richelieu, Rueil-Malmaison

Dominique SANTONI
Collège-Lycée Buffon, Paris

Véronique JAUBERT
Lycée Jacques Prévert, Longjumeau

Pascale CAMPS-VAQUER
Collège Les Vallées, La Garenne-Colombes
Formatrice DAFPEN

Françoise LAVEILLE
Université Paris Descartes, Paris V

Paul LARREYA
Professeur en linguistique

Avec la participation de
Ruth PHAN,
Lycée Charles de Gaulle, Poissy

et de **Philip BENZ,**
Lycée Pierre et Marie Curie, Châteauroux

Hatier

Les auteurs tiennent à remercier Hannah Faye Wood pour sa précieuse collaboration.

Conception maquette et mise en page : Marc & Yvette

Illustrations : Bruno Marivain

Cartographie : Corédoc

Iconographie : Nadine Gudimard

Édition : Catherine de Bernis

ISBN : 978-2-218-95333-0

AVANT-PROPOS

Broaden your horizons

Quel est le programme officiel ?

Le programme du cycle terminal va se décliner autour d'un thème fédérateur sur l'année de Première et celle de Terminale : **gestes fondateurs** et **mondes en mouvement**.
Cette entrée est structurée autour de quatre notions : **mythes et héros • espaces et échanges • lieux et formes du pouvoir • idée de progrès**.
En classe de Première, les programmes en vigueur prévoient la consolidation du niveau **B1** et la mise en route vers **B2**, le niveau attendu au baccalauréat.

Approfondissez votre connaissance du monde anglo-saxon.

Les unités ont été conçues pour vous donner envie de découvrir le monde anglophone, de mieux appréhender la culture et l'histoire de différents pays, de vous ouvrir à de nouveaux horizons. Apprendre une langue étrangère, c'est voyager dans le temps et dans l'espace, vous initier à d'autres modes de vie, de nouveaux auteurs, ainsi qu'à la peinture, au cinéma, à la littérature de pays très divers.

Trying is the safest way to achieving.

Soyez acteur de votre apprentissage.

Les documents sont variés afin de solliciter votre curiosité et votre réflexion.
Des mises en situation authentiques, concrètes et vivantes vous sont proposées au cours et à la fin de chaque unité (YOUR TASK). Ces tâches finales vous aideront à mobiliser vos connaissances, à faire preuve de créativité et à améliorer vos aptitudes à communiquer.
N'hésitez pas à vous appuyer sur les encadrés **Help!** Les pages de réflexion sur la langue et les exercices vous permettront d'enrichir votre lexique et de fixer les points de grammaire étudiés.
Vous prendrez peu à peu la parole de façon plus naturelle. Vous vous sentirez confiant(e) face à des documents nouveaux et / ou des interlocuteurs différents.

Speak! Don't let the others speak for you!

Get help when you're not sure.

Entraînez-vous.

– Les fiches de compréhension écrite et orale du **Workbook** vous aideront à mettre au point des stratégies d'écoute et de lecture, à découvrir des documents de façon autonome.
– Des documents très divers ont été enregistrés pour faciliter votre travail personnel. Ils sont signalés par ce picto : MP3 1
– Des **pages de méthodologie** serviront à développer et consolider vos compétences en compréhension écrite et orale ainsi qu'en production écrite et orale ou en traduction.
– Le **précis grammatical** à la fin du manuel vous permettra de revoir et d'approfondir certains points de grammaire dont vous avez besoin pour communiquer.

Évaluez-vous.

– Sur le site compagnon, vous trouverez des **documents audio** que vous pourrez télécharger pour vous entraîner à la compréhension de l'oral. Ces enregistrements sont accompagnés de fiches à travailler individuellement.
– Des entraînements avec corrigés vous sont fournis pour préparer les évaluations finales dans chacune des compétences.

Now turn your brain on!

Teachers open the door, but you must enter by yourself.

Les auteurs

DÉROULEMENT

OUVERTURE

Annonce de la tâche finale, détaillée à la fin de l'unité

Introduction de la thématique et du champ lexical de l'unité

AIDES LEXICALES

Pour développer la prise de parole

Vocabulaire à mémoriser

Voyelle accentuée

Noms

Phonétique

Traduction

Adjectifs

Verbes

Help!

Setting

the woods
pool of water
stream: *ruisseau*
narcissus / daffodil

Narcissus

laurel wreath /ri:θ/: *couronne de lauriers*
perfect features: *traits parfaits*
well-shaped
vain: *vaniteux*
self-centred: *égocentrique*
be amazed at / by one's beauty
be mesmerized / hypnotized by
see one's own reflection

Amorces de phrases pour guider la production

– If...
– You'd better + V
– You'd better not + V
– You have to...
– As soon as you enter the shop, you will / should...

LES DOCUMENTS (DE 4 À 7 PAGES)

Renvoi aux CD classe

La ou les compétences langagières travaillées sur l'ensemble de la page ou de la double page

Tâche intermédiaire préparant à la tâche finale

Renvoi au DVD-Rom

La compétence langagière en jeu lors de cette activité

Renvoi au *Workbook*

PICTOS UTILISÉS DANS CE MANUEL

- Lire
- Écrire
- Écouter
- Parler en continu
- Parler en interaction
- WB Renvoi au *Workbook*
- CD Renvoi aux CD classe
- Video Renvoi au DVD-Rom

MP3 1 À télécharger sur le site compagnon : www.editions-hatier.fr/meetingpoint/. Les fichiers comprennent tous les exercices labellisés MP3 dans le manuel ainsi que 15 documents supplémentaires.

D'UNE UNITÉ

LANGUAGE AT WORK

Objectifs linguistiques liés à la thématique de l'unité

Réflexion sur la langue : observation et déduction

Mise en pratique en contexte

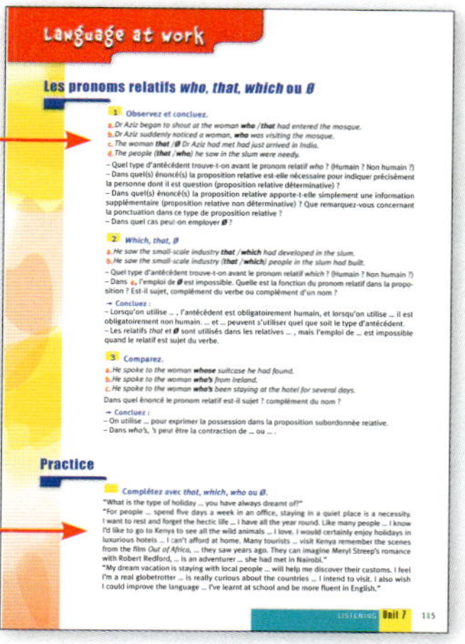

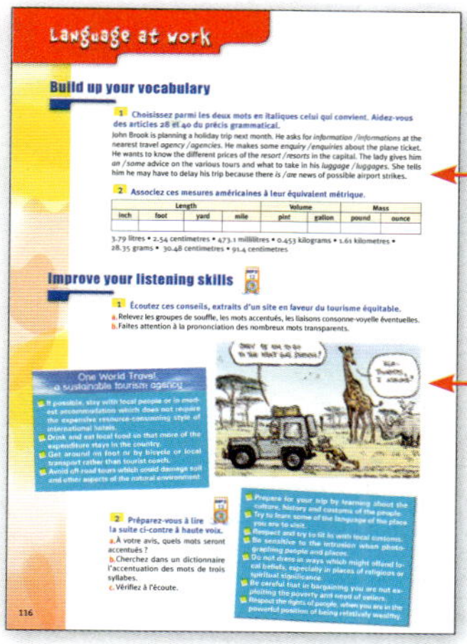

Lexique : enrichissement et renforcement

Exercices de phonologie s'appuyant sur des enregistrements disponibles sur les MP3 élève (travail individuel)

YOUR TASK

Reprise de l'énoncé de la tâche

Mise en œuvre concrète et guidée de la tâche finale

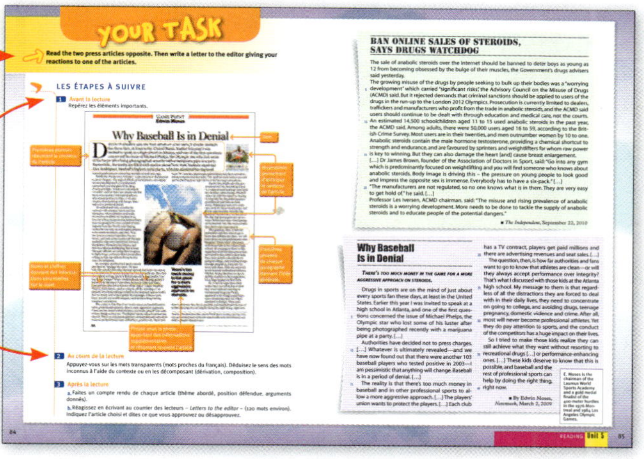

Documents servant à la mise en œuvre de la tâche

EN FIN D'UNITÉ

selon l'activité langagière dominante

Des double-pages de **lectures suivies** *(Reading Corner)* pour s'initier à la lecture autonome d'œuvres littéraires

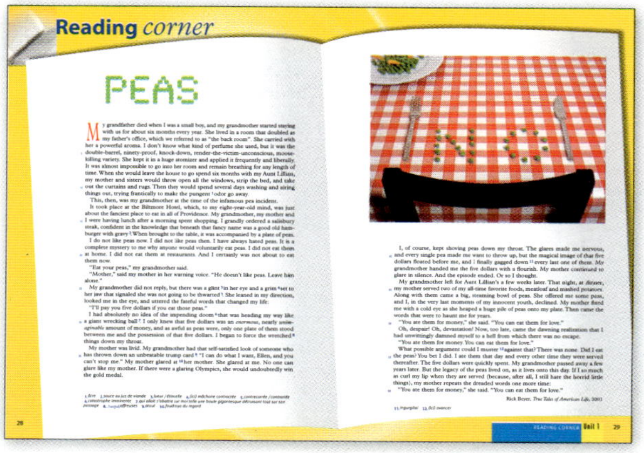

Des double-pages de documents déclencheurs pour l'entraînement à la production orale *(Speaking Corner)*

ÉVALUATIONS DIAGNOSTIQUES

Découvrir ce qu'est l'évaluation diagnostique à l'entrée en Première

Qu'est-ce qu'une évaluation diagnostique ?
Dans quel but ?

Grille des compétences évaluées par le CECRL

Entrée dans le thème des évaluations

Déroulement des évaluations diagnostiques

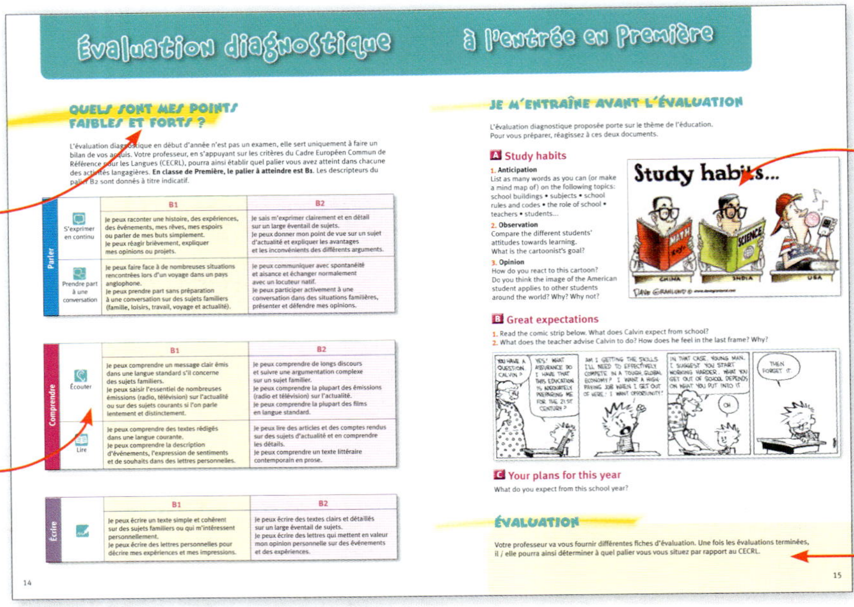

Évaluation diagnostique à l'entrée en Première

QUELS SONT MES POINTS FAIBLES ET FORTS ?

L'évaluation diagnostique en début d'année n'est pas un examen, elle sert uniquement à faire un bilan de vos acquis. Votre professeur, en s'appuyant sur les critères du Cadre Européen Commun de Référence pour les Langues (CECRL), pourra ainsi établir quel palier vous avez atteint dans chacune des activités langagières. **En classe de Première, le palier à atteindre est B1.** Les descripteurs du palier B2 sont donnés à titre indicatif.

		B1	B2
Parler	S'exprimer en continu	Je peux raconter une histoire, des expériences, des événements, mes rêves, mes espoirs ou parler de mes buts simplement. Je peux réagir brièvement, expliquer mes opinions ou projets.	Je sais m'exprimer clairement et en détail sur un large éventail de sujets. Je peux donner mon point de vue sur un sujet d'actualité et expliquer les avantages et les inconvénients des différents arguments.
	Prendre part à une conversation	Je peux faire face à de nombreuses situations rencontrées lors d'un voyage dans un pays anglophone. Je peux prendre part sans préparation à une conversation sur des sujets familiers (famille, loisirs, travail, voyage et actualité).	Je peux communiquer avec spontanéité et aisance et échanger normalement avec un locuteur natif. Je peux participer activement à une conversation dans des situations familières, présenter et défendre mes opinions.

		B1	B2
Comprendre	Écouter	Je peux comprendre un message clair émis dans une langue standard s'il concerne des sujets familiers. Je peux saisir l'essentiel de nombreuses émissions (radio, télévision) sur l'actualité ou sur des sujets courants si l'on parle lentement et distinctement.	Je peux comprendre de longs discours et suivre une argumentation complexe sur un sujet familier. Je peux comprendre la plupart des émissions (radio et télévision) sur l'actualité. Je peux comprendre la plupart des films en langue standard.
	Lire	Je peux comprendre des textes rédigés dans une langue courante. Je peux comprendre la description d'événements, l'expression de sentiments et de souhaits dans des lettres personnelles.	Je peux lire des articles et des comptes rendus sur des sujets d'actualité et en comprendre les détails. Je peux comprendre un texte littéraire contemporain en prose.

	B1	B2
Écrire	Je peux écrire un texte simple et cohérent sur des sujets familiers ou qui m'intéressent personnellement. Je peux écrire des lettres personnelles pour décrire mes expériences et mes impressions.	Je peux écrire des textes clairs et détaillés sur un large éventail de sujets. Je peux écrire des lettres qui mettent en valeur mon opinion personnelle sur des événements et des expériences.

14

JE M'ENTRAÎNE AVANT L'ÉVALUATION

L'évaluation diagnostique proposée porte sur le thème de l'éducation. Pour vous préparer, réagissez à ces deux documents.

A Study habits

1. Anticipation
List as many words as you can (or make a mind map of) on the following topics: school buildings • subjects • school rules and codes • the role of school • teachers • students...

2. Observation
Compare the different students' attitudes towards learning. What is the cartoonist's goal?

3. Opinion
How do you react to this cartoon? Do you think the image of the American student applies to other students around the world? Why? Why not?

B Great expectations

1. Read the comic strip below. What does Calvin expect from school?
2. What does the teacher advise Calvin to do? How does he feel in the last frame? Why?

C Your plans for this year

What do you expect from this school year?

ÉVALUATION

Votre professeur va vous fournir différentes fiches d'évaluation. Une fois les évaluations terminées, il / elle pourra ainsi déterminer à quel palier vous vous situez par rapport au CECRL.

15

FICHES D'ÉVALUATION DIAGNOSTIQUE

Évaluer les activités langagières à l'entrée en Première

Fiches distribuées par le professeur

Compréhension de l'écrit

- **Extrait de roman et extrait d'un journal**
- Fiches d'évaluation accompagnées d'un barème (en anglais et français)
- Critères de répartition en groupes de compétences

Compréhension de l'oral

Discours de Barack Obama

- Fiches d'évaluation accompagnées d'un barème (en anglais et français)
- Critères de répartition en groupes de compétences

Expression écrite

- Écrire un mot d'excuse
- Écrire un récit à partir d'une bande dessinée
- Barème et critères de répartition en groupes de compétences

Prise de parole en continu

Monologue

- Réagir à un dessin humoristique (sujets différents)
- Barème et critères de répartition en groupes de compétences

Prise de parole en interaction

Dialogue

- Débattre avec quelqu'un sur des sujets différents
- Barème et critères de répartition en groupes de compétences

MODE D'EMPLOI

ÉVALUATIONS SOMMATIVES

Évaluer les compétences langagières à la fin de chaque partie

Activités d'entraînement préparant l'évaluation, avec des conseils méthodologiques

Un sujet d'auto-évaluation pour faire le point

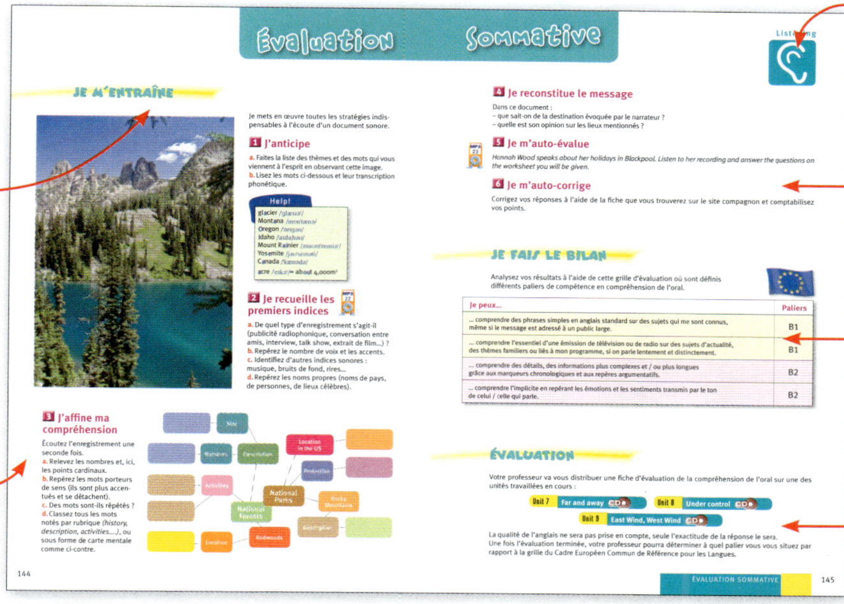

L'activité langagière testée dans cette évaluation

Corrigé fourni pour repérer ses erreurs

Grille d'évaluation du CECRL pour faire le point sur ses acquis et prendre conscience des progrès à accomplir

Déroulement des évaluations sommatives (avec au minimum trois sujets par activité langagière)

FICHES D'ÉVALUATION SOMMATIVE

Fiches distribuées par le professeur

Compréhension de l'écrit

Extraits de roman

- Fiches d'évaluation (en anglais et français) accompagnées d'un barème
- Critères de répartition en groupes de compétences

Compréhension de l'oral

Interview et reportages radio

- Fiches d'évaluation (en anglais et français) accompagnées d'un barème
- Critères de répartition en groupes de compétences

Expression écrite

Expression libre

- Deux types de production écrite
- Barème et critères de répartition en groupes de compétences

Prise de parole en continu

Monologue

- Réagir à un dessin humoristique (sujets différents)
- Barème et critères de répartition en groupes de compétences

Prise de parole en interaction

Dialogue

- Débattre avec quelqu'un sur des sujets différents
- Barème et critères de répartition en groupes de compétences

Spoken production

Unit 1 YOU ARE WHAT YOU EAT • Espaces et échanges

Unit 2 ADVERT-TEASING • Espaces et échanges • Lieux et formes de pouvoir

Unit 3 INCREDIBLE INDIA • Espaces et échanges • Lieux et formes de pouvoir • Idée de progrès

Sommaire Méthodologie et Vidéos, p. 13

Reading

Unit 4 DEALING WITH THE DEVIL • Mythes et héros

Unit 5 THE FOURTH POWER • Lieux et formes de pouvoir • Idée de progrès

Unit 6 BLACK IS BEAUTIFUL • Lieux et formes de pouvoir

Listening

Unit 7 FAR AND AWAY • Espaces et échanges

YOUR TASK

Select your five favourite activities in and around Denver. (p. 117)

Unit 8 UNDER CONTROL • Lieux et formes de pouvoir • Idée de progrès

YOUR TASK

Leave a message on a radio station voicemail. (p. 129)

Unit 9 EAST WIND, WEST WIND • Lieux et formes de pouvoir • Espaces et échanges

YOUR TASK

Post a comment about three videos on a museum forum page. (p. 143)

Sommaire Méthodologie et Vidéos, p. 13

Speaking interaction

Unit 10 KING ARTHUR REVISITED • Mythes et héros • Lieux et formes de pouvoir

Unit 11 WHATEVER WORKS • Lieux et formes de pouvoir • Espaces et échanges

Unit 12 BORN TO SHOP? • Lieux et formes de pouvoir • Espaces et échanges

Writing

Unit 13 EVERLASTING YOUTH • Mythes et héros

YOUR TASK
Write an interview. (p. 197)

Unit 14 GUNS OR ROSES? • Lieux et formes de pouvoir • Mythes et héros

YOUR TASK
Write an article on the life of soldiers. (p. 208)

Unit 15 THE LAND OF OZ • Mythes et héros

YOUR TASK
Post an entry on your blog about your holidays in Australia. (p. 223)

Histoire des arts · Art Project

Unit 16 THE POWER OF LOVE • Mythes et héros

Video — Documents vidéo disponibles dans le DVD-Rom

Le DVD-Rom contient, en plus des vidéos, 16 images fixes à vidéoprojeter en classe.

Évaluation diagnostique

QUELS SONT MES POINTS FAIBLES ET FORTS ?

L'évaluation diagnostique en début d'année n'est pas un examen, elle sert uniquement à faire un bilan de vos acquis. Votre professeur, en s'appuyant sur les critères du Cadre Européen Commun de Référence pour les Langues (CECRL), pourra ainsi établir quel palier vous avez atteint dans chacune des activités langagières. **Au cycle terminal, le palier à atteindre est B1 / B2.**

		B1	B2
Parler	S'exprimer en continu	Je peux raconter une histoire, des expériences, des événements, mes rêves, mes espoirs ou parler de mes buts simplement. Je peux réagir brièvement, expliquer mes opinions ou projets.	Je sais m'exprimer clairement et en détail sur un large éventail de sujets. Je peux donner mon point de vue sur un sujet d'actualité et expliquer les avantages et les inconvénients des différents arguments.
Parler	Prendre part à une conversation	Je peux faire face à de nombreuses situations rencontrées lors d'un voyage dans un pays anglophone. Je peux prendre part sans préparation à une conversation sur des sujets familiers (famille, loisirs, travail, voyage et actualité).	Je peux communiquer avec spontanéité et aisance et échanger normalement avec un locuteur natif. Je peux participer activement à une conversation dans des situations familières, présenter et défendre mes opinions.

		B1	B2
Comprendre	Écouter	Je peux comprendre un message clair émis dans une langue standard s'il concerne des sujets familiers. Je peux saisir l'essentiel de nombreuses émissions (radio, télévision) sur l'actualité ou sur des sujets courants si l'on parle lentement et distinctement.	Je peux comprendre de longs discours et suivre une argumentation complexe sur un sujet familier. Je peux comprendre la plupart des émissions (radio et télévision) sur l'actualité. Je peux comprendre la plupart des films en langue standard.
Comprendre	Lire	Je peux comprendre des textes rédigés dans une langue courante. Je peux comprendre la description d'événements, l'expression de sentiments et de souhaits dans des lettres personnelles.	Je peux lire des articles et des comptes rendus sur des sujets d'actualité et en comprendre les détails. Je peux comprendre un texte littéraire contemporain en prose.

		B1	B2
Écrire		Je peux écrire un texte simple et cohérent sur des sujets familiers ou qui m'intéressent personnellement. Je peux écrire des lettres personnelles pour décrire mes expériences et mes impressions.	Je peux écrire des textes clairs et détaillés sur un large éventail de sujets. Je peux écrire des lettres qui mettent en valeur mon opinion personnelle sur des événements et des expériences.

à l'entrée en Première

JE M'ENTRAÎNE AVANT L'ÉVALUATION

L'évaluation diagnostique proposée porte sur le thème de l'éducation.
Pour vous préparer, réagissez à ces deux documents.

A Study habits

1. Anticipation
List as many words as you can (or make a mind map of) on the following topics: school buildings • subjects • school rules and codes • the role of school • teachers • students...

2. Observation
Compare the different students' attitudes towards learning.
What is the cartoonist's goal?

3. Opinion
How do you react to this cartoon?
Do you think the image of the American student applies to other students around the world? Why? Why not?

B Great expectations

1. Read the comic strip below. What does Calvin expect from school?
2. What does the teacher advise Calvin to do? How does he feel in the last frame? Why?

C Your plans for this year

What do you expect from this school year?

ÉVALUATION

Votre professeur va vous fournir différentes fiches d'évaluation. Une fois les évaluations terminées, il / elle pourra ainsi déterminer à quel palier vous vous situez par rapport au CECRL.

Everything You Always Wanted to Know about Sex, a film by Woody Allen (1973)

Spoken production

Unit 1 YOU ARE WHAT YOU EAT

- The birth of fast food restaurants
- A growing trend: obesity
- New lifestyles
- Eating animals? For or against?

→ YOUR TASK

You have just joined the improvisation club in your school. The first session will be about food. Candidates will pick a card and get ready to speak.

→ p. 27

Unit 2 ADVERT-TEASING

- Learn how to analyse ads or awareness campaigns
- Discover a new form of marketing
- What influence do ads have on teenagers?

→ YOUR TASK

You are working for an advertising agency. Choose a product or a cause, and make a radio spot.

→ p. 41

Unit 3 INCREDIBLE INDIA

- Explore a huge country and learn about the challenges it still faces
- Tradition versus modernity
- Has the status of women improved?

→ YOUR TASK

You are a journalist working for the BBC World Service. You will prepare a report entitled *India, a Land of Contrasts*.

→ p. 55

ÉVALUATION SOMMATIVE *SPOKEN PRODUCTION* → p. 56-57

Unit 1

YOU ARE WHAT YOU EAT

YOUR TASK AT THE END OF THIS UNIT

You have just joined the improvisation club in your school. The first session will be about food. Candidates will pick a card and get ready to speak. → p. 27

TUNE IN!

1 What's wrong here?

a. Look at the cartoon for one minute then close your book. List all the elements you remember.

b. What can the viewer guess about this family's lifestyle?

c. Read what is written in the balloon and the newspaper headline. What event is the woman referring to? According to her what is the problem?

d. What contrast is the cartoon based on? Do you find it effective or not?

e. Who is the target? What are the cartoonist's goals?

f. Is the message effective or not? Why?

Help!

Reactions

It's gross /grəʊs/ (fam.) = disgusting!
How pathetic!: *Comme c'est navrant !*
It's over the top = too much.
I am aware of this issue = topic.
at stake /steɪk/: *en jeu*
I approve / disapprove of...

Consequences

obesity /əʊˈbiːsɪti/
health /helθ/: *santé*
overweight
couch /kaʊtʃ/ potato
unbalanced diet
put on ≠ lose weight
be addicted to

2 Dropping litter

a. React to this document.

b. What sort of document is this?

c. What is the message?

d. Who is the target? Justify your answer with elements from the document.

e. Are you aware of this problem? Why? Why not?

f. Do you find the message effective? Why? Why not?

Help!

Junk food items
slice / portion of
extra large / jumbo size soft drink
takeaway container
helping = portion
litter or rubbish (GB) = trash (US)
dustbin (GB) = garbage can (US)

PREPARE YOUR TASK

3 Five mistakes

a. Each group prepares an oral account of one of the two documents studied (p. 18 and 19). Include five wrong statements. The other group observes the picture carefully and spots the mistakes.

b. In your opinion, which document is funnier, more shocking or more critical of people's attitude to food?

4 A worrying trend CD WB

a. Obesity: a world problem. Listen to a journalist report on the causes of obesity in the world. Turn to your Workbook for help.
b. Change your habits. Listen to the recording and list the problems and solutions mentioned. Turn to your Workbook to understand more.
c. Use the information collected to make posters for an awareness campaign against obesity.

5 Watch a video

Hidden reality

Turn to your worksheet for help.

I. THE McDONALD BROTHERS

Part 1

By the end of the 1940s the McDonald brothers had grown dissatisfied with the drive-in business. [...] The brothers thought about selling the restaurant. Instead they tried something new.

The McDonalds fired all their carhops[1] in 1948, closed their restaurant, installed larger grills, and reopened three months later with a radically new method of preparing food. It was designed to increase the speed, lower prices, and raise the volumes of sales. The brothers eliminated almost two-thirds of the items[2] of their old menu. They got rid of everything that had to be eaten with a knife, spoon or fork. The only sandwiches now sold were hamburgers or cheeseburgers. The brothers got rid of their dishes and glassware, replacing them with paper cups, paper bags, and paper plates. They divided the food preparation into separate tasks performed by different workers. To fill a typical order, one person grilled the hamburger; another "dressed" and wrapped it; another prepared the milk shake; another made the fries; and another worked the counter. For the first time, the guiding principles of a factory assembly line were applied to a commercial kitchen. The new division of labor meant that a worker only had to be taught how to perform one task. Skilled and expensive short-order cooks were no longer necessary. All of the burgers were sold with the same condiments: ketchup, onions, mustard, and two pickles. No substitutions were allowed. The McDonald brothers' Speedee Service System revolutionized the restaurant business. An ad of theirs seeking franchisees later spelled out the benefits of the system: "Imagine – No Carhops – No waitresses – No dishwashers – No Bus Boys[3] – The McDonald's System is Self-Service!"

1. people who serve customers at a drive-in restaurant 2. (here) dishes 3. people whose job is to set or clear tables in a restaurant

Part 2

Richard McDonald designed a new building for the restaurant hoping to make it easy to spot from the road. Though untrained as an architect, he came up with a design that was simple, memorable, and archetypal. On two sides of the roof he put golden arches, lit by neon at night, that from a distance formed the letter *M*. The building effortlessly fused[1] advertising with architecture and spawned[2] one of the most famous corporate[3] logos in the world.

The Speedee Service System, however, got off to a rocky start[4]. Customers pulled up to the restaurant and honked their horns[5], wondering what had happened to the carhops, still expecting to be served. People were not yet accustomed to waiting in line and getting their own food. Within a few weeks, however, the new system gained acceptance, as word spread about the low prices and good hamburgers. The McDonalds now aimed for a much broader[6] clientele. They employed only young men, convinced that female workers would attract teenage boys to the restaurant and drive away other customers. Families soon lined up to eat at McDonald's. Company historian John F. Love explained the lasting significance of McDonald's new self-service system: "Working-class families could finally afford to feed their kids restaurant food."

Eric Schlosser, *Fast Food Nation,* 2001

1. mixed **2.** created **3.** of a company **4.** had a difficult beginning **5.** *klaxonnaient* **6.** (here) more diverse

1 Find the key information

Read the text and say what you have understood. Then read again for more details.

Part 1

a. What do these dates and time references correspond to?
• 1940s • three months later • 1948 • for the first time

b. Organize your notes. List all the words connected with the different changes introduced in the restaurant: work organization • menu • food preparation • type of service • staff.

c. Pick out two phrases in the text corresponding to this definition:

> "A system for making products in a factory in which each worker or machine is responsible for adding or checking a particular part."

Who do these words remind you of? In what sector? When?

Part 2

a. List the main characteristics of the building: impact on the viewer • advantages of the design. Quote keywords only.

b. Classify the information given in a grid. Use the following headings: Old habits • New habits • Reputation • Type of customers. Write keywords only.

c. Explain in your own words what the last two lines mean.

PREPARE YOUR TASK →

2 On the air

You are in charge of a radio programme about the big changes in eating habits in the 20th century. Make a short presentation of the beginnings of "McDonald's".

PREPARE YOUR TASK →

3 Act out

You are the McDonald brothers (Richard and Maurice). You have decided to try something new. Deal with the following themes in your conversation:

– situation of the restaurant at that time
– reasons for changing
– possible changes: impact on customers
– final decision

4 Tell me more

What does the word "McDonald's" mean to you?

2. COOKING, CLUBBING

Text 1

Mrs Patton is shopping at the supermarket with Arun, the Indian boy she is hosting.

Mrs Patton, with her hand on the cart that Arun is rolling as rapidly as he can along the aisles of tinned soup[1], pasta and rice, tries to slow him down. "We haven't enough yet, Ahroon," she protests. "You should have seen the way I'd[2] load a shopping cart when the children were small. I'd have Melanie sitting up here on the shelf[3], and there'd be such a heap of groceries[4] under her, she'd have to stick her feet right up on top." [...]

"And do you know, that load wouldn't last us even a week. Three days and I'd be back for more," she chuckles[5], hurrying to keep up with him. The wheels of the cart squeal, the rubber-soled shoes squeak[6], Arun swivels[7] to avoid another loaded cart trundling past[8].

"Do they eat less now?" he asks. There is scarcely room[9] in the cart for another package. He feels revulsion rising in his throat as if from too gigantic a meal.

"My no, they eat all the time," she laughs, a little out of breath. "But – it's different now. We don't sit down to meals like we used to. Everyone eats at different times and wants different meals. We just don't get to eating together much now they're grown. So I just fill the freezer and let them take down what they like, when they like. Keeping the freezer full – that's my job, Ahroon," she declares, and grasps the handle to stop him so she can study the labels on the soup cans.

Anita Desai, *Fasting, Feasting,* 1999

1. *rayons des soupes en conserve* **2.** = would *(ici) marque l'habitude dans le passé*
3. *(ici) siège escamotable* **4.** *monticule de provisions* **5.** *glousse* **6.** *crissent*
7. *pivote sur lui-même* **8.** rolling past **9.** *il reste à peine assez de place*

Text 2

My wife and I have started telling people to drop by[1] at dinnertime, even if they have plans for later in the evening. They come. I offer them some frittata[2] or scrambled eggs or sometimes just grilled cheese and homemade sauerkraut[3]. Our food is not complicated.

Friends come and we eat and talk, and then they might cancel[4] their plans and sit. We play Scrabble. Even better, we've rediscovered charades. Teams of four face off in our living room and we laugh, I swear, till tears are just pouring down[5] our cheeks. The rhythm of our life is changing.

It's not based on electronic entertainment. It's based on home-cooked food, and not especially good home-cooked food, either. [...] It's based on the fact that our house has become a home. [...]

But, still, I enjoy feeling a little like a grandmother, feeding all my friends. There is something wonderful about it, and wonderful about playing host and everybody just being able to kick their shoes off[6] and relax.

This rush we're in—I don't think people like it. At least for this year my family has opted out of it[7]. Is that why people flock to us lately?

Colin Beavan, *No Impact Man,* 2009

1. *passer à l'improviste* **2.** *omelette* **3.** *choucroute* **4.** *annuler* **5.** *coulent le long de*
6. *retirer ses chaussures d'un coup de pied* **7.** *a décidé d'y échapper*

1 Find the key information

	Text 1	Text 2
Shopping?		
Cooking?		
Eating (when, where)?		
Fun involved?		

a. Each group reads one text and fills in the corresponding column of the grid (use a separate sheet of paper).

PREPARE YOUR TASK

b. Oral account: A reporter in each group presents one of the passages to the class.

Text 1
- To me these children represent... / act as if...
- Unlike Mrs Patton, we...
- Mrs Patton doesn't seem to... , whereas in our family...
- You... , contrary to what people usually do...
- It's not surprising that people should...

Text 2
- My text deals with...
- It focuses / concentrates on...
- Since the narrator..., it reveals that...
- The narrator and his wife embody...

2 Writing workshop

Group 1: Arun writes an email to his brother to tell him about the eating habits in his host family and gives his reactions.

Group 2: One of the guests writes a thank-you letter in which he / she explains why he / she enjoyed the evening.

PREPARE YOUR TASK

3 Debate

Choose one of the following topics, find arguments and illustrate them with examples.

a. *It's the company, not the cooking that makes the meal.*
Kirby Larson. Discuss.

b. *I've been on a diet for two weeks and all I've lost is two weeks.*
Totie Fields. Discuss.

c. Takeaway food is becoming more and more popular. Explain this evolution in today's society.

4 News flash CD WB

a. Listen to the true story of Steve Vaught.
Turn to your Workbook for help.

PREPARE YOUR TASK

b. Speak from your notes and include the following points:
- person: name, age, original problem(s), physical consequence(s);
- reaction / decision;
- American people's reactions: explanation(s) given;
- new philosophy / vision of the world: two examples.

3. FOOD FOR THOUGHT

1 Nuggets

a. Give your immediate reactions.
b. Identify the different elements.
c. What makes you feel it is a personal message?
d. Find the goals and the target of this campaign.
e. Do you find this ad effective? Why? Why not?

PREPARE YOUR TASK

2 Make a speech

You are a spokesman for one of the following organizations: the Vegetarian Society • the Balanced Diet • the RSPCA *(SPA)* • the 100% Protein Fans.

Make a punchy speech to convince your listeners to join in (2 minutes).

Help!

vegetarianism /ˌveʒəˈteərɪənɪzəm/
vegetarian /ˌveʒəˈteərɪən/
provoking
disgusting = revolting = gross (fam.)
rescue
address sb directly
appeal to: *faire appel à*
I can't stand + V-ING
It puts me off: *ça me dégoûte.*
stop or start or go on + V-ING

Language at work

Infinitif et gérondif (V-*ING*)

1 Observez et comparez.

a. *Children always **fancy** / **feel like** buying colourful food packaging!*
b. *Most teenagers **can't stand** / **bear** eating hot and spicy dishes.*
c. *She really **resents** shopping alone. She **enjoys** going to the market with her husband.*
d. *Unlike many friends, we **don't mind** cooking every day.*

– Qu'expriment les mots en gras : une décision que l'on prend • une contrainte • un sentiment ou un goût ?
– Quelle forme grammaticale suit ces mots en gras ?

→ **Concluez :** les verbes exprimant ... ... sont suivis d'un verbe à la forme ... .

2 Observez.

a. *Doctors are fed up **with** trying to convince their patients not to go on drastic diets.*
b. *Why are people so fond **of** / keen **on** having their meals in front of a screen?*
c. *Sociologists are interested **in** understanding people's new eating habits.*
d. *More and more people are getting used **to** consuming healthy food again.*
e. *Fewer young people look forward **to** sharing family meals at weekends.*
f. *I don't object **to** having lunch in a fast food restaurant now and then.*

– Les éléments en gras sont des prépositions. De quelle forme grammaticale sont-ils suivis ?
– Observez le fonctionnement de *to* dans les trois derniers énoncés. En quoi ce *to* diffère-t-il du *to* qui est à la suite d'un verbe comme *want* ou *promise* ?

→ **Concluez :** quand une ... est suivie d'un verbe, ce verbe est obligatoirement à la forme ... .

3 Observez et comparez.

a. *He has decided to go to the supermarket and he intends to buy some organic food.*
b. *Remember to buy bread.*
c. *I complained about the food, but I didn't like doing that.*
d. *They remembered eating in the same restaurant when they first visited London.*
e. *He expects his guests to come before 8 a.m.*
f. *He plans to do more sport next year.*

Relevez les formes en V-*ING* et celles en *to* + V. Le choix entre V-*ING* et *to* + V dépend du sens du verbe qui précède.
– Dans quels cas le verbe indique-t-il que l'on a pour but l'accomplissement d'une action ?
– Dans quel cas exprime-t-il une opinion ou un sentiment sur une action ?

→ **Concluez.**

Practice

Écrivez un paragraphe sur le document ci-contre en utilisant un maximum de structures étudiées dans l'unité.

Language at work

Build up your vocabulary

Observez ces deux documents et réagissez.

a. Gagnez l'attention de votre interlocuteur en utilisant ces structures :
– *What I find striking / unusual / shocking / interesting in this picture is that...*
– *What strikes me most about the picture is that...*
– *The problem is that...*
– *What is worth noticing is that...*

b. Comparez les deux illustrations : quels sont les points communs et les différences ? Utilisez les structures du contraste et de l'opposition :
compared ***with*** • *similar* ***to*** • *same ...* ***as*** • *different* ***from / to*** • *while.*

Edward Hopper, *Automat*, 1927 (71.4cm x 91.4cm)

Improve your pronunciation

1 Trouvez à quels mots correspondent ces transcriptions phonétiques.

/ˈvɪtəmɪns/ /ˈfaɪbəʳz/ /ˈprəʊtiːnz/ /ˈkæləriz/ /kəˈlestərɒl/ /ɔːˈgænɪk/
Lisez-les maintenant à haute voix.

2 Écoutez les phrases suivantes. MP3 1

Chaque phrase va être lue de deux façons différentes. Laquelle est la plus percutante ? Pourquoi ?

a. *I can't believe they spend so much time eating.*
b. *Family dinners are long and boring.*
c. *Family gatherings are exceptional moments.*
d. *I can't stand having turkey every Christmas.*
e. *What a huge waste of time!*
f. *The art of cooking has been lost.*

YOUR TASK

You have just joined the improvisation club in your school. The first session will be about food. Candidates will pick a card and get ready to speak.

PRÉPAREZ-VOUS

1 **Relisez ce que vous avez appris au cours de l'unité.**

2 **Entraînez-vous avec ces cartes d'improvisation.**

The hamburger fan

Homemade food

The best fast food

No more meat

5 ADay
(five portions of fruit and vegetables every day)

– Dites ce que vous savez du thème proposé.
– Donnez votre opinion et celle de vos amis ou de votre famille sur le sujet.
– Notez seulement des mots clés sur une feuille, pas de phrases entières.

Peter Menzel, *Hungry Planet*, 2007

VOTRE PRESTATION

1 **Tirez une carte d'improvisation.**

– Vous avez 5 minutes de préparation.
– Notez sur une feuille des mots clés uniquement.

2 **Le jury (formé par le reste de la classe) choisira la meilleure improvisation en fonction de ces critères :**

a. La prononciation (rythme de la phrase, accentuation des mots, réalisation des phonèmes) permet-elle de comprendre le message ?
b. Le message et les idées sont-ils intéressants ?
c. Les structures et le lexique sont-ils suffisamment riches et variés ?

CONSEILS

– Gardez la **parole le plus longtemps possible**. Utilisez des *gap fillers* si vous hésitez ou souhaitez vous reprendre (voir p. 249).
– Soignez votre **prononciation** pour que votre message soit compréhensible.
– Mettez-vous **en scène** :
• regardez votre auditoire en parlant ;
• parlez fort pour qu'on vous entende au fond de la classe ;
• soyez souriant(e) et convaincu(e).

PEAS

My grandfather died when I was a small boy, and my grandmother started staying with us for about six months every year. She lived in a room that doubled as my father's office, which we referred to as "the back room". She carried with her a powerful aroma. I don't know what kind of perfume she used, but it was the double-barrel, ninety-proof, knock-down, render-the-victim-unconscious, moose-killing variety. She kept it in a huge atomizer and applied it frequently and liberally. It was almost impossible to go into her room and remain breathing for any length of time. When she would leave the house to go spend six months with my Aunt Lillian, my mother and sisters would throw open all the windows, strip the bed, and take out the curtains and rugs. Then they would spend several days washing and airing things out, trying frantically to make the pungent[1] odor go away.

This, then, was my grandmother at the time of the infamous pea incident.

It took place at the Biltmore Hotel, which, to my eight-year-old mind, was just about the fanciest place to eat in all of Providence. My grandmother, my mother and I were having lunch after a morning spent shopping. I grandly ordered a salisbury steak, confident in the knowledge that beneath that fancy name was a good old hamburger with gravy[2]. When brought to the table, it was accompanied by a plate of peas.

I do not like peas now. I did not like peas then. I have always hated peas. It is a complete mystery to me why anyone would voluntarily eat peas. I did not eat them at home. I did not eat them at restaurants. And I certainly was not about to eat them now.

"Eat your peas," my grandmother said.

"Mother," said my mother in her warning voice. "He doesn't like peas. Leave him alone."

My grandmother did not reply, but there was a glint[3] in her eye and a grim[4] set to her jaw that signaled she was not going to be thwarted[5]. She leaned in my direction, looked me in the eye, and uttered the fateful words that changed my life:

"I'll pay you five dollars if you eat those peas."

I had absolutely no idea of the impending doom[6] that was heading my way like a giant wrecking ball[7]. I only knew that five dollars was an *enormous*, nearly *unimaginable* amount of money, and as awful as peas were, only one plate of them stood between me and the possession of that five dollars. I began to force the wretched[8] things down my throat.

My mother was livid. My grandmother had that self-satisfied look of someone who has thrown down an unbeatable trump card[9]. "I can do what I want, Ellen, and you can't stop me." My mother glared at[10] her mother. She glared at me. No one can glare like my mother. If there were a glaring Olympics, she would undoubtedly win the gold medal.

1. *âcre* **2.** *sauce au jus de viande* **3.** *lueur / étincelle* **4.** *(ici) mâchoire contractée* **5.** *contrecarrée / contrariée* **6.** *catastrophe imminente* **7.** *qui allait s'abattre sur moi telle une boule gigantesque détruisant tout sur son passage* **8.** /retʃɪd/ *affreuses* **9.** *atout* **10.** *foudroya du regard*

I, of course, kept shoving peas down my throat. The glares made me nervous, and every single pea made me want to throw up, but the magical image of that five dollars floated before me, and I finally gagged down[11] every last one of them. My grandmother handed me the five dollars with a flourish. My mother continued to glare in silence. And the episode ended. Or so I thought.

My grandmother left for Aunt Lillian's a few weeks later. That night, at dinner, my mother served two of my all-time favorite foods, meatloaf and mashed potatoes. Along with them came a big, steaming bowl of peas. She offered me some peas, and I, in the very last moments of my innocent youth, declined. My mother fixed me with a cold eye as she heaped a huge pile of peas onto my plate. Then came the words that were to haunt me for years.

"You ate them for money," she said. "You can eat them for love."

Oh, despair! Oh, devastation! Now, too late, came the dawning realization that I had unwittingly damned myself to a hell from which there was no escape.

"You ate them for money. You can eat them for love."

What possible argument could I muster[12] against that? There was none. Did I eat the peas? You bet I did. I ate them that day and every other time they were served thereafter. The five dollars were quickly spent. My grandmother passed away a few years later. But the legacy of the peas lived on, as it lives on to this day. If I so much as curl my lip when they are served (because, after all, I still hate the horrid little things), my mother repeats the dreaded words one more time:

"You ate them for money," she said. "You can eat them for love."

Rick Beyer, *True Tales of American Life*, 2001

11. *ingurgitai* **12.** *(ici) avancer*

ADVERT-TEASING

YOUR TASK AT THE END OF THIS UNIT

You are working for an advertising agency. Choose a product or a cause, and make a radio spot. → p. 41

TUNE IN!

1 React

a. What immediately strikes you?
b. Name the logo, the slogan and the catchphrase.
c. What is advertised?
d. Do you like this advert? Why? Why not?

– This **a**dvert prom**o**tes...
– It **a**dvertises...
– The ad t**a**rgets...
– The **a**dvertiser has used...
– He / She rel**i**es on...
– The l**ay**out **u**nderlines...
– The eff**e**ct prod**u**ced is...
– Since the c**o**lours are bright, g**a**rish, this ad attr**a**cts...

2 Check your vocabulary

Match each definition with the corresponding word below:

target audience | layout | goal | brand

– the name of the product
– the group of people who may be interested in the product advertised
– an objective or aim, something you hope to achieve
– the way the printed ad is designed.

1. RADIO DAYS

PREPARE YOUR TASK

1 Radio ad #1 CD

a. Listen and find the product advertised.

b. – Identify the voice(s): How many? Male? Female? Adult? Child?
– What effects are used to catch the listeners' attention? Choose from the list: sound effects? soundtrack? noises? shouts?
– What types of music are used? What for?
– What stressed words did you pick out?

c. Do you find the ad effective? Why? Why not?

2 Radio ad #2 CD WB

a. Focus

Group 1
– Find information about the new product, the price, the country, the brand.
– What aspect of everyday life is this ad based on?

Group 2
Concentrate on:
– The goals, the target and the slogan.
– The catchy effects. What makes this ad lively?

b. Class work
Prepare an oral account of this ad and don't forget to give your reactions.

3 Radio ad #3 CD WB

Listen to this third ad and tell the class what you have understood.
Turn to your Workbook for help.

PREPARE YOUR TASK

4 Karaoke CD WB

a. Listen to this extract from the third ad script and work on the rhythm and sounds.

On FRIDAYS some THINGS JUST HAVE to BE.
SOMEONE HAS to SAY "OOH, it's FRIDAY!" as if it's UNUSUAL for it to COME STRAIGHT after THURSDAY.
The JOURNEY HOME HAS to TAKE for EVER, and WHEN you GET HOME, you HAVE to SLUMP DOWN on the SOFA and GO "AGH".

– What do the words in capital letters correspond to on the recording?
– What links *(= liaisons)* are made? Explain why in French (→ see p. 247).
– Focus on the intonation and turn to your Workbook.
– Where will you make pauses and breathe?

b. Read these three sentences aloud.

2. BUZZ MARKETING

1 Get ready

a. Look at this picture then select the words you expect to find in the text you will read below:

> accidents • cab • pedestrians • influence • communicate • inform • traffic • promote • park • billboard *(panneau publicitaire)*

b. What do you think the text is about? Make at least three or four sentences.

Part 1

Now London's famously talkative black cab[1] drivers are offering more than simple solutions to the great questions of our time: they may also be trying to sell something.

As companies scramble[2] for new channels to communicate commercial messages, black cab drivers have been recruited to serve in the brave new world of word-of-mouth[3] advertising.

Adrian Torlini, 41, from Aylesbury, Buckinghamshire, has been a cab driver for nine years, and feels able to talk about any subject. Lately, however, he has persistently informed his passengers of the delights of Bangkok.

"It's not all ping-pong shows you know," he says as he manœuvres up the Old Kent Road. "There's the floating market, the tiger—the temples are out of this world. The food's fantastic."

This part of Mr Torlini's repertoire has been paid for out of the marketing budget of the Tourism Authority of Thailand. He would quibble with[4] the idea that his conversation has been bought for advertising. "It's not like I'm paid anything for doing it," he says. Instead he was flown out to Bangkok for five days, all expenses paid.

"I suppose that's payment of a sort," he says. "But I have never seen it as a job. They have just given me an experience. No one said I had to talk about it. They just know that if you send someone somewhere and they like it they are going to talk about it, and if they are a cab driver they are going to talk to lots of people about it." [...]

1. *taxi* **2.** *se bousculent, se battent* **3.** *de bouche à oreille* **4.** *chicanerait sur*

Part 2

Mr Torlini is an "ambassador driver" for Taxi Promotions UK. It is now launching a new service: Womad (Word of Mouth Advertising) Taxis, and Asher Moses, the managing director, believes that all kinds of products could eventually find a slot[1] in the discourses of his drivers. [...]

People are asking themselves, "How the hell do we reach people?" [...]

The next big thing in word-of-mouth advertising, however, is "buzz" marketing. Consumers fill out a questionnaire to prove themselves an influential "agent", and receive free products that are not yet in the shops. Much like Mr Torlini's free holidays, it is thought that these free products have an inherent "talkability"—agents discuss them with friends and relatives and report back.

■ *The Times*, January 14, 2008

1. *créneau*

Help!

salesman /ˈseɪlzmən/
adman
bright side of
promote /prəˈməʊt/
encourage /ɪnˈkʌrɪdʒ/ sb to + V
urge /ɜːdʒ/ sb to + V
reach /riːtʃ/: *atteindre*
be in contact /ˈkɒntækt/ with

2 Find the key information WB

Read the text and say what you have understood.
Turn to your Workbook if necessary.

PREPARE YOUR TASK

3 Radio report

You are a journalist making a radio report on a new form of advertising. Include the following points:

a. Introduce Adrian Torlini (age, residence, job, last holidays, new occupation, opinion about it).
b. Explain what this new occupation consists in and why Adrian Torlini was recruited to do it.
c. Sum up what you have learnt about the past and the latest "channels to communicate". Explain the evolution from one "channel to communicate" to another.

PREPARE YOUR TASK

4 Info search on brands

Group work

a. Choose a brand from the following list: Levi's • Coke • Disney • Ford • Chrysler • General Motors • Kellogg's • Apple • Gap • Abercrombie • Rolls-Royce • Burberry • Cadbury.

b. Go on the Internet and on the brand website, read about the history of the firm. Find information about the founder and the different stages of the firm's development. Take notes (keywords only) and report to your group.

Class work

a. What did you discover? What was the most interesting report? Why?

b. Choose a brand and with the help of your notes write a paragraph summing up the key information.

3. PICTURE ME

Part 1

Heather has landed a modeling job at a department store in the mall. She says she was buying socks with her mother the week after her braces[1] came off and some lady asked if she modeled. I suspect the fact that her dad works for the mall management company had something to do with it. […]

She asks me to go with her for the bathing suit shoot. I think she's afraid to screw up[2] in front of them. Heather's mother drives us. […]The scabs[3] on my lips are especially gross in that little rectangle mirror.

Of course I want to be a model. I want to paint my eyelids gold. I saw that on a magazine cover and it looked amazing—turned the model into a sexy alien that everyone would look at but nobody dared touch.

1. appareil dentaire 2. se planter 3. croûtes

Part 2

I like cheeseburgers too much to be a model. Heather has stopped eating and complains about fluid retention. She should worry more about brain retention, the way she's dieting away her gray matter. At last check, she was wearing a size one and a half, and she just *has* to get down to a size one.

The photo shoot is in a building cold enough to store ice. Heather looks like our Thanksgiving turkey wearing a blue bikini. Her goose bumps[1] are bigger than her boobs[2]. I'm shivering and I'm wearing my ski jacket and a wool sweater. The photographer turns up the radio and starts bossing the girls around. Heather totally gets into it. She throws her head back, stares at the camera, flashes her teeth. The photographer keeps saying, "Sexy, sexy, very cute. Look this way. Sexy, think beach, think boys." It creeps me out. Heather sneezes in the middle of a group pose and her mother runs in with tissues. It must be catching. My throat is killing me. I want a nap[3].

Laurie Halse Anderson, *Speak*, 1999

1. chair de poule 2. seins (familier) 3. sieste

1 Find the key information WB

a. Read the passage and say what you have understood. Turn to your Workbook if necessary.
b. Speak from your notes and include the following points:

Group 1
- Different characters
- Type of job, where
- The narrator's physical appearance

Group 2
- The narrator's image of the model
- The two main characters' attitude to food
- Shooting conditions
- The narrator's reaction(s)

PREPARE YOUR TASK

2 Act it out!

You are talking with a friend who wants to join a model agency. Discuss the pros and cons.

Video

3 Watch a video

The living doll

Learn more about a top model's life.
Turn to your worksheet for help.

4. AD CRITIC

1 Parody ad campaign

You want to create a gallery of parody advertisements in a satirical magazine.

A Analyse a spoof ad (= parody ad) before you start.

a. What first caught your eye?

b. Find the product and say what it is usually used for.

c. Read the catchphrase. Is it a real ad?

d. What does the packaging make you think of?
– What camera angle is used (→ see p. 245)? Why?
– What aspect of the product is underlined? Quote elements of the ad to justify your answer.
– Who is the target audience?
– What is being made fun of here?

e. Do you think this document is: ironic • depressing • comical • critical • serious • useful • old-fashioned?

Help!

Spoof ad	Situation
antidepressant pun = play on words washing powder treat feel down ≠ be cheered up	parody / spoof ad make fun of: *se moquer de* laugh /lɑːf/ at denounce = expose criticize sb for sth / V-ING convey the idea / impression that

PREPARE YOUR TASK → **B** Find more information about spoof ads. Select one you particularly like and explain your choice to your team members.

C Create a print spoof ad.
– Choose a real ad and work carefully on the layout: Make collages, draw, cut, paste and paint to create a new ad. You may scan an existing ad and use computer software to make changes to the original.
– Don't forget a catchphrase, a punchy slogan and a logo.
PREPARE YOUR TASK → – Then present your spoof ad to the rest of the class.

WEB BOX
www.adbusters.org/gallery/spoofads
parody.organique.com/
www.funny-adverts.com/spoof-ads/index.php

2 Writing workshop

Discuss this quotation (180 words).

> *Advertising is the art of convincing people to spend money they don't have for something they don't need.*
> Will Rogers (American journalist, 1879-1935)

5. SUPPORTING A CAUSE

PREPARE YOUR TASK

1 Group work

Each group will deal with one of the two documents (p. 36 and 37).

a. React to the document (colours, place, country, people, looks, activity).

b. Prepare an oral account of this campaign. Include the following points: layout • message • goal • target • techniques. Then give your reactions.

c. What device is used (→ see p. 245)? What is the effect produced?

Help!

Reactions	Document 1	Document 2
weird /wɪəd/ = odd: *étrange* awful striking humorous ironic /aɪˈrɒnɪk/ eye-catching disturbing: *troublant* effective thought-provoking make sb a laughing stock: *se moquer de qqn*	couch /kaʊtʃ/ = sofa couch potato: *légume vautré devant la télé* remote control oversized distorted glued to / hooked on: *accro à* addicted to dumb /dʌm/ ≠ smart, clever stare at: *regarder fixement*	mat: *natte* sole /səʊl/: *semelle* equipment /ɪˈkwɪpmənt/ low wages /ləʊ ˈweɪdʒɪz/: *faible salaire* awful working conditions workshop: *atelier* glass case handmade squat /skwɒt/: *être accroupi* bend (bent, bent): *courber*

2 Class work

a. Which of the two campaigns, p. 36 and 37, do you find better (more effective, more useful, more informative, etc.)? Justify your choice.

b. Confront your opinion with the class.

3 Watch a video

Video

Child labour

a. Watch an awareness campaign about child labour (by Radiohead) and learn more about some Asian children's way of life.
b. Turn to your worksheet for help.
c. React to what you have seen.

PREPARE YOUR TASK

4 On stage!

You have decided to support a cause. Try to convince a friend to join in. He/she may not agree.
Visit the following websites to find ideas:

WEB BOX

- child soldiers: www.unicef.org
- health: www.gotmilk.com
- save the Planet: www.wwf.org

« Faire faire quelque chose à quelqu'un » / « agir sur quelqu'un »

1 Observez et classez.

a. *The commercial I saw last night* ***urged*** *citizens to protect our planet against pollution.*
b. *The poster on this billboard* ***encourages*** *us to re-use, recycle and reduce our waste.*
c. *Market pressures* ***force*** *producers to reduce costs and launch aggressive campaigns.*
d. *The last WWF campaign* ***made*** *them think about the necessity of saving water resources.*
e. *That ad really* ***made*** *me laugh!*
f. *The kid* ***had*** *his mum buy the cereals he had seen on TV.*

→ Classez ces verbes en deux colonnes en fonction des éléments qui les suivent :
... + *V* (= base verbale) ou ... + *TO* + *V*.

2 *Make* ou *have* ?

– Parmi les énoncés ci-dessus, lesquels peuvent être traduits en français à l'aide du verbe « faire » ?
– Quel(s) énoncé(s) exprime(nt) une contrainte forte ?
– Quel(s) énoncé(s) indique(nt) que l'on a eu recours à la persuasion ?

→ ... + nom ou pronom + ... exprime une cause directe ou une contrainte forte.
→ ... + nom ou pronom + ... peut exprimer une cause indirecte, telle que la persuasion.

Les énoncés exclamatifs

1 Observez et concluez.

a. ***What*** *a humorous commercial!*
b. ***What*** *an eye-catching poster about Yellowstone Park!*
c. ***What*** *wonderful visual effects!*
d. *It's* ***such*** *an extravagant idea!*
e. ***Such*** *ads are very expensive!*

De quels éléments grammaticaux sont suivis les mots en gras ?
→ *What* et *such* sont suivis de l'article ... s'ils introduisent un nom **dénombrable au singulier**.
→ *What* et *such* sont suivis de l'article ... s'ils introduisent un nom **dénombrable au pluriel**.

2 Observez et déduisez.

a. *All these commercials!* ***What*** *nonsense!* ***What*** *irrelevant information!*
b. *Advertising can cause* ***such*** *damage!*

De quels éléments grammaticaux sont suivis les mots en gras ?
→ *What* et *such* sont suivis de l'article ... si le nom est ... .

3 Comparez.

a. ***How*** *brilliant (this advert is)!*
b. ***How*** *cleverly done!*
c. *This ad is (ever)* ***so*** *brilliant!*

De quels éléments grammaticaux sont suivis les mots en gras ?
→ *How* introduit un ... ou un ... .
→ Une exclamation en *How* (qui appartient à un style plutôt recherché) peut être reformulée avec ... .

Practice

1 Réécrivez ces énoncés à l'aide de *what* et, lorsque c'est possible, de *how*.

a. This ad is hilarious.
b. These commercials are a waste of money.
c. The punch line is very funny.
d. It's so clever of them!
e. The soundtrack is most original.
f. This campaign on drinking and driving gives useful advice.
g. It's such a luxurious product!

2 Rédigez un paragraphe à propos de cette affiche en essayant d'utiliser les mots suivants.

Verbs		Nouns
– buy	– consume	– exotic fruit and vegetables
– pollute	– pay	– carbon dioxide /daɪˈɒksaɪd/
– curb	– import	– petrol (GB) / gas (US)
– change	– produce	– greenhouse gases
– modify		– consumption
		– habit: *habitude*
		– carbon footprint: *empreinte carbone*

3 Traduisez ces phrases.

a. Les publicitaires nous contraignent à changer nos habitudes en créant de nouveaux besoins.
b. Ils nous font croire que nous avons réellement besoin du portable dernier cri.
c. Cette campagne de sensibilisation contre le gaspillage de l'eau fait réfléchir les citoyens.
d. Cette affiche encourage les gens à essayer cette nouvelle marque de vêtements de sport.
e. Regarder cette vidéo sur les dégâts causés par le réchauffement climatique les a persuadés de prendre des mesures rapidement.
f. Tout le battage publicitaire autour de ce concert m'a poussé à acheter un billet.

Language at work

Improve your pronunciation

1 Écoutez et comparez l'intonation utilisée dans les énoncés exclamatifs en anglais. MP3 2

– This cake is so good!
– What a shocking advert!
– How surprisingly cheap!
– It's such a trendy colour!

a. Quels mots sont particulièrement accentués ?
b. Lisez les phrases suivantes.

– What a wonderful idea for a cause!
– I just need this car; it's so neat!
– Wear a watch that's such a jewel!
– How unfair! You must act now!

c. Écoutez-les et imitez l'enregistrement.

2 Travaillez l'accent de phrase. MP3 3

a. Lisez et écoutez cette phrase :

I think natural fruit juice is good for you.

En accentuant un mot en particulier, le locuteur veut signifier quelque chose. Trouvez le mot accentué associé à chaque intention du locuteur et reliez-le à chaque bulle.

1- C'est sans produits chimiques.

2- Pas des jus de légumes.

3- J'insiste, c'est vraiment bon et nécessaire.

4- C'est mon opinion à moi.

5- Toi, tu n'es pas très en forme, tu en as besoin.

b. Écoutez les phrases enregistrées. Repérez le mot accentué dans chacune d'elles. Quelle est l'intention du locuteur dans chacune ?

3 Mise en voix CD WB

Dans votre *Workbook*, soulignez les mots porteurs de sens, marquez les liaisons consonne-voyelle et délimitez les groupes de souffle à l'aide d'une barre. Lisez ensuite le script à haute voix, enfin vérifiez à l'écoute.

YOUR TASK

You are working for an advertising agency. Choose a product or a cause, and make a radio spot (30, 60 seconds or maximum 90 seconds).

LES ÉTAPES À SUIVRE

1 Relisez vos notes sur l'unité.

Faites la liste des techniques utilisées pour rendre une publicité à la radio attrayante et efficace.

2 Préparez votre script.

a. Choisissez un produit ou une cause. Vous pouvez inventer un nouveau produit ou parler d'une cause peu connue.
b. Faites la liste des qualités de votre produit ou de votre cause, ou au contraire des aspects à dénoncer. Gardez en tête le public ciblé.

Contexte : moment de la scène, lieu ? Est-ce une scène de la vie quotidienne ? Activités successives des personnages ?

Le narrateur est une voix off, un utilisateur du produit, quelqu'un qui recherche une solution à un besoin, un témoin…

Type de script possible :
– dialogue entre deux personnages
– réponse à une question posée dès le début
– récit / reportage

Informations pratiques :
– le nom de la marque doit être entendu ou moins deux fois
– contacts (numéro de téléphone, site, adresse…)

Effets sonores : musique de fond, bruitages ?

Déroulé du spot :
– partie 1 : le problème à résoudre, souvent sous forme de question
– partie 2 : les difficultés rencontrées
– partie 3 : les solutions miracle

3 Outils grammaticaux

Incluez des exclamations et des superlatifs.

4 Sur les ondes

a. Vous pouvez soit vous enregistrer et présenter votre travail en MP3, soit jouer le sketch en classe.
b. Pensez à moduler votre voix. Certains mots doivent être particulièrement accentués.

ATTENTION!
– Pour être plus convaincant(e), faites des phrases courtes et percutantes et accentuez les mots importants.
– Respectez les intonations surtout dans les exclamatives.

SPEAKING CORNER

A Read and comment

"*Many a small thing has been made large by the right kind of advertising.*"
Mark Twain (1835-1910)

"*A product is something made in a factory; a brand is something that is bought by the customer. A product can be copied by a competitor; a brand is unique. A product can be quickly outdated; a successful brand is timeless.*"
Stephen King (born in 1947)

B Observe and react

C Podcast

Listen to these six London Underground spoof ads.

D Observe and react

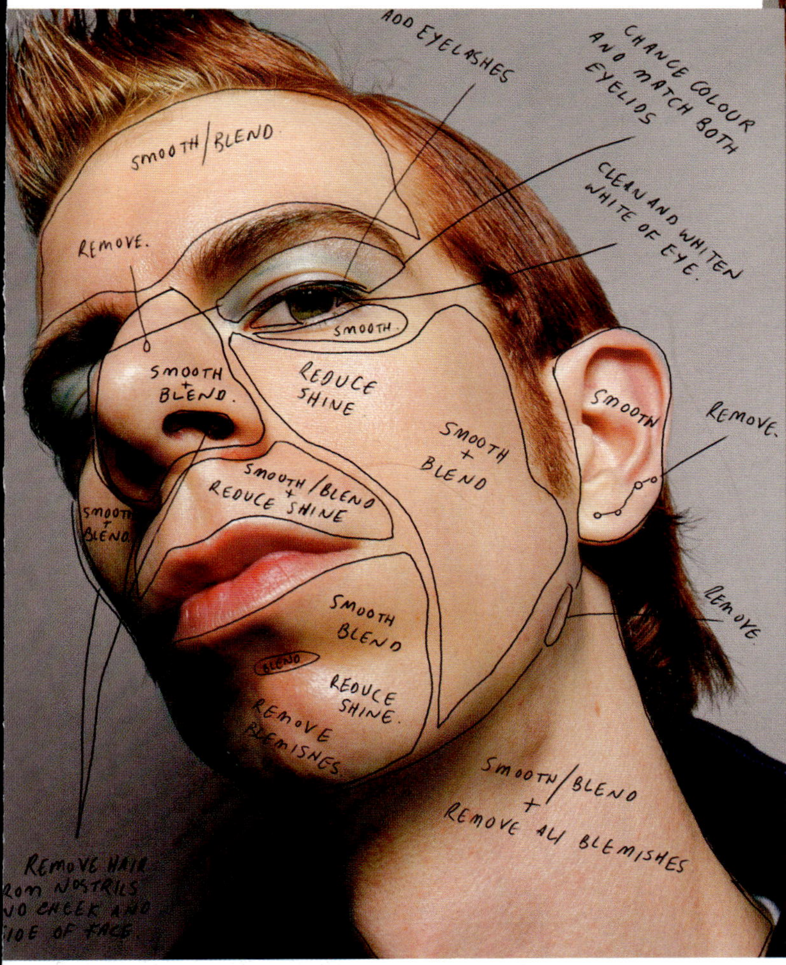

E Watch videos

Go to: www.dove.co.uk/cfrb/videos.html
Select the videos “Amy” and “Evolution”.

Unit 3

INCREDIBLE INDIA

YOUR TASK AT THE END OF THIS UNIT

You are a journalist working for the BBC World Service. You will prepare a report entitled *India, a Land of Contrasts*.
→ p. 55

TUNE IN!

Women in Jaysalmer (State of Rajahstan)

1 Discover

a. When you think of India, what immediately comes to your mind? What do you associate India with?

b. What strikes you in this photo? What are your impressions? What image of the country is given here?

Help!

Landscapes	Activities	Life
desert /dezət/ sand dunes drought /draʊt/: *sécheresse* deserted uninhabited ≠ populated barren landscape: *paysage dénudé*	jar: *cruche* daily chores /tʃɔːʳz/: *corvées journalières* running water well: *puits* fetch water or wood: *chercher de l'eau ou du bois*	slum: *taudis* shanty town: *bidonville* Hinduism /ˈhɪndʊˌɪzəm/ the Ganges /ˈgændʒiːz/ spices: *épices* destitute = needy suffer from starvation

2 India today WB

a. Skim through the documents below and list the changes and obstacles to the future development of India.

b. What did you learn and what struck you most?

A AT A GLANCE

Population: 1.15 billion today; 1.6 billion by 2030
Capital city: New Delhi (pop. 12.8 million)
Most populated cities: Mumbai, formerly Bombay (16.4 million); Kolkata, formerly Calcutta (13.2 million)
Languages: Hindi, English, Urdu, Tamil, Bengali, Kashmiri, Telugu, Marathi, Gujarati, Malayalam
Religions: 80% Hindu, 14% Muslim, 2.4% Christian, 2% Sikh, 0.7% Buddhist, 0.5% Jains, 0.4% other
Government: democracy, federal republic
Currency: rupee
Major economic sectors: agricultural products, textile goods, gems and jewellery, software services and technology, engineering goods, chemicals, leather products
Popular games: hockey, cricket

By the 19th century, Britain had assumed political control of virtually all Indian lands. Indian armed forces in the British army played a vital role in both World Wars. Non-violent resistance to British colonialism led by Mohandas Gandhi and Jawaharlal Nehru brought independence in 1947. The subcontinent was divided into two States: India and Pakistan.

B India rising

The country is now in a process of rapid economic development, but it faces complex and enduring internal problems, such as those around the caste system. India's massive overpopulation, poverty and environmental problems, as well as widespread corruption, are major challenges. [...]

Despite its burgeoning economy, the gap between rich and poor in India is vast.

About 35% of people live on less than US$1 a day. Poverty is at its worst in rural areas and is often accompanied by high levels of illiteracy and poor health.

Nationally, almost half of children suffer from malnourishment, although infant mortality rates have declined. Almost 60% of people in towns and 20% in rural areas do not have access to proper sanitation.

Despite such problems, India has seen overall poverty decline—a shift which has been accompanied by more general improvements to living standards.

Life expectancy rose from 59 to 63 between 1990 and 2004. Adult literacy rose from 50% to 61% over the same period.

■ *BBC News*, January 22, 2007

3 Who wants to be a millionaire?

Prepare ten questions on India to test your classmates' knowledge of the country. For each question write down four possible answers the show host will read.
The players will choose the right one.

PREPARE YOUR TASK

4 Seven years in India CD WB

Listen to Simon Robinson with *Time Magazine* in New Delhi, India. He is talking with Prashant Panjiar, a photographer who has been working for seven years on a photo project on India.

WEB BOX
www.time.com/time/photoessays/2007/pan_india_multimedia/

I. THE QUIET REVOLUTION

A A WORLD POWER

Since the late 1980's, India has become increasingly attractive to foreign investors. Multinationals see its huge, cheap English-speaking labour force as an asset. The success of high-tech industries in particular has attracted many overseas Indians who return to work in their native country. This "brain gain" results in a growing number of middle-class potential consumers.

Changes are striking, especially for women. The majority of small-town girls may still be married at an early age, but a significant number of them are driving vehicles and seeking higher education.

The media's role has been crucial. Mobiles, Internet cafés and cable TV are obvious markers of this economic transformation.

B Not enough

The India of today is vibrant, confident and ambitious – and not afraid to show it.

Take Rishi Rajani for example. The 30-something garment[1] tycoon[2] based in Mumbai and Denmark is a self-confessed workaholic[3] who also loves the good life.

His latest acquisition is a black Porsche sports car, which he drives through the streets of Mumbai.

In the money capital of India, flaunting your wealth[4] is now fashionable.

Mr Rajani has always dreamed of owning the mean[5] machine, and now his dream is a reality thanks to the success of the economy and his business.

"I work hard, you know, for my money," he says. "And I need a reward. This is my reward. But it's not enough. My next goal? A yacht. That's when I'll know I've really made it. I'm already working towards it."

■ *BBC News*, August 14, 2007

1. *(formel) vêtement, habillement* **2.** a person who is successful in business and has become rich and powerful **3.** somebody addicted to working **4.** *étaler sa richesse* **5.** extremely powerful

1 Group 1

Read the two articles

a. What explains the economic development of India? What is the key sector?

b. What consequences does this transformation have (role of women, consumer goods, education)?

c. Explain the "brain gain" in your own words.

d. Draw the portrait of Rishi Rajani (age, job, values in life, goals, what he symbolizes).

Help!

standard /ˈstændəd/ of living
status symbol
wealthy /ˈwelθɪ/ = well-off
privileged
self-satisfied
show off: *faire étalage de*
can afford sth / to + V: *avoir les moyens de*
embody: *incarner*
fulfil one's dreams: *réaliser ses rêves*
achieve success

C Mumbai's shadow city

I live in a corner of Mumbai called Dharavi, in a cramped hundred-square-foot shack[1] which has no natural light or ventilation, with a corrugated metal[2] sheet serving as the roof over my head. It vibrates violently whenever a train passes overhead. There is no running water and no sanitation. This is all I can afford. But I am not alone in Dharavi. There are a million people like me, packed in a two-hundred hectare triangle of swampy[3] urban wasteland, where we live like animals and die like insects. Destitute migrants from all over the country jostle with[4] each other for their own handful of sky in Asia's biggest slum. There are daily squabbles[5]– over inches of space, over a bucket of water – which at times turn deadly. Dharavi's residents come from the dusty backwaters[6] of Bihar and UP and Tamil Nadu and Gujarat. They came to Mumbai, the city of gold, with dreams in their hearts of striking it rich and living upper-middle-class lives. But that gold turned to lead[7] a long time ago, leaving behind rusted hearts and gangrenous minds. Like my own. […] But for the starving residents of Dharavi, this is home.

Amidst[8] the modern skyscrapers and neon-lit shopping complexes of Mumbai, Dharavi sits like a cancerous lump in the heart of the city. And the city refuses to recognize it. So it has outlawed it. All the houses in Dharavi are "illegal constructions", liable to be demolished at any time. But when the residents are struggling simply to survive, they don't care. So they live in illegal houses and use illegal electricity, drink illegal water and watch illegal cable TV. They work in Dharavi's numerous illegal factories and illegal shops, and even travel illegally – without ticket – on the local trains which pass directly through the colony.

Vikas Swarp, *Q and A: Slumdog Millionaire*, 2005

1. *cabane* **2.** *tôle ondulée* **3.** *marécageux* **4.** *se bousculent* **5.** *querelles*
6. *zones reculées* **7.** /led/ *plomb* **8.** in the middle of

2 Group 2 WB

Read the text and say what you have understood. Then turn to your Workbook for help.

a. Who migrates to Mumbai and why?
b. What are their living conditions?
c. What threatens them?

PREPARE YOUR TASK

3 Class work: Oral account

Prepare a two-minute oral account on Mumbai with the help of these documents.

Help!

living conditions
needy / destitute people
bright / better future
opportunities
below the poverty line

attract
improve: *améliorer*
flee to: *fuir vers*
settle down: *s'installer*
be threatened /θretnd/ with

2. THE DREAM INDUSTRY

1 Planet Bollywood CD WB

a. Listen to a Bollywood fan who explains what Bollywood is.
Turn to your Workbook for help.

PREPARE YOUR TASK → b. Prepare a two-minute oral account of the document you have heard.

c. Read these two reviews. Which of these two films would you like to see? Why?

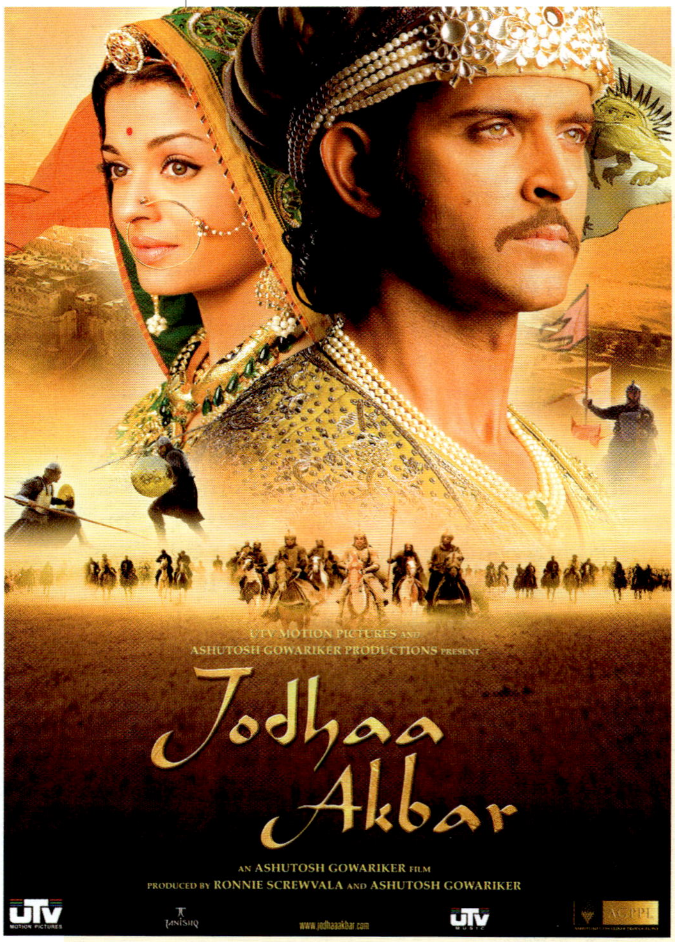

A love story set in the 16th century between the Mughal Emperor who ruled Hindustan (now India), Jalaluddin Mohammad Akbar, and a fiery young Rajput princess, Jodhaa. It is a story of battles, love, tolerance and respect.

Mohan Bhargava is an NRI (non-resident Indian) working at NASA in a prestigious position. After twelve years in the US, he returns to India to find his nanny. While he soon adapts to his new life, he is faced with harsh realities: poverty, caste discrimination, child marriage, illiteracy and a general disregard for education. He tries to bring about some changes…

PREPARE YOUR TASK →

2 Watch a video

Swades

What did the passenger realize?
Turn to your worksheet for help.

Video

3. FIRST MEETING

My mother called me one day into a side room and told me to be prepared to be inspected by a prospective bridegroom. They had a shock at home when I told my people that I'd not allow anyone to inspect me as a bride and that I'd rather do the inspection of the groom! They felt outraged and my father's younger brother, my father being too angry to speak to me, took me aside and said: "Don't be mad! Don't you know that it's not done?" I replied: "If it is not done, it's better that someone starts doing it now."

"What's the matter with you, my dear, why do you want to spoil[1] your chance of settling down[2] in life?" I had to explain that that was not my aim in life. I had other aims. I said I would like to work, rather than be a wife. [...]

I was finally persuaded. I was particularly fond of that uncle and could not brush him aside. I decided to go through the ceremony of being viewed and assessed[3]. I had made up my mind that I'd hate the young fellow and discourage him publicly. They decked me[4] in all the jewellery pieces borrowed from my sister-in-law in the house, diamonds and gold all over my ears, neck, nose, and wrist, and clad me[5] in a heavy sari crackling with gold lace[6]. I felt suffocated with all that stuff over me. I felt sick and felt that I was losing my identity. But I bore it all patiently as they fitted me out in the side room, and stood around and exclaimed at how well I looked, and the children gaped and cheered and joked. I hated the whole scene. I was seized with a feeling that I was in a wrong world, and that I was a stranger in their midst[7]. I saw my mother's face beaming with satisfaction and I was irritated at her simplicity. Although I was only thirteen, I had my own notions of what was good for me and what I should do in life. Although they admired me, I dreaded to look into the mirror myself. And then they seated me like a doll, and I had to wait for the arrival of the eminent personage with his parents. What a fuss they made when they arrived. It's hard to get a bridegroom, and when one is available parents treat him as a hard-won prize.

R.K. Narayan, *The Painter of Signs*, 1976

1. *gâcher* **2.** *t'installer* **3.** *évaluée* **4.** *m'ont parée* **5.** *m'ont revêtue* **6.** *dentelle* **7.** *parmi eux*

PREPARE YOUR TASK

1 Find the key information WB

Read the text once and say what you have understood. Then turn to your Workbook for help.

2 Recap (use your notes only)

a. Who is the narrator? How old was the narrator at the time of the scene?
b. What was the narrator told? What were her reactions? Why? How did the narrator's family respond to her behaviour? Why?
c. What did the narrator finally decide?
d. Compare the narrator's and the parents' attitudes before the meeting.
Say what marriage meant to them.
e. Draw the narrator's portrait.

PREPARE YOUR TASK

3 Role play

Imagine the conversation during the meeting. Act the dialogue out.

4 Listen to Savithri Amman CD WB

Learn more about the caste system in India.

4. BECAUSE I'M A GIRL

INDIA IS MISSING 10 MILLION DAUGHTERS

Over the last 20 years, about 10 million female fetuses may have been selectively aborted following ultrasound[1] results in India, suggest Prabhat Jha at the University of Toronto, Canada, and colleagues.

Their study of 1.1 million households[2] across India reveals that in 1997, far fewer girls were born to couples if their preceding child or children were also female. "There was about a 30% gap in second females following the birth of any earlier females," Jha told *New Scientist*. [...] The gap in births equates to about 0.5 million missing female births a year, says the team. Assuming the practice has been common in the two decades since ultrasound became widely available, this adds up to 10 million missing girls.

"Female infanticide of the past is refined [...] to a fine skill in this modern guise," says Shiresh Sheth of the Breach Candy Hospital in Mumbai.

[...] Sheth notes that in India's patriarchal society, a daughter is regarded as a "liability[3]", as she will belong to the family of her future husband. [...]

Jha warns that the preference for boys is likely to have "profound long-term consequences". In China, the cultural preference for boys and restrictions on family size are already having effects. Some reports suggest there are 40 million bachelors unable to find brides.

But there could be other serious consequences, Jha speculates, such as an impact on the spread of HIV. "If there are fewer females to marry and form stable sexual partnerships then males may resort to the use of paid sex," he suggests. Selective abortion on the basis of sex has been illegal in India since 1994. But there must be "diligence in enforcing[4] existing laws, which is not commonly done," says Jha.

■ www.newscientist.com, January 2006

1. *échograhie* **2.** *foyers* **3.** *handicap* **4.** *il faut veiller à faire appliquer*

1 Main facts WB

What do you learn about the situation of girls in India? Turn to your Workbook for help.

Help!

Pregnancy	Prejudice	Law
(have an) abortion: *avortement* expect a baby = be pregnant resort to modern techniques get rid of: *se débarasser de*	burden: *fardeau* equal rights ≠ inequalities male-dominated society dowry /daʊri/: *dot* be discriminated against despise: *mépriser*	professional ethics get round the law: *contourner la loi* close one's eyes to sth check: *vérifier* control: *gérer, diriger* select

PREPARE YOUR TASK →

2 A radio spot

Prepare a one-minute radio spot for an awareness campaign to prevent female infanticide.

5. RESIST

A twelve-year-old stops child marriages

Pratibha Patil, President of India (on the left)

In a village with the lowest female literacy in the country, a 12-year-old bidi-roller[1] has done what the government has been trying for years—stopped child marriage. Rekha Kalindi (12) has become a household name in her district for refusing to get married in November last year. "Since Rekha's revolt, there's been no child marriage in the village," said Prosenjit Kundu, assistant labour commissioner, Purulia, West Bengal government. "Now all girls want to be like her and some others, like Afsana Khatoon (13) from a neighbouring village, also said no."

Rekha seems an unlikely hero. The frail girl lives in a one-room home with seven others in Bararola village in the Jhalda-2 block of West Bengal's Purulia district. Her home has no electricity, no running water and no toilet.

She's never watched a film [...] or owned a toy. "We don't play. Little children in nursery play," says the 12-year-old, who looks no older than 7.

She and her friends spend their evenings collecting firewood and tendu leaves in the forest to sell at the weekly market in Kotshila town, seven kilometres away.

Rekha belongs to the Kalindi tribe, a scheduled tribe[2] in which girls are traditionally married at the age of 12. "My sister Jyotsna, now 15, got married at 12 and has already had four dead babies. She now lives with her second husband because the first one left her. Still, my parents wanted me to also get married but I said no, I want to study. They finally agreed," said Rekha.

Though her father Jagdish Kalindi stopped her food, water and soap for some days, she stood firm and he finally came around. "We told our teacher that Rekha wanted to study and together we made her *baba* (father) agree. We will all marry after turning 18," said her friend, classmate and neighbour Budhamani Kalindi (12). Forty per cent of the world's child marriages take place in India, leading to 78,000 women dying at childbirth each year.

According to UNICEF, teenage pregnancy and motherhood is nine times higher among women with no education than among women with 12 or more years of education.

■ *Hindustan Times*, April 12, 2009

1. *personne qui roule des feuilles de bétel à mâcher* **2.** *tribu recensée dans la Constitution indienne*

1 Find the key information WB

Read the text and say what you have understood. Then turn to your Workbook for help.

PREPARE YOUR TASK →

2 Argue your case

Rekha is invited to make a speech against child marriages before the UNICEF. Imagine her speech and deliver it in front of the class.

Help!

Father	Daughter
clash showdown: *confrontation* in dire poverty compel = oblige = force sb to do sth expect sb to do sth obey sb deter sb from V-ING: *dissuader qqn de*	bold = daring: *audacieuse* object to sth / V-ING challenge = defy stand up against claim one's rights dare: *oser*

Language at work

Quantité et comparaison

1 Dans les énoncés suivants, classez les éléments en gras selon la notion exprimée :

quantité nulle • insuffisante / faible • grande

a. *Indian girls do not have as **many opportunities** as Indian boys.*
b. ***Very few people** marry outside their caste.*
c. *In **a few cases** young people resist family pressure.*
d. *There are **fewer girls** than boys in India today.*
e. ***Less money** is invested to educate girls.*
f. ***Many women** are still illiterate. They have very **little hope** of escaping poverty.*
g. *Some States are fighting against sex discrimination, in others **not much** is done.*
h. ***Most parents** in India dream of having a boy rather than a girl.*
i. *A lot of pressure is put on girls to marry as early as possible. **Many girls** have **no** other **solution** than to obey their parents.*

2 Traduisez les énoncés ci-dessus.

3 Comparez.

a. *Many women have **little** hope of escaping poverty.*
b. ***Few** girls rebel against their parents in rural areas.*
– Les énoncés a et b expriment-ils une notion différente (quantité faible, forte, etc.) ?
– Les noms qui suivent *little* et *few* sont-ils dénombrables ou indénombrables ?
– Qu'en déduisez-vous sur l'emploi des deux formes ?
– Associez chaque énoncé à la question *how much...?* ou *how many...?*

4 Posez-vous les mêmes questions et expliquez ces constructions.

a. *Less money is invested to educate girls.*
b. *There are fewer girls than boys in India today.*
c. *Many women are uneducated.*
d. *Because of the dowry, many parents don't want to spend much money on their daughters' education.*

5 Observez.

a. ***More than half of** the population is literate.*
b. *There are **three times as** many inhabitants in Mumbai as in Bangalore.*
c. *There are **five times as** many people in Mumbai as in Jaipur.*
Associez chaque forme en gras à son équivalent français :
plus de la moitié de • moins de cinq fois • cinq fois plus • trois fois moins • trois fois plus.

6 Comparez.

a. *There are fewer and fewer baby girls because of the use of ultrasound scans.*
b. *The higher the level of education, the better.*
c. *The more education girls get, the older they marry.*
– Quelle forme ces trois énoncés ont-ils en commun : un comparatif, un superlatif ?
– Comment sont reliés les énoncés b et c ?
– Traduisez les trois énoncés en français. Que remarquez-vous concernant l'ordre des mots en b et c ?

7 Écoutez et imitez. MP3 4

Écoutez les énoncés ci-dessus (5 et 6), puis lisez-les à haute voix. Veillez à bien réaliser les formes réduites.

Language at work

Practice

1 Complétez ces phrases avec *some*, *many*, *most*, *little* ou *few*.

In India, ... people are destitute and ... of them try to improve their condition. But not ... of them succeed. ... people thought that outsourcing from rich countries would be very beneficial to India, but in fact very ... Indians have derived substantial advantages from it. There is ... hope that things are going to change in a near future for ... of the population. People who migrate to big cities have ... chance of making big money, yet ... of them are hopeful. Besides, ... girls are still married by their parents at a very young age, and very ... women dare to resist. ... parents in rural areas give ... importance to their education.

2 Traduisez ces phrases en anglais.

a. La population indienne est dix-huit fois plus nombreuse que la population française.
b. Il y a sept fois plus de musulmans que de sikhs en Inde.
c. Plus les filles sont instruites, plus elles se marient tard *(marry /old)*.
d. Plus vite les gens deviennent riches à Mumbai, plus ils sont satisfaits.
e. Plus les gens se battront pour leurs droits, plus les choses changeront.

3 The Pink Saris

a. Read the beginning of a newspaper article below.

In the poorest part of Uttar Pradesh, a region of Northern India, a group of women is fighting for equality. They wear pink saris and carry sticks in self-defence. They fight against discrimination, dowry demands, domestic violence and the corruption of officials.

A woman, Sampa Pal Devi, is at the head of the movement.

"Nobody comes to our help in these parts. The officials and the police are corrupt and anti-poor. So sometimes we have to take the law in our hands. Village society is loaded against women…"

b. Imagine the rest of the interview and write the rest of the article. Talk about the condition of women, child marriages, a male-dominated society, the lower castes (= the Untouchables)... Use expressions of quantity in your written production.

Build up your vocabulary

1 Classez les mots suivants en trois colonnes.

condition des femmes • buts • moyens mis en œuvre

ban • be on an equal footing • campaign for / against • curse • eradicate prejudices • get a fair deal • have the same opportunities • hold sb inferior • household chores • improve • upgrade people's education • take steps • get rid of • submissive • tackle / address an issue

2 Complétez ces phrases à l'aide d'un mot choisi dans la liste.

burden • dowry • bring up • put an end • take • measures • shame • second-class citizens • outnumber

a. In India, girls are considered a ... on their family.
b. Having a girl is a source of ... even today because girls are considered ... .
c. Parents have to ... the girl and give a ... to get her married.
d. The government should ... drastic ... to prevent female infanticide.
e. The government should also ... to child marriages.
f. The situation is alarming because men will soon ... women.

Improve your speaking skills

How to be more fluent

Si vous ne trouvez pas vos mots, utilisez les stratégies suivantes.

Ⓐ Évitez de dire « euh »

Essayez au contraire d'utiliser des *gap fillers* pour meubler le silence ou les pauses pendant votre prise de parole.

I mean... — *What I mean to say is...* — *Well, actually...*

How shall I put it? — *... now what's the word...?*

Ⓑ Quand vous cherchez vos mots

a. Trouvez un équivalent ou un mot de sens proche.

Deux des trois solutions proposées pour exprimer les morceaux de phrases soulignés sont correctes. Lesquelles ?

Dans de nombreux foyers indiens (1) les femmes ont pour tâche de (2) chercher (3) de l'eau et du bois.
Les femmes indiennes doivent affirmer (4) leurs droits.
Quand elles se marient elles ont du mal à s'adapter (5) à leurs beaux-parents.

1. ☐ in many Indian States	☐ in many Indian houses	☐ in many Indian households
2. ☐ the women's role is to	☐ women have many tasks	☐ it is the duty of women to
3. ☐ carry	☐ get	☐ fetch
4. ☐ give up	☐ fight for	☐ stand up for
5. ☐ can't adapt	☐ find it hard to adapt	☐ have trouble adapting

b. Pensez à des synonymes ou périphrases.

Sans chercher dans le dictionnaire, trouvez des mots proches, des synonymes ou périphrases pour dire ce qui est souligné. Quand on est bloqué(e) par un mot, il y a toujours une solution !

J'ai écouté, effarée, une étudiante m'annoncer qu'elle serait ravie d'épouser un inconnu choisi par ses parents. « Le concept d'amour nous est étranger. Je suis plus pragmatique, et de toutes les manières, qu'est-ce que l'amour ? »

c. Passez par la négative.

Exemple : Beaucoup de femmes indiennes ont du mal à s'adapter à leurs beaux-parents.
→ ont du mal : *can't / are unable to*

À vous : Cette campagne de prévention a échoué. Beaucoup de familles sont réticentes à avoir des filles.

YOUR TASK

You are a journalist working for the BBC World Service. You will prepare a report entitled *India, a Land of Contrasts* (two to three minutes).

LES ÉTAPES À SUIVRE

1 Revoyez les documents étudiés au cours de l'unité.

Classez les informations récoltées en deux colonnes : tradition et facteurs de changements. Lequel de ces deux aspects voulez-vous mettre en valeur dans votre reportage ?

2 N'oubliez pas d'aborder les points suivants.

Economic and social changes
- economic boom, leading sectors, film industry
- consumer society, emergence of a middle-class

Challenges India faces today
- caste system
- dowry, sex discrimination, arranged marriages
- overpopulation, poverty

Women in India
- signs of change?

3 Vous pouvez inclure des témoignages.

Un de vos camarades pourra jouer le rôle de la personne interviewée : un homme d'affaires qui a réussi, un médecin indien, une jeune femme qui va se marier...

4 Travaillez la prononciation à l'avance.

a. Soulignez, dans vos notes sur papier libre, le(s) mot(s) à accentuer.
b. Repérez la voyelle de la syllabe accentuée.
c. Marquez les liaisons consonne-voyelle.

LES CONSEILS POUR VOTRE PRESTATION

- Parlez distinctement, lentement et assez fort.
- Regardez votre auditoire.
- Respirez et marquez des pauses.
- Utilisez des *gap-fillers* si vous hésitez (→ p. 249).
- Réalisez correctement les formes réduites (→ p. 247).

JE M'ENTRAÎNE

1 Avant de prendre la parole

Ne rédigez pas des phrases complètes mais prenez des notes :
– mobilisez le vocabulaire dont vous allez avoir besoin (mots clés uniquement) ;
– organisez votre prise de parole (utilisez des abréviations, des mots de liaison, des flèches, des symboles...).

a. Transformez ce paragraphe en notes.

This ad promotes a beauty cream. First, it shows a woman with a wrinkled face. Then it shows the same woman who looks much younger because she has used the cream advertised. The contrast between the two women is striking. The goal is to attract our attention. This method is very effective because many women want to look more attractive. The target of this ad may be middle-aged women who worry about their looks.

b. Transformez ces notes en phrases.

MP3 5

Indian girls more educated today → Get jobs in international firms + and + easily.
Earn their living → + and + independent → major changes in rural areas.
Comparez votre production à l'enregistrement proposé.

2 Je m'entraîne

Observez cette publicité et préparez votre présentation. Aidez-vous des conseils ci-dessus.

→ **Temps de préparation :** de 5 à 10 minutes
→ **Temps de parole :** de 2 à 3 minutes

N'oubliez pas :
– Si vous hésitez, utilisez des *gap fillers : er / um..., ... you see / you know...* (→ p. 249)
– Donnez votre opinion personnelle : *in my view..., in my opinion...* (→ p. 248-249)
– Utilisez une structure de conclusion : *To conclude..., in short...* (→ p. 249)

3 Pendant la prise de parole

a. Tenez-vous droit, posez vos mains sur la table et non sur vos genoux.
Tenez compte de votre interlocuteur, assurez-vous :
– qu'il est prêt à vous écouter : *Shall I start?*
– qu'il vous comprend : *Would you like me to repeat? Do you see what I mean?* (→ p. 248)
Parlez à voix haute et intelligible. Marquez des pauses pour respirer.
Regardez votre interlocuteur le plus souvent possible, ne lisez pas vos notes.

MP3 6

b. Attention à la prononciation : pensez à accentuer les mots importants, pensez aux formes réduites et aux liaisons consonne-voyelles. (→ p. 246-247)
Adoptez un débit régulier et parlez sans précipitation.
Entraînez-vous en écoutant cet enregistrement. Répétez chaque phrase dans les blancs prévus à cet effet.

MP3 7

4 Je m'auto-corrige

Écoutez l'enregistrement correspondant à la publicité page 56 et comparez votre production à celle enregistrée par un anglophone.

JE FAIS LE BILAN

Analysez votre prestation à l'aide de cette grille d'évaluation où sont définis différents paliers de compétence en production orale en continu.

Je peux...	Paliers
... introduire, défendre et nuancer mon propos sur des sujets plus abstraits. ... faire part de mes réactions et de mes sentiments. ... utiliser un vocabulaire adapté au sujet choisi. ... être compréhensible malgré un léger accent français.	B1
... parler en ne faisant que quelques erreurs qui ne gênent pas la compréhension. Je parviens parfois à me corriger. ... m'exprimer avec une certaine aisance, mon discours s'enchaîne malgré des pauses et des reprises.	B1
... regarder mon interlocuteur et tenir compte de ses réactions, en reformulant au besoin mon propos.	B1
... introduire, défendre et nuancer mon propos sur une vaste gamme de sujets. ... parler de façon fluide, entendre mes erreurs et les corriger moi-même. ... tenir compte des réactions de mon interlocuteur et adapter ma prestation.	B2

ÉVALUATION

Votre professeur va vous demander de réagir à un document en lien avec l'une des trois unités travaillées :

Unit 1 You are what you eat — Unit 2 Advert-teasing — Unit 3 Incredible India

→ **Temps de préparation :** de 5 à 10 minutes
→ **Temps de parole :** de 2 à 3 minutes
Une fois l'évaluation terminée, votre professeur pourra déterminer à quel palier vous vous situez par rapport à la grille du Cadre Européen Commun de Référence pour les Langues.

Reading

Unit 4 DEALING WITH THE DEVIL

- Read extracts from English Gothic novels
- Analyse the characteristics of the Gothic novel
- Discover the Gothic novel today

→ YOUR TASK

You will read one extract from a collection of short stories and write the back cover for a new edition of the book.

→ p. 69

Unit 5 THE FOURTH POWER

- Changes in the printed press over the past few decades
- Tabloids versus quality press
- What dangers threaten the freedom of the press?

→ YOUR TASK

Read two press articles. Then write a letter to the editor giving your reactions to one of the articles.

→ p. 84

Unit 6 BLACK IS BEAUTIFUL

- Learn more about the Civil Rights Movement in the USA
- Listen to Martin Luther King and Malcolm X
- From the Jim Crow laws to the White House

→ YOUR TASK

You are a film director. Write the scenario based on the scene you will read.

→ p. 100

ÉVALUATION SOMMATIVE *READING* → p. 104-105

Unit 4

DEALING WITH THE DEVIL

YOUR TASK AT THE END OF THIS UNIT

You will read one extract from a collection of short stories (p. 70-71) and write the back cover for a new edition of the book. → p. 69

TUNE IN!

Matching

a. Look at the three front covers.
Can you identify two of the novels from their summaries (A or B, p. 60)? Justify your choice.

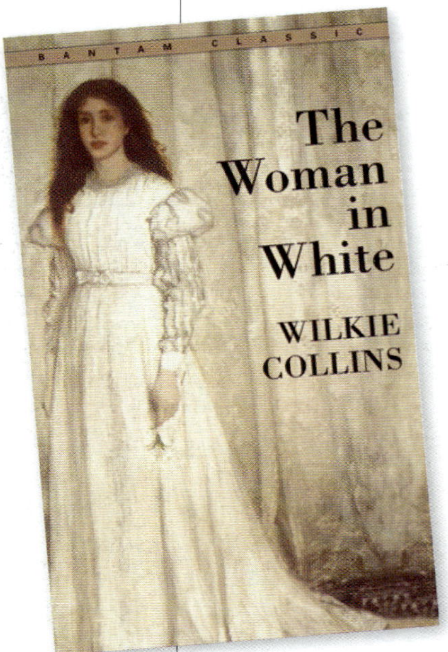

A In the first pages, the reader discovers an isolated gray stone manor on the windswept Cornish coast, as the second Mrs Maxim de Winter remembers the chilling[1] events she experienced when she began her new life as the young wife of a husband she did not know very well. With an eerie[2] presentiment of evil in her heart, the second Mrs de Winter walks in the shadow of her mysterious predecessor, determined to uncover the darkest secrets and shattering[3] truths about Maxim's first hauntingly beautiful[4] wife.

1. *glaçants* **2.** mysterious **3.** *dévastatrices*
4. *d'une beauté envoûtante*

B Set in a Roman Catholic Europe of violent passions and extreme oppression, the novel follows Adeline, who is mysteriously placed under the protection of a family escaping Paris and their debts. They take refuge in a ruined abbey in the middle of the woods in the south-east of France, where a skeleton, a manuscript, and a rusty dagger[1] are discovered in concealed[2] rooms. Adeline finds herself at the mercy of the abbey's owner, a Marquis whose attentions finally force her to run away.

1. *poignard* **2.** hidden

b. In your opinion which of the novels do the following extracts come from? Justify.

1 *Having reached the door, he stopped for some moments, listening in apprehensive anxiety—no sound was heard but that of the wind, which swept in hollow gusts[1] over the waste[2]. At length he ventured to knock, and, having waited some time, during which he indistinctly heard several voices in conversation, someone within inquired what he wanted. La Motte answered, that he was a traveller who had lost his way, and desired to be directed to the nearest town. "That," said the person, "is seven miles off, and the road bad enough, even if you could see it: If you only want a bed, you may have it here and had better stay." [...] The door was now opened by a tall figure with a light, who invited La Motte to enter. [...] The forlorn[3] and desolate aspect of this apartment made La Motte shrink involuntarily, and he was turning to go out when the man suddenly pushed him back, and he heard the door locked upon him.*

1. rafales 2. (ici) lande déserte
3. à l'abandon

2 *Last night I dreamed I went to Manderley again. It seemed to me that I was passing through the iron gates that led to the driveway. The drive was just a narrow track now, its stony surface covered with grass and weeds. Sometimes, when I thought I had lost it, it would appear again, beneath a fallen tree or beyond a muddy[1] pool formed by winter rains. The trees had thrown out new low branches which stretched across my way. I came to the house suddenly, and stood there with my heart beating fast and tears filling my eyes.*

There was Manderley, our Manderley, secret and silent as it had always been, the grey stone shining in the moonlight of my dream. [...]

Then a cloud came over the moon, like a dark hand across a face.

1. boueuse

3 *"Is this the road to London?" she asked.*

Her face looked thin and pale in the moonlight, and there was something very sad about her expression. She had fair hair and large trusting eyes, and in her hand she carried a small bag. I guessed her to be about twenty-two years old.

What on Earth was such a woman doing all by herself in the lonely place?

"Please, sir," she repeated, "is this the road to London?"

"Yes," I replied. "But where did you come from? I didn't see you until you touched me. You gave me quite a shock."

"I was hiding among those trees," she replied. [...] "Will you help me?"

c. In these five texts, list all the words referring to the place, the general atmosphere and the characters (name, sex, age and feelings).

I. CARMILLA

While travelling to Karnstein, an abandoned village in Styria, Laura and her father meet one of her father's oldest friends, General Spielsdorf.

Part 1

"I have been made the dupe of a preternatural conspiracy."

Notwithstanding[1] his professions of confidence in the General's penetration, I saw my father, at this point, glance at the General, with, as I thought, a marked suspicion of his sanity.

The General did not see it, luckily. He was looking gloomily and curiously into the glades[2] and vistas of the woods that were opening before us.

"You are going to the Ruins of Karnstein?" he said. "Yes, it is a lucky coincidence; do you know I was going to ask you to bring me there to inspect them. I have a special object in exploring. There is a ruined chapel, ain't there, with a great many tombs of that extinct family?"

"So there are—highly interesting," said my father. "I hope you are thinking of claiming the title and estates?"

My father said this gaily, but the General did not recollect the laugh, or even the smile, which courtesy exacts[3] for a friend's joke; on the contrary, he looked grave and even fierce, ruminating on a matter that stirred[4] his anger and horror.

"Something very different," he said, gruffly. "I mean to unearth some of those fine people. I hope, by God's blessing, to accomplish a pious sacrilege here, which will relieve our Earth of certain monsters, and enable honest people to sleep in their beds without being assailed by murderers. I have strange things to tell you, my dear friend, such as I myself would have scouted[5] as incredible a few months since."

My father looked at him again, but this time not with a glance of suspicion—with an eye, rather, of keen intelligence and alarm.

1. *malgré* 2. clearings in the forest 3. *exige* 4. provoked 5. *(ici) jugées*

Part 2

"The house of Karnstein," he said, "has been long extinct: a hundred years at least. My dear wife was maternally descended from the Karnsteins. But the name and title have long ceased to exist. The castle is a ruin; the very village is deserted; it is fifty years since the smoke of a chimney was seen there; not a roof left."

"Quite true. I have heard a great deal about that since I last saw you; a great deal that will astonish you. But I had better relate everything in the order in which it occurred," said the General. "You saw my dear ward[1]—my child, I may call her. No creature could have been more beautiful, and only three months ago none more blooming."

"Yes, poor thing! When I saw her last she certainly was quite lovely," said my father. "I was grieved and shocked more than I can tell you, my dear friend; I knew what a blow it was to you."

He took the General's hand, and they exchanged a kind pressure. Tears gathered in the old soldier's eyes. He did not seek to conceal[2] them. He said:

"We have been very old friends; I knew you would feel for me, childless as I am. She had become an object of very near interest to me, and repaid my care by an affection that cheered my home and made my life happy. That is all gone. The years that remain to me on Earth may not be very long; but by God's mercy I hope to accomplish a service to mankind before I die, and to subserve[3] the vengeance of Heaven upon the fiends[4] who have murdered my poor child in the spring of her hopes and beauty!"

Sheridan Le Fanu, *Carmilla*, 1872

1. adopted child **2.** hide **3.** *(ici) faciliter* **4.** monsters or very bad people

1 Find the key information WB

Read the text and say what you have understood. Then read again for more details. Turn to your Workbook if you have any vocabulary problems.

a. List all the characters present and mentioned in the passage. What are their relationships?

b. Find all the words and phrases linked to emotions, ways of speaking and ways of looking, for each of the main characters. Make a chart or a mindmap in your notebook.

	The General	Laura's father
Emotions		
Ways of speaking		
Ways of looking		

c. What characteristics of the Gothic novel can you find here (location, atmosphere, characters)?

2 From another angle

Imagine you are Laura's father, and you want to tell a friend about meeting the General and about how you felt during your conversation.

3 Solve the mystery

a. What could have caused the death of the General's child?

b. Why did the General plan to "unearth" the people of Karnstein?

c. Why did Laura's father doubt the General's sanity?

d. According to the general who are the "fiends" that murdered his niece?

4 Radio reading

You work for a radio programme entitled *Mysterious Encounters*. Record this passage (or a part of it) including a voice over, a soundtrack and sound effects to create a Gothic atmosphere.

PREPARE YOUR TASK

5 Writing fiction

Write your own conclusion to this extract from *Carmilla*. Include as many elements as possible from the Gothic tradition.

2. AN UNEXPECTED ENCOUNTER

1 Get ready

a. Observe the photo and react to it: What atmosphere is created here? What elements of the Gothic novel do you recognize?
b. Judging from the title and the photo, what do you think may be happening in this passage?

Part 1

How lucky that I was alone!

Alone. I repeated the word with grim[1] satisfaction as I wrenched myself to my feet despite the pain. At precisely that moment, a figure stepped out from the trees to the north, some thirty paces away.

A dizzying[2] array of emotions shot through me in a second. The first was surprise; I was far from any trail here, and I didn't expect company. Then, as my eyes focused on the motionless figure, seeing the utter stillness, the pallid skin, a rush of piercing hope rocked through me. I suppressed it viciously, fighting against the equally sharp lash of agony as my eyes continued to the face beneath the black hair, the face that wasn't the one I wanted to see. Next was the fear; this was not the face I grieved for[3], but it was close enough for me to know that the man facing me was no stray hiker[4].

And finally, in the end, recognition.

"Laurent!" I cried in surprised pleasure. It was an irrational response. I probably should have stopped at fear. […]

1. sinister **2.** *étourdissant* **3.** *pleurais* **4.** *randonneur égaré*

Part 2

Yes, fear would have made more sense, but all I felt was an overwhelming satisfaction. The meadow was a magic place again. A darker magic than I'd expected, to be sure, but magic all the same. Here was the connection I'd sought. The proof that – somewhere in the same world where I lived – he *did* exist. […]

"Bella?" he asked, looking more astonished than I felt.

"You remember." I smiled. It was ridiculous that I should be so elated because a vampire knew my name.

He grinned[1]. "I didn't expect to see you here." He strolled toward me, his expression bemused[2]. […]

"Did Victoria ever find you?" I asked, breathless, desperate to distract him. It was the first question that popped into my head, and I regretted it as soon as the words were spoken. Victoria – who had hunted me with James, and then disappeared – was not someone I wanted to think of at this particular moment.

But the question did not stop him. "Yes," he said, hesitating on that step. "I actually came here as a favor to her." He made a face. "She won't be happy about this."

"About what?" I said, eagerly, inviting him to continue. He was glaring into the trees, away from me. I took advantage of his diversion, taking a furtive step back.

He looked back at me and smiled, the expression made him look like a black-haired angel. "About me killing you," he answered with a seductive purr[3].

Stephenie Meyer, *New Moon,* 2006

1. *fit un grand sourire* **2.** perplexed **3.** *en susurrant*

2 Find the key information WB

Read the text and say what you have understood. Then read again for more details. Turn to your Workbook for help.

3 Recap

Who is the narrator?

Part 1

a. What is the situation at the beginning of the passage: place, characters, time of day...?
b. Who does the narrator discover?
c. What is the narrator's first reaction? Why?
d. What do the last three sentences (l. 16-17) suggest? What effect is produced on the reader?

Part 2

a. List the characters who are present or mentioned. What can we guess about their relationship? Quote the relevant words.
b. Read lines 1 to 4 again and explain the narrator's feeling at the beginning of this part. How can you explain it?
c. What does the narrator suddenly understand?
d. List the different elements (setting and characters) that create suspense and tension.

PREPARE YOUR TASK

4 What's next?

Group 1: If you already know the story, make an oral account of what happens next in the novel or the film.
Group 2: Imagine a possible sequel to the story if you haven't read it. You may use the poster on the right. Confront your version with the real story.

PREPARE YOUR TASK

5 Reader's review

Write an attractive headline and a few lines to present the novel on a bookshop shelf. Use adjectives and superlatives to catch the readers' attention.

Help!

Vampirism	Atmosphere
werewolf /ˈweəʳwʊlf/ (pl. -wolves): *loup-garou*	eerie: *sinistre*
bat: *chauve-souris*	scary
garlic: *ail*	unsettling: *dérangeant*
cross: *croix*	disquieting /dɪsˈkwaɪətɪŋ/: *troublant*
coffin: *cercueil*	mysterious
stake /steɪk/: *pieu*	gloomy: *lugubre*
feed on	weird /wɪəʳd/: *étrange*
suck blood /blʌd/	bloodcurdling: *qui vous fige le sang*
vanish = disappear	hair-raising
	give sb the creeps: *donner la chair de poule à qqn*

6 Movie fan

You want to buy a DVD because you love Gothic stories. You have heard of Kenneth Branagh's version of Mary Shelley's *Frankenstein*. Go on the Internet and watch the trailer.
Convince a friend to watch the film with you.

3. Crime story

You enter a competition for the best Gothic story. Use the stills below and the elements of the Gothic novel you have studied in this unit in order to write a story (200 words).

Help!

edge of the cliff: *bord de la falaise*
thunder: *tonnerre*
flash of lightning: *éclair*
dimly lit: *éclairé faiblement*
ajar: *entrebâillé*
break the news to sb: *annoncer une nouvelle à qqn*
commit suicide / a murder

Exprimer des degrés de probabilité dans le présent, le passé et le futur

1 Degré de probabilité.

Associez chaque modal en gras à sa traduction. Plusieurs réponses sont parfois possibles.

– *She **may** want to escape.*
– *She **might** be in love with him.*
– *She **must** be scared to death.*
– *She **could** be dead in a year from now.*

– Il se peut qu'elle…
– Elle est sans doute…
– Peut-être qu'elle…
– Il est presque certain que…
– Il se pourrait qu'elle…
– Elle doit être…

2 Observez.

– *"The General is mad. He **must have had** a shock when his daughter died."*
– *"What **could have happened**?"*
– *"I don't know. His daughter **may have met** a dangerous man, she **may have fallen** in love with him. She **might not have told** her parents anything. He **may have killed** her afterwards."*
– *"The General **must feel** miserable. He **may be dreaming** of taking his revenge. He **could want** to kill the murderer. He **may spend** the rest of his life looking for him."*

a. Dites pour chaque forme verbale en gras si elle porte sur un fait présent, passé ou futur.
b. Quel élément (contexte, forme verbale) vous permet de justifier votre réponse ?
c. Quelle forme verbale est utilisée après le modal : base verbale • forme *BE* + *-ING* • *have* + participe passé ?
d. Récapitulez :

Pour exprimer un degré de **probabilité** sur un **fait présent** on emploie :	Pour exprimer un degré de **probabilité** sur un **fait passé** on emploie :	Pour exprimer la **possibilité d'un fait futur** on emploie :
Modal + … ou, pour action en cours de déroulement : modal + … + …	Modal + … + …	Modal + … + (repère futur)

3 Comparez.

a. *He **may know** who the murderer is.*
b. *"He looks sad." "Yes, he **must be thinking** about the past."*
c. *"His eyes are red." "He **must have been crying** a lot."*

– Dans quel énoncé le modal en gras se rapporte-t-il à une action en cours ?
– Dans quel énoncé le modal se rapporte-t-il à une action qui vient de se passer et laisse des traces visibles dans le présent ?

Language at work

Practice

1 Mettez le verbe entre parenthèses à la forme qui convient : base verbale, forme *BE* + V-*ING* ou *have* + participe passé, puis réécrivez les phrases en entier.

a. Why did he react so violently? I believe he must (be scared).
b. The General believes that he may (free) the Earth of some monsters forever if he commits a sacrilege.
c. She must (be) beautiful when she was a young woman.
d. As they are alone in the forest, he may (take) advantage of the situation to kill her.
e. I wonder what is going on. He might (spy on) her.

2 Pour chacun des énoncés, repérez si le fait décrit est passé, présent ou futur et décidez quelle forme doit être utilisée après le modal en anglais. Décidez du degré de probabilité puis traduisez.

a. Il l'avait certainement suivie.
b. Elle ne l'a peut-être pas entendu.
c. Elle pense peut-être à son ancien petit ami.
d. Elle est certainement très triste.
e. Il se peut que les loups-garous attaquent.
f. Il est possible que l'un des personnages meure.
g. L'un des personnages pourrait mourir bientôt.

Build up your vocabulary

1 Exprimer la peur et la surprise.

a. Lisez ce paragraphe.

She was walking in the woods when suddenly she heard a noise. It ***made her jump****. She kept cool and thought it was just an animal. Later she heard footsteps behind her and she* ***was startled*** *again. She* ***had the shock of her life****. When she saw him she* ***caught her breath*** *and was* ***speechless****. This time she* ***was scared*** *stiff. Her face was* ***as white as a sheet*** *and she* ***panicked****. Her hair stood on end. She* ***shuddered*** *when she heard his voice. Her legs started shaking. She nearly fainted. But she ran away to escape.*

b. Vérifiez que vous comprenez le sens de tous les mots ou expressions en gras. Utilisez un dictionnaire si nécessaire.
c. Classez les mots ou expressions en gras en deux colonnes selon qu'ils expriment la peur ou la surprise.

2 Dérivation.

a. Sachant que le suffixe ***-ful*** signifie « plein de », que ***-less*** signifie « sans », « dépourvu de », que ***-some*** signifie « qui provoque » et que le suffixe ***-en*** indique une transformation, trouvez les équivalents anglais des mots suivants :
– à partir de *fear* : peureux / craintif • intrépide • aspect redoutable / effroyable
– à partir de *fright* : effrayer • effroyable
b. Traduisez ces adverbes : de manière craintive • avec intrépidité.
Puis vérifiez vos réponses à l'aide d'un dictionnaire si nécessaire.

3 Traduisez les mots en gras. Utilisez un dictionnaire si nécessaire.

Kathleen **dreaded** going back home in the middle of the night. She was walking **unaware of** a **threatening** presence behind the trees when she suddenly heard footsteps. **It made her skin crawl**. She **shrieked** with terror and **ran for her life**. Fortunately, she managed to escape from her **unknown assailant**.

YOUR TASK

First read one extract from a collection of short stories p. 70-71. Then write the back cover for a new edition of the book.

PRÉPARATION À LA LECTURE

1. Mobilisez toutes les stratégies de lecture.
a. Appuyez-vous sur les mots transparents du texte (mots que l'on peut reconnaître grâce au français).
b. Déduisez le sens des mots inconnus à partir des indices contenus dans le contexte.
c. Appuyez-vous sur les procédés de dérivation et de composition pour comprendre le sens des mots.

2. Procurez-vous un dictionnaire que vous pourrez utiliser en dernier recours ou utilisez un dictionnaire en ligne.

LECTURE ET COMPRÉHENSION

1. Relisez tous les textes de l'unité.

2. Lisez l'extrait p. 70-71 en utilisant les stratégies de lecture étudiées.

3. Repérez les personnages principaux et les liens qu'ils entretiennent, leurs sentiments, les émotions qu'ils ressentent.

4. Listez les lieux, les éléments du décor, les éléments qui créent l'atmosphère.

5. Rassemblez tous les éléments qui paraissent étranges ou surnaturels.

6. Déterminez les points essentiels de l'intrigue.

RÉDACTION DE LA 4e DE COUVERTURE

Une quatrième de couverture doit donner envie de lire le roman. Le résumé doit accrocher le lecteur et l'inciter à ouvrir le livre.

1. Relisez les deux débuts de quatrième de couverture p. 60.

2. Dressez la liste des adjectifs rencontrés dans l'extrait (atmosphère, émotion) et à réutiliser dans votre texte.

3. Préparez un texte de présentation *(blurb)* de 80 mots environ : personnages principaux, liens entre eux, quelques éléments clés de l'intrigue.

4. Imaginez quelques commentaires de critiques pour inciter les lecteurs potentiels à lire le roman. Pensez à utiliser des adjectifs au superlatif.

5. Vous pourrez créer votre quatrième de couverture sur papier ou sur ordinateur sur le site : www.readwritethink.org/files/resources/interactives/bookcover/

6. Relisez-vous avec attention.

Revelations in Black

One day the narrator finds a book in an antiques shop. The owner refuses to sell it because it was written by his brother just before he died in an institution for the insane. He finally agrees to lend it and the narrator discovers a very strange story. He feels so uneasy he goes out for an evening walk. He is immediately attracted to a garden where he notices a woman.

The Woman in Black, a film by James Watkins (2011)

"I suppose you are the owner here. I... I really didn't know the place was occupied, and the gate... well, the gate was unlocked. I'm sorry I trespassed."

She made no reply to that, and the dog merely gazed at me in dumb silence. No graceful words of polite departure came to my lips, and I moved hesitatingly toward the gate.

"Please don't go," she said suddenly, looking up. "I'm lonely. Oh, if you but knew how lonely I am!" She moved to one side on the bench and motioned that I sit beside her. The dog continued to examine me with its big eyes.

Whether it was[1] the nearness of that odor of heliotrope, the suddenness of it all, or perhaps the moonlight, I did not know, but at her words a thrill of pleasure[2] ran through me, and I accepted the proffered seat. [...]

Then the woman said to me in English which was slightly stilted[3] and marked with an accent:

"It has been ages since I have spoken to anyone... We are strangers. I do not know you, and you do not know me. Yet... strangers sometimes find in each other a bond[4] of interest. Supposing... supposing we forget customs and formality of introduction? Shall we?"

For some reason I fell my pulse quicken as she said that. "Please do," I replied. "A spot like this is enough introduction in itself. Tell me, do you live here?"

She made no answer for a moment, and I began to fear I had taken her suggestion too quickly. Then she began slowly:

"My name is Perle von Mauren, and I am really a stranger to your country, though I have been here now more than a year. My home is in Austria near what is now the Czechoslovakian frontier. You see, it was to find my only brother that I came to the United States. During the war he was a lieutenant under General Mackensen, but in 1916, in April I believe it was, he... he was reported missing."

"War is a cruel thing. It took our money; it took our castle on the Danube, and then—my brother. Those following years were horrible. We lived always in doubt, hoping against hope that he was still living."

1. *(ici) était-ce à cause de* **2.** *un frisson de plaisir* **3.** *légèrement guindé* **4.** *(ici) lien*

"Then after the Armistice a fellow officer claimed to have served next to him on grave-digging detail[5] at a French prison camp near Monpré. And later came a thin rumor that he was in the United States. I gathered together as much money as I could and came here in search of him."

Her voice dwindled off[6], and she sat in silence staring at the brown weeds. When she resumed, her voice was low and wavering[7].

"I... found him... but would to God I hadn't! He... he was no longer living."

I stared at her. "Dead?" I asked.

The veil trembled as though moved by a shudder[8], as though her thoughts had exhumed some terrible event of the past.

What do we learn about Perle's past?
What is strange about this woman?

Unconscious of my interruption she went on:

"Tonight I came here—I don't know why—merely because the gate was unlocked, and there was a place of quiet within. Now have I bored you with my confidences and personal history?"

"Not at all," I replied. "I came here by chance myself. Probably the beauty of the place attracted me. I dabble in[9] amateur photography occasionally and react strongly to unusual scenes. Tonight I went for a midnight stroll to relieve my mind from the bad effect of a book I was reading."

She made a strange reply to that, a reply away from our line of thought and which seemed an interjection that escaped her involuntarily.

"Books," she said, "are powerful things. They can fetter[10] one more than the walls of a prison."

She caught my puzzled stare at the remark and added hastily[11]: "It is odd that we should meet here."

For a moment I didn't answer. I was thinking of her heliotrope perfume, which for a woman of her apparent culture was applied in far too great a quantity to show good taste. The impression stole upon me that the perfume cloaked[12] some secret, that if it were removed I should find... but what?

The hours passed, and still we sat there talking, enjoying each other's companionship. She did not remove her veil, and though I was burning with desire to see her features, I had not dared to ask her to. A strange nervousness had slowly seized me. The woman was a charming conversationalist, but there was about her an indefinable something which produced in me a distinct feeling of unease.

It was, I should judge, but a few moments before the first streaks of a dawn when it happened. [...]

A thin shadow moving across the garden attracted my gaze once again into the night about me. I looked up over the spire of the deserted house and started as if struck by a blow. For a moment I thought I had seen a curious cloud formation racing low directly above me, a cloud black and impenetrable with two wing-like ends strangely in the shape of a monstrous flying bat.

I blinked my eyes hard and looked again.

"That cloud!" I exclaimed, "that strange cloud! Did you see—"

I stopped and stared dumbly.

The bench at my side was empty. The woman had disappeared.

Carl Jacobi, *Revelations in Black*, 1933

What happened? What mysterious elements did the narrator notice?

5. a group of soldiers or police officers given a particular job **6.** *(ici) mourut* **7.** *mal assurée*
8. *frisson* **9.** *tâte de* **10.** *enchaîner* **11.** *précipitamment* **12.** *masquait*

Unit 5

THE FOURTH POWER

YOUR TASK AT THE END OF THIS UNIT

Read two press articles. Then write a letter to the editor giving your reactions to one of the articles. → p. 84

TUNE IN!

Help!

capital letters
at stake: *en jeu*
wrap up: *envelopper*
threaten /ˈθretn/: *menacer*
alert sb to
make sb aware of

1 Observe the magazine front cover

a. What immediately strikes you: picture, layout *(mise en page)*, headline? Who is the target? What visual devices are used here?

b. What does the front cover reveal about the press today?

c. Are you aware of this problem? Why? Why not?

PREPARE YOUR TASK

2 The crisis

Read the following extracts and fill in the grid below. Use a separate sheet of paper.

A The disappearance of traditional newspapers is increasingly regarded as inevitable. [...]

The conventional answer, of course, is that the Internet is the culprit. Readers by the millions have migrated to the Web, where news and information are supplied for free. In their wake[1], newspaper subscriptions[2] have evaporated, advertisers have decamped, and print revenues have plummeted[3].

But is the rise of the Internet really the cause of the exodus from newspapers? When I signed on 20 years ago, the slide in readership was already underway. Daily circulation was already falling.

The absence of a newspaper habit among young readers was already prompting concern. Today the crisis may be more acute[4], but the symptoms appeared before the World Wide Web did.

So if the Internet isn't at the root of the newspapers' woes[5], what is? I nominate not the computer screen, but the TV screen.

Newspapers have been undone by the rise of television, which emphasizes[6] stimulation over substance and fast-paced imagery over focused thought. [...]

■ *The Boston Globe*, October 2007

1. *sillage* **2.** *abonnements* **3.** *ont chuté dramatiquement* **4.** *aiguë, grave* **5.** /wəʊz/ *(formel) maux* **6.** *privilégie*

B Newspaper and magazine publishers have been looking for an effective micropayment system for years, without much success, both due to public resistance to the idea of paying for online content and due to the technical hurdle[1] of excessive transaction costs. Now, with the popularity of mobile devices like smartphones and the iPad, more people seem willing to accept subscription services like Apple's, and Google has just rolled out "One Pass", a micropayment scheme that may satisfy both publishers and consumers.

1. *obstacle*

	Situation	Causes	Solution
Extract A			
Extract B			

3 Weigh the pros and cons

In groups, discuss the advantages and drawbacks of the online and the printed press.

Help!

Online press	Printed press
on the spot: *sur-le-champ* interactive communication free: *gratuit* superficial /suːpəˈfɪʃəl/ = shallow filter out: *passer au crible*	in-depth (information): *en profondeur* thorough /ˈθʌrə/: *minutieux, détaillé* expensive investigate check facts: *vérifier les faits*

4 New challenges CD WB

Listen to Barack Obama's speech at the White House Correspondents' Association Dinner.

a. Get ready and read the phonetic transcriptions aloud and write the words they correspond to.
/pəˈsuː/ /ˈswiːpɪŋ/ /ˈreslɪŋ/ /dɪˈmɒkrəsi/ /kənˈtend/ /tʌf/ /kəˈmɪtmənts/

b. What is President Obama's message here?

c. List the problems President Obama mentions in his speech.

d. Is the overall tone of his speech: pessimistic • optimistic • confident • distrustful • threatening • serious • light *(léger)* • supportive • critical? Justify your choices.

1. TABLOIDS VS. QUALITY PRESS

1 Newspapers

a. Each group will concentrate on one front page. Observe it and fill in the following grid on a separate sheet of paper.

b. Then compare your results.

01EU INT

SLIP

Daily Mail

PRINTED IN EUROPE SATURDAY

SATURDAY, JUNE 27, 2009

www.dailymail.co.uk

€2.50

After 25 years under lock and key, the memoirs that could rock the Royals

Last secrets of the Queen Mum's favourite spy

PAGES 44-45

Was star killed by an injection to ease his pain?

POLICE TO QUESTION JACKSON DOCTOR

By **Michael Seamark** and **David Gardner** in Los Angeles

POLICE in Los Angeles were preparing to question one of Michael Jackson's doctors last night.

The move followed claims that, only minutes before he died, the star was given an injection of a painkiller which can cause cardiac arrest. The doctor, named as cardiologist Conrad Robert Murray, was said to have tried to revive Jackson, then disappeared for several hours.

Sources said the singer had been using the drug, Demerol, as he battled to be fit for his first London show next month. The heart specialist had been living at his rented house.

The new mystery over Jackson's sudden death came as:

- Debbie Rowe, the mother of two of his three children, vowed to fight 'tooth and nail' for custody against the singer's mother Katherine;
- Creditors began staking their

Turn to Page 2

Mourned by millions: Makeshift shrines were set up around the world after Michael Jackson's death

Name of the paper
Date of publication
Topic(s) dealt with
Layout: - Space given to the article - Space given to the photographs - Size of the characters - Colours
Adjectives to qualify the headline
Aspect(s) focused on
Target audience
Conclusion: quality paper or popular paper / tabloid?

Help!

The press

news *(indénombrable): nouvelle*
tabloid /tæblɔɪd/
gossip *(indénombrable): ragot*
sensational event
story involving public figures
in-depth (information): *en profondeur*
spectacular detail
headline
subheading: *sous-titre*
bold characters: *lettres en gras*
capital letters
inquisitive: *curieux*
biased /baɪəst/ ≠ neutral
unearth/dig out: *déterrer*
stalk /stɔːk/: *traquer sans relâche*
hint: *insinuer*

PREPARE YOUR TASK

2 Your press review

Go on the following websites:

WEBBOX

The Times: www.thetimes.co.uk/tto/news
The Guardian: www.guardian.co.uk
The Mirror: www.mirror.co.uk
USA Today: www.usatoday.com

Skim through the homepage, select one news item you are interested in. Read the whole article. Then make a short oral account of it, and justify your choice.

A GROWING SCARCITY MOTIVATES ART BUYERS
PAGE 16 | WEEKEND ARTS

DREAMS DIE AS DETROIT GEARS DOWN
PAGE 12 | BUSINESS

International Herald Tribune
WEEKEND

NEW BABY? COLLEGE BILLS LOOM
INSIDE | SPECIAL REPORT

THE STORY OF HOW GOD GREW UP AND MELLOWED
PAGE 20 | WEEKEND ARTS

VARDA'S CINEMATIC MEMOIR
PAGE 17 | WEEKEND ARTS

International Herald Tribune

THE GLOBAL EDITION OF THE NEW YORK TIMES

SATURDAY-SUNDAY, JUNE 27-28, 2009

GLOBAL.NYTIMES.COM

Michael Jackson performing during his "HIStory World Tour" concert in Vienna. The pop star, one of the best-selling artists of all times, died before he could stage a comeback tour.

U.S. and Russia split on cyber peril

Both see urgent threat but differ on way to fight criminal activity online

BY JOHN MARKOFF AND ANDREW E. KRAMER

Superstar, recluse and a paradox

NEW YORK

BY JON PARELES

Michael Jackson at 13, singing in his home.

A kinder view at the end of a troubled life

LONDON

BY JULIA WERDIGIER, MATTHEW SALTMARSH AND SHARON OTTERMAN

Iran authorities say vote is 'healthiest' in 3 decades

TEHRAN

BY NAZILA FATHI AND ALAN COWELL

Saturday 27 June 2009

International Edition

THE INDEPENDENT

Jackson: the plot thickens

> Police seal off home amid reports prescription drugs caused his death

> Doctors await results of toxicology tests to establish what he had taken

> Performer had complained about physical strain of upcoming tour

News and analysis 2-11
Andy Gill 8-9
David Hepworth 10-11

PLUS WIN THE COMPLETE SET OF MICHAEL JACKSON'S ALBUMS. SEE PAGE 46

PREPARE YOUR TASK

3 You are the editor

a. Decide what type of paper you work for: quality paper or tabloid.

b. Choose a recent event.

c. Find a photo to illustrate this event and write the caption under the photo.

d. Write the headline and the first paragraph.

2. A MEDIA STAR

1 Get ready

a. Read the definition of the expression "media training":

> preparation, including counselling and rehearsal, given to somebody before an interview by the media or an appearance on radio or television.

b. What tips would you give to somebody appearing on TV for the first time?

Part 1

Ten years ago this month I got a phone call from an American publisher telling me that they had just bought one of my books and were going to send me on a three-week, sixteen-city publicity tour.

"We're going to make you a media star," he said brightly.

"But I've never been on TV," I protested in mild panic.

"Oh, it's easy. You'll love it," he said with the blithe assurance[1] of someone who doesn't have to do it himself.

"No, I'll be terrible," I insisted. "I have no personality." "Don't worry, we'll give you a personality. We're going to fly you to New York for a course of media training." [...]

1. *(ici) tranquille certitude*

Part 2

So I flew to New York and, as it turned out, the media training was less of an ordeal[1] than I had feared. I was put in the hands of a kindly, patient man named Bill Parkhurst, who sat with me for two days in a windowless studio somewhere in Manhattan and put me through an endless series of mock[2] interviews. [...]

In one five-day period, I flew from San Francisco to Atlanta to Chicago to Boston and back to San Francisco. I once flew from Denver to Colorado Springs in order to do a 30-second interview which – I swear – went like this:

Interviewer: "Our guest today is Bill Bryson. So you've got a new book out, have you, Bill?"

Me: "That's right."

Interviewer: "Well, that's wonderful. Thanks so much for coming." [...]

In three weeks I gave over 250 interviews of one type or another and never once met anyone who had read my book or had the faintest[3] idea who I was. At one radio station the interviewer covered the microphone with his hand just before we went on and said: "Now tell me, are you the guy who was abducted[4] by aliens or are you the travel writer?"

The whole point, as Bill Parkhurst taught me, is to sell yourself shamelessly, and believe me, you soon learn to do it.

Bill Bryson, *Notes from a Big Country*, 1998

1. *épreuve* 2. *fausses / fictives*
3. *la moindre* 4. was kidnapped

PREPARE YOUR TASK

2 Main facts

Read the text and discuss with the class what you have understood.

3 Recap

a. Part one

Sum up all the information given about the narrator: name • job • his media experience • his worries and feelings.

b. Part two

What have you learnt about the publicity tour?
Explain why the two anecdotes related are surprising.

c. What image of the media is given here?

d. Conclude

Is the text: critical • dramatic • thrilling • humorous • poetic • informative (several answers possible)? Justify your answers.

e. Speak in chains

Give an oral account of the text with the help of your notes only.

- He doesn't believe he will...
- He fears that he might + V
- He finds it... that people should...
- He is worried about V-ING...
- He ends up thinking that...

Help!

Narrator	Publicity tour	Interpretation
inexperienced /ɪnɪks'pɪərɪənst/ shy: *timide* dumbfounded /dʌm'faʊndɪd/: *abasourdi* dread: *redouter* narrate one's experience fear + ... + might + V: *craindre que*	entertaining /entə'teɪnɪŋ/ last: *durer* promote /prə'məʊt/ give an account /ə'kaʊnt/ of talk sb into + V-ING: *persuader qqn de faire qqch*	fake / sham: *faux / artificiel* superficial = shallow reliable /rɪ'laɪəbl/: *sur lequel on peut compter* pathetic: *minable* make fun of = laugh at

4 Translation workshop WB

Translate from "So I flew to New York..." (Part two, l. 1) down to the end of the paragraph.
Turn to your Workbook for help.

Video

5 Watch a video

News on the march

Watch this extract from *Citizen Kane* (Orson Welles, 1941).

Get ready

a. What immediately strikes you in the photo?

b. What angle shot is used? What is the impact on the viewer? (→ see p. 245)

c. Concentrate on the man (job • looks • feelings • personality • career • achievements • ambitions).

d. Judging from the photo, imagine what the scene deals with.
Turn to your worksheet for help.

3. IF IT BLEEDS, IT LEADS

1

2

"Oh, my God—I'm having an affair!"

3

1 Group work: Look and analyse one cartoon

What are the artist's goals in each document?

2 Class work: React

a. What do these cartoons have in common? Justify the title at the top of the page.
b. Which of these three cartoons do you find the most: striking • shocking • true-to-life • cynical? Justify your answers.

REPARE OUR TASK →

3 Writing workshop WB

Turn to your Workbook for help.
a. You are a reporter in a country devastated by an earthquake or a hurricane. Write the article corresponding to what you have seen (120 words).
b. The media (television, newspapers, the Internet...) do not always respect people's sufferings and private lives. Do you share this view? Give examples (200 words).

Help!

Cartoon 1	Cartoon 2	Cartoon 3
hype: *médiatisation* numerous /ˈnjuːmərəs/: *nombreux* sensational /senˈseɪʃənl/ invade tell lies ≠ tell the truth denounce /dɪˈnaʊns/ = expose /ɪkˈspəʊz/ investigate: *enquêter* be eager to: *être impatient de* hit the headlines: *faire la une* what matters...: *ce qui importe*	gossip: *commérages* stunned: *abasourdi* inquisitive: *curieux / fureteur* have an affair with sb: *avoir une liaison avec qqn* cheat on / be unfaithful to: *tromper / être infidèle à* disclose: *révéler* exploit (the public taste for) increase the circulation harm / ruin sb's reputation	earthquake: *tremblement de terre* on the look-out for...: *à l'affût de...* desperate /ˈdespərɪt/ upset: *bouleversé* be in dire straits: *être dans le plus grand besoin* cover an event: *couvrir un événement* focus /ˈfəʊkəs/ on = concentrate on boost sales: *développer les ventes* make a profit

4. THE TRUTH

Folarin is a journalist, whose wife has just been killed. Sade and her little brother listen to the conversation between their uncle and father.

"They're not finished with you, Folarin! They won't stop until they've shut you up. You know what that means! You've gone too far with them now."

Their father always took chances with what he wrote. He said nothing now, but Sade knew his words.

The truth is the truth. How can I write what's untrue?

Sade knew how worried Mama had been about his latest article. But Sade had never heard Mama try to stop him, like Uncle Tunde did.

Their uncle stretched across the desk to pick up a newspaper. One hand resting on their father's shoulder, he began to read aloud: "Why do the Brass Buttons[1] who rule over us spend millions of naira[2] sending their children to the most expensive schools and colleges in England and America? How does a soldier – even a general – acquire so much money? And what about our own schools and colleges here in Nigeria? Our Brass Button generals shut them down when teachers complain they have not been paid and when students complain they have no books. It seems they can still sleep easily in their beds even though hundreds of thousands of our own children are not being taught. What a disgrace for a country that held some of the finest universities and schools in Africa! But then our Commander-in-Chief believes more in buttons than brains."

Normally Papa would have flared up[3].

Every word of that is true.

But today he was mute. His face was turned to the window that overlooked the front gate where the car had stopped. Their uncle slid the newspaper back on to the desk.

"You call your article 'Our Children's Future'. What do you imagine will happen to your own, Folarin?" [...]

"Look, Folarin, we all know how brave you are. Braver than most of us. But are you wise? You say our country must have writers to tell the truth. But tell me, what can you write from the grave[4]?"

Beverley Naidoo, *The Other Side of Truth*, 2000

1. the Nigerian army **2.** Nigerian currency / money **3.** *serait entré dans une violente colère* **4.** *tombe*

PREPARE YOUR TASK

1 Find the key information WB

a. Read the text and discuss with the class what you have understood. Then read the text again and turn to your Workbook for help.

b. Recap.

– Concentrate on the article written by Folarin. Explain the situation in his country.
– How does Uncle Tunde react to this article? What does he think of his brother? Why?
– Focus on Sade's comments about her father's attitude. What are her feelings?

PREPARE YOUR TASK

2 Jumbled text WB

The paragraphs of an essay have been jumbled. Reorder them.

Build up your vocabulary

1 **Recopiez cette carte mentale et complétez-la avec les mots correspondant aux définitions.**

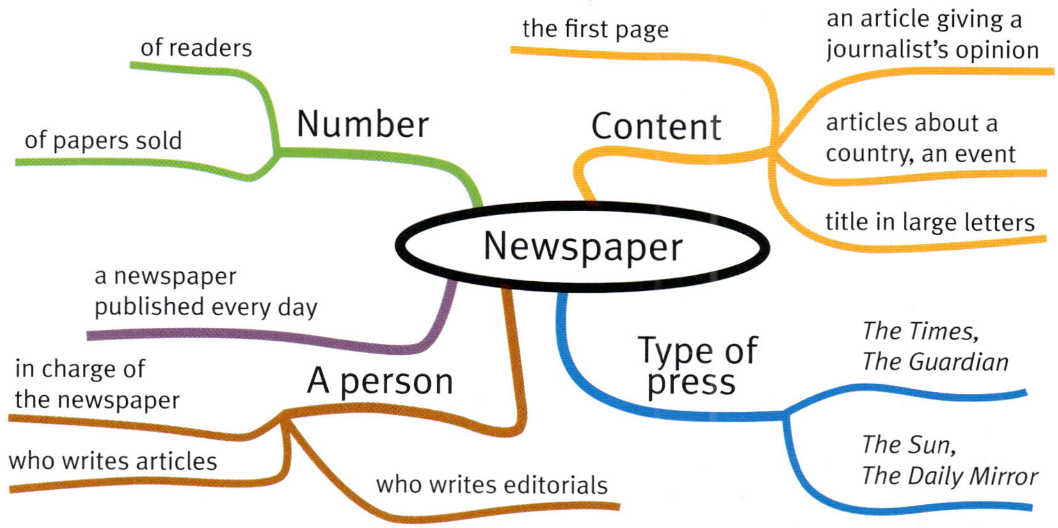

2 **Classez ces mots en deux colonnes. Utilisez un dictionnaire si nécessaire.**

- investigate
- break sth
- cover an event
- exploit the public's taste for scandals
- check a source
- inform
- reveal / disclose the truth
- cover up a scandal
- libel
- intrude upon people's private lives

Devoirs des journalistes	Dérives possibles

3 **Il manque certains mots dans ces titres. Lesquels ? À quelles catégories grammaticales appartiennent-ils ? Réécrivez les phrases complètes.**

MEDIA FREEDOM THREATENED

> French footballer expelled from team

French accused of Pacific nuclear cover-up

Asylum seekers claim abuse on flight

Footballer jailed for false injury claim

4 **Transformez ces énoncés complets en titres de journaux.**

a. *Computers are blamed because more and more pupils are illiterate.*
b. *There is a big row over the new carbon tax.*
c. *Talks will soon resume between the two countries at war.*
d. *New measures will be taken to cut drug abuse.*

Les subordonnées de cause, de concession (bien que, malgré) et de contraste (alors que)

1 **Structurez une phrase.**

Dites quelle est la relation exprimée par chacun des mots en gras dans les énoncés suivants (opposition • cause • concession). Puis classez-les dans le tableau ci-dessous :

Phrase	Relation	Mots de liaison en anglais

a. ***Although*** *there is an epidemic, the sales are not increasing.*
b. ***In spite of*** *the epidemic, sales are not increasing.*
c. ***Even though*** *everybody is concerned, people are not interested.*
d. *The epidemic should scare people,* ***however*** *they don't panic.*
e. *The editor expected people to be scared,* ***and yet*** *they weren't.*
f. *He expected sales to increase,* ***whereas*** *they have dropped.*
g. ***As*** *the news was important, it made the headlines.*
h. ***Since*** *everybody was concerned, the journalists decided to warn the public.*

2 **Observez et comparez.**

a. *In spite of the big headlines, people are not attracted by the newspaper.*
b. *Although the headlines are big, people are not attracted by the newspaper.*
c. *Despite all the editor's efforts, his strategy has failed.*
d. *Although the editor has made a lot of effort, his strategy has failed.*

– *In spite of* et *despite* sont-ils suivis d'un groupe nominal seul ou d'une proposition complète (GN + GV + ...) ?

– *Although* /ɔːlˈðəʊ/ est-il suivi d'un groupe nominal seul, d'un groupe verbal ou d'une proposition complète (GN + GV + ...) ?

3 **Traduisez tous les énoncés de l'exercice 2. en français.**

4 ***Whereas*** /wɛərˈæz/ **ou *although* ?**

Traduisez ces deux phrases puis comparez leur sens.

a. *Although it is a big event, very few journalists will cover it.*
b. *The editor thought it was a big event, whereas the other journalists did not.*

"THE PUBLIC AREN'T PANICKING ABOUT BIRD FLU!!!"

Practice

1 Complétez ces phrases avec : *although* • *in spite of* • *despite* • *however* • *and yet* • *since*.

A journalist is reporting live while a fire is raging, and firemen are trying to put out the fire.
... many people may die or be seriously injured, the journalist is only focusing on media stars.
... there will be a lot of casualties, the journalist is only concerned with celebrities.
... the danger, the reporter is only interested in the stars' fate.
He is not worried about the ordinary people living in this building. ... their families are.
The journalist should cover the event and give information about the extent of the damage, ... he highlights an insignificant detail.
The report is ridiculous, ... many people will watch it.
... many people are only interested in stars, the report will attract an audience.
... the cartoon is a negative and pessimistic view of journalism, I think it is quite true.

"Luckily, none of the people inside appear to be celebrities."

2 Traduisez ces phrases.

a. Malgré le prix, je continuerai à acheter un journal chaque jour.
b. Il existe de nombreux journaux gratuits, et cependant les gens lisent de moins en moins de presse.
c. Il lit le journal chaque jour, alors que ses enfants ne lisent pas la presse.
d. Bien que cela soit dangereux, de nombreux journalistes se battent pour défendre la liberté de la presse dans les dictatures.
e. Comme ils veulent attirer plus de lecteurs, certains journaux publient des articles sur les gens célèbres.
f. Comme la presse a beaucoup de pouvoir, on l'appelle souvent le quatrième pouvoir.

Improve your pronunciation

1 À quel mot correspond chacune des transcriptions phonétiques suivantes ? Transcrivez-les sur papier libre.

a. /ˈdʒɜːnəlɪzəm/
b. /fəˈtɒgrəfə^{r}/
c. /ˈɑːtɪkl/
d. /ˈpʌblɪʃ/
e. /ɪˈvent/
f. /məˈnɪpjʊleɪt/
g. /ˈtæblɔɪd/
h. /ˈkwɒlɪti peɪpə^{r}/
i. /mægəˈziːn/
j. /rɪˈvjuː/
k. /ɪnˈtruːʒən/
l. /ˈkʌvərɪdʒ/

2 Utilisez les transcriptions phonétiques pour classer ces mots dans un tableau de ce type. Sont-ils accentués sur la première, la seconde ou la troisième syllabe ?

Première syllabe	Deuxième syllabe	Troisième syllabe

3 Lisez ces mots à haute voix. Puis vérifiez à l'écoute. MP3 8

YOUR TASK

Read the two press articles opposite. Then write a letter to the editor giving your reactions to one of the articles.

LES ÉTAPES À SUIVRE

1 Avant la lecture

Repérez les éléments importants.

GAME POINT
Edwin Moses

Why Baseball Is in Denial

Titre

Premières phrases résumant le contenu de l'article

DRUGS IN SPORTS ARE ON THE MIND OF JUST ABOUT EVERY SPORTS fan these days, at least in the United States. Earlier this year I was invited to speak at a high school in Atlanta, and one of the first questions concerned the issue of Michael Phelps, the Olympic star who lost some of his luster after being photographed recently with a marijuana pipe at a party. Meanwhile, the media are filled with stories about New York Yankees superstar Alex Rodriguez, baseball's highest-paid player, who has admitted having used banned performance-enhancing steroids several years ago.

Illustrations permettant d'anticiper le contenu de l'article

While the Phelps story will pass—authorities have decided not to press charges—the saga of A-Rod, as he is known, once again throws baseball and U.S. professional sports back into the glare of the drug-testing spotlight. Whatever is ultimately revealed—and we have now found out that there were another 103 baseball players who tested positive in 2003—I am pessimistic that anything will change. Baseball is in a period of denial.

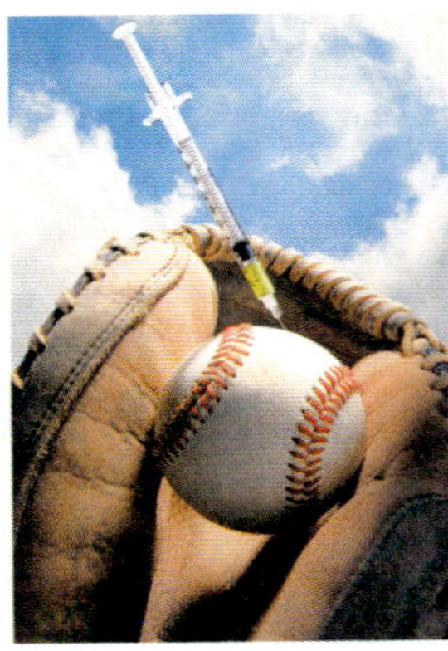

To understand why, consider the contrast with amateur sports and the Olympics, where athletes must make themselves available for random drug tests by telling the governing bodies where they are going to be over a period of time. Experts from the World Anti-Doping Authority can turn up and require athletes to be tested anywhere, any time. True, the system remains imperfect. For evidence, just look at the number of Olympic medalists who were sanctioned between the Sydney Olympics and Athens, and between Athens and Beijing. But at least Olympic officials are using their weapons to fight drugs, and have shown themselves willing to ban top athletes for up to two years for violations.

By contrast, professional sports merely attempts to "manage the issue." In baseball, the penalty for using banned steroids has been increased to a minimum 50-game suspension for a first offense. But with no random testing, there is little chance of being caught. Can anything change? When I helped devise anti-doping policies for the U.S. Olympic Committee, between 1989 and 1994, Donald Fehr, executive director of the Major League Baseball Players Association, used to come to all the meetings. I explained how drug testing worked in the amateur-sports world. But he seems not to have gotten the message. Fifteen years later, steroid use is still rampant, and random drug testing remains a nonstarter.

Noms et chiffres donnant des informations essentielles sur le sujet

The reality is that there's too much money in baseball and in other professional sports to allow a more aggressive approach. There are too many vested interests, too many people who want to keep things as they are. The players' union wants to protect the players. There are corporate sponsors of baseball parks who don't want to see their home team sullied by a positive test. Each club has a TV contract, players get paid millions and there are advertising revenues and seat sales. The need for more home runs and power pitching goes right down to the hot-dog concessions.

Sports fans might ask why government can't do something about it. Congressional hearings were held last summer, after George Mitchell came out with his report on doping in baseball, but the politicians just pontificated and then sat back down. Politicians want new stadiums built for their constituents, and photo opportunities with the big-name pro sports stars. At the end of the day, big sports generate tax revenue. Politicians know what's going on in baseball, but, like most people, they don't want to go near it.

The question, then, is how far authorities and fans want to go to know that athletes are clean—or will they always accept performance over integrity? That's what I discussed with those kids at the Atlanta high school. My message to them is that regardless of all the distractions they are forced to deal with in their daily lives, they need to concentrate on going to college, and avoiding drugs, teenage pregnancy, domestic violence and crime. After all, most will never become professional athletes. Yet they do pay attention to sports, and the conduct of the competitors has a huge impact on their lives.

Premières phrases de chaque paragraphe donnant l'idée générale

So I tried to make those kids realize they can still achieve what they want without resorting to recreational drugs (as Phelps appeared to be doing) or performance-enhancing ones (as A-Rod admitted to doing). These kids deserve to know that this is possible, and baseball and the rest of professional sports can help by doing the right thing, right now.

There's too much money in the game for a more aggressive approach on steroids.

Phrase sous la photo apportant des informations supplémentaires et résumant souvent l'article

MOSES *is the chairman of the Laureus World Sports Academy (laureus.com), and a gold-medal winner of the 400-meter hurdles in the 1976 Montreal and 1984 Los Angeles Olympic Games.*

54

MIKE POWELL—ALLSPORT-GETTY IMAGES, DEBORAH VAN KIRK—GETTY IMAGES

2 Au cours de la lecture

Appuyez-vous sur les mots transparents (mots proches du français). Déduisez le sens des mots inconnus à l'aide du contexte ou en les décomposant (dérivation, composition).

3 Après la lecture

a. Faites un compte rendu de chaque article (thème abordé, position défendue, arguments donnés).

b. Réagissez en écrivant au courrier des lecteurs – *Letters to the editor* – (120 mots environ). Indiquez l'article choisi et dites ce que vous approuvez ou désapprouvez.

BAN ONLINE SALES OF STEROIDS, SAYS DRUGS WATCHDOG

The sale of anabolic steroids over the Internet should be banned to deter boys as young as 12 from becoming obsessed by the bulge of their muscles, the Government's drugs advisers said yesterday.
The growing misuse of the drugs by people seeking to bulk up their bodies was a "worrying development" which carried "significant risks", the Advisory Council on the Misuse of Drugs (ACMD) said. But it rejected demands that criminal sanctions should be applied to users of the drugs in the run-up to the London 2012 Olympics. Prosecution is currently limited to dealers, traffickers and manufacturers who profit from the trade in anabolic steroids, and the ACMD said users should continue to be dealt with through education and medical care, not the courts.
An estimated 14,500 schoolchildren aged 11 to 15 used anabolic steroids in the past year, the ACMD said. Among adults, there were 50,000 users aged 16 to 59, according to the British Crime Survey. Most users are in their twenties, and men outnumber women by 10 to one.
Anabolic steroids contain the male hormone testosterone, providing a chemical shortcut to strength and endurance, and are favoured by sprinters and weightlifters for whom raw power is key to winning. But they can also damage the heart [and] cause breast enlargement.
[...] Dr James Brown, founder of the Association of Doctors in Sport, said: "Go into any gym which is predominantly focused on weightlifting and you will find someone who knows about anabolic steroids. Body image is driving this – the pressure on young people to look good and impress the opposite sex is immense. Everybody has to have a six-pack." [...]
"The manufacturers are not regulated, so no one knows what is in them. They are very easy to get hold of," he said. [...]
Professor Les Iversen, ACMD chairman, said: "The misuse and rising prevalence of anabolic steroids is a worrying development. More needs to be done to tackle the supply of anabolic steroids and to educate people of the potential dangers."

■ *The Independent*, September 22, 2010

Why Baseball Is in Denial

There's too much money in the game for a more aggressive approach on steroids.

Drugs in sports are on the mind of just about every sports fan these days, at least in the United States. Earlier this year I was invited to speak at a high school in Atlanta, and one of the first questions concerned the issue of Michael Phelps, the Olympic star who lost some of his luster after being photographed recently with a marijuana pipe at a party. [...]

Authorities have decided not to press charges. [...] Whatever is ultimately revealed—and we have now found out that there were another 103 baseball players who tested positive in 2003—I am pessimistic that anything will change. Baseball is in a period of denial. [...]

The reality is that there's too much money in baseball and in other professional sports to allow a more aggressive approach. [...] The players' union wants to protect the players. [...] Each club has a TV contract, players get paid millions and there are advertising revenues and seat sales. [...]

The question, then, is how far authorities and fans want to go to know that athletes are clean—or will they always accept performance over integrity? That's what I discussed with those kids at the Atlanta high school. My message to them is that regardless of all the distractions they are forced to deal with in their daily lives, they need to concentrate on going to college, and avoiding drugs, teenage pregnancy, domestic violence and crime. After all, most will never become professional athletes. Yet they do pay attention to sports, and the conduct of the competitors has a huge impact on their lives.

So I tried to make those kids realize they can still achieve what they want without resorting to recreational drugs [...] or performance-enhancing ones. [...] These kids deserve to know that this is possible, and baseball and the rest of professional sports can help by doing the right thing, right now.

■ By Edwin Moses, *Newsweek*, March 2, 2009

E. Moses is the chairman of the Laureus World Sports Academy and a gold medal finalist of the 400-meter hurdles in the 1976 Montreal and 1984 Los Angeles Olympic Games.

Reading *corner*

SEVEN O'CLOCK NEWS

Folarin Solaja is a Nigerian journalist. After the murder of his wife, he sent his two children to Great Britain to save their lives. He later entered the UK illegally and was sent to a detention centre. His two children managed to contact a BBC journalist to help their father get political asylum.

Sade sank into the sofa. Mr. Seven O'Clock was behind his desk waiting for the fanfare of music to stop. If nothing else, she liked his tie. It was pleasantly bright – pawpaw orange shading into a sunset of red, pink and purple. Papa disliked wearing ties, but even he might like this one. They hadn't spoken for a couple of days. Was he still bothering[1] to get people to watch this news?

Suddenly Sade sat bolt upright[2]. Papa was smiling from a large square behind Mr. Seven O'Clock! A much younger Papa, but definitely their father!

"Femi! Look!"

Femi swivelled around[3].

"A Nigerian journalist, Mr. Folarin Solaja, currently being detained after attempting to enter Britain illegally, is at the centre of a growing dispute. A spokesman for the Nigerian government has said that Mr. Solaja is wanted for murder and should be returned to Nigeria. Mr. Solaja, however, is claiming political asylum. Coming so soon after the execution of the Nigerian writer Mr. Ken Saro-Wiwa[4], the case is politically sensitive. Mr. Nelson Mandela, President of South Africa, has continued to urge a tougher line against Nigeria's military dictators. But here in Britain the government has been taking a tougher line against asylum seekers[5] claiming that many are not genuine[6] refugees. To discuss the situation, we have in the studio Tara Mosam, a writer and film-maker, who has recently returned from Nigeria where she followed the case of Ken Saro-Wiwa. Tara Mosam, first of all, what do you know of Folarin Solaja?" [...]

"Folarin Solaja is well known within Nigeria as one of a small band of very courageous journalists who still dare to tell the truth about abuses of human rights by the Military Government. He writes for the small but important weekly paper *Speak*, which has been playing a dangerous cat and mouse game with the authorities. The newspaper's staff have moved their offices several times to avoid being closed down by the police. But unlike Ken Saro-Wiwa, Mr. Solaja is not well known outside Nigeria."

"What events actually led him to seek asylum here?" Mr. Seven O'Clock leaned slightly forward like he had done across the table a few nights earlier.

"About five weeks ago there was an attempt on his life[7]. Unknown gunmen called at his house, fatally shooting his wife instead of him. Apparently he had been receiving death-threats for some time but had ignored them. However, after the assassination of his wife, he went into hiding. The Home Office[8] say that he was arrested a couple of weeks ago trying to enter through London Airport on a false passport. They say that he did not declare on arrival that he was a political refugee and that he did not ask for political asylum until his identity was challenged. So they intend to deport him."

"Is there anything stopping them?"

1. *s'évertuait* **2.** *se redressa* **3.** *se retourna* **4.** a well-known opponent to the Nigerian government who was executed in 1995
5. *demandeurs d'asile* **6.** *vrais* **7.** *on a attenté à sa vie* **8.** *le Ministère de l'Intérieur*

"Mr. Solaja has appealed on the grounds that his life will be in danger if he is returned to Nigeria and also that his children are here in England. He says they were smuggled[9] here immediately after their mother's death. But the Home Office claims to have no record of them."

Mr. Seven O'Clock looked grave. Was he going to say that he had actually met them? Tell everyone watching that the Home Office was wrong. Sade felt blood flush to her face.

"I gather that there is a warrant[10] out for Mr. Solaja's arrest in Nigeria." Mr. Seven O'Clock was straightening up.

"Yes, a further twist. Mr. Solaja has now been accused of murdering his wife and Nigeria wants him extradited. Already some Nigerians are saying that the murder charge is an attempt to throw a cloak over[11] the real assassins. But of course it would be extremely dangerous for Folarin Solaja if he were to be deported. As you know, there was a great deal of criticism about the trial of Ken Saro-Wiwa and his colleagues."

"Well, I imagine we shall be hearing more of this case. Thank you very much, Tara Mosam. After the break we shall – "

Uncle Roy began to clap.

"Congratulations, children! My goodness! You actually did it!"

"But he didn't say it was us – that we told him!" Femi looked confused.

"Our English teacher says you have to stick to the main points," explained Sade.

"That was probably it," Aunt Gracie said gently. "But now that your daddy is in the news, it won't be so easy for them to send him straight back!"

Beverley Naidoo, *The Other Side of Truth*, 2000

9. *on les a fait entrer illégalement* **10.** *mandat d'arrêt* **11.** *(ici) couvrir*

Unit 6

BLACK IS BEAUTIFUL

YOUR TASK AT THE END OF THIS UNIT

You are a film director. Write the scenario based on the scene you will read. → p. 100

TUNE IN!

1 Observe and react

a. What elements immediately strike you?
b. Where (country, place) and when do you think this picture was taken?
c. Explain the situation.
d. What is the impact on the viewer? What were the photographer's goals?
e. What laws are enforced here? Turn to your Workbook for help. WB

Help!

Setting	Situation	Impact
drinking fountain /ˈdrɪŋkɪŋ ˈfaʊntɪn/ = water cooler restroom (US) = lavatory (GB) sink (US): *lavabo* tap /tæp/ (GB) = faucet /ˈfɑːsɪt/ (US): *robinet* lean over /liːn ˈəʊvəʳ/: *se pencher sur* drink from: *boire à*	law-abiding: *respectueux des lois* ban sb from V-ING ≠ allow sb to + BV have the right to be compelled to = be forced to be allowed to ≠ be forbidden to be segregated be separated /ˈsepəreɪtɪd/ share: *partager*	harsh reality: *dure réalité* shocking unbelievable degrading = humiliating amazing: *étonnant* remind sb of sth: *rappeler qqch à qqn*

2 Merry-Go-Round

Where is the Jim Crow section
On this merry-go-round[1],
Mister, cause I want to ride?
Down South where I come from
White and colored
Can't sit side by side.
Down South on the train
There's a Jim Crow car.
On the bus we're put in the back–
But there ain't[2] no back
To a merry-go-round!
Where's the horse
For a kid that's black?

Langston Hughes, *The Collected Poems of Langston Hughes*, 1994

1. *manège* 2. /eɪnt/ = isn't

Jean-Michel Basquiat, *Jim Crow*, 1986 (206cm x 244cm)

a. Who is the narrator (approximate age, ethnic group)?

b. Where does he / she come from? Guess where he / she is now.

c. Explain the situation in trains and on buses in the South. What laws are referred to here? Turn to your Workbook for help. WB

d. What is unusual from the narrator's point of view? Why? What are his / her feelings and reactions?

3 A historical landmark

a. Look at the photo. Where and when does the scene take place? Who are the two people? What are they doing?

b. Focus on the title and the sentence in red.
– What does the "v." stand for? What is a "Board of Education"? Guess who "Brown" refers to.
– Explain what happened and why it marks a turning point in US history.

REPARE OUR TASK

c. Learn more: Read the text below and find the three words that are missing.

What caused the case?

In 1951, Linda Brown was denied admission to an all-[1] elementary [2] in Topeka, Kansas. Instead, she was told to attend an all-[3] [2] in another neighborhood. Her father sued[1] the [2] district for not letting his daughter attend the [2] closest to their home. […] The case was appealed to the Supreme Court under the title Brown v. Board of Education of Topeka. Thurgood Marshall, who later became the Supreme Court's first [3] Justice[2], argued that the segregated [2]s violated the 14th Amendment's guarantee of equal protection to all citizens.

1. *poursuivit en justice*
2. *juge de la Cour Suprême*

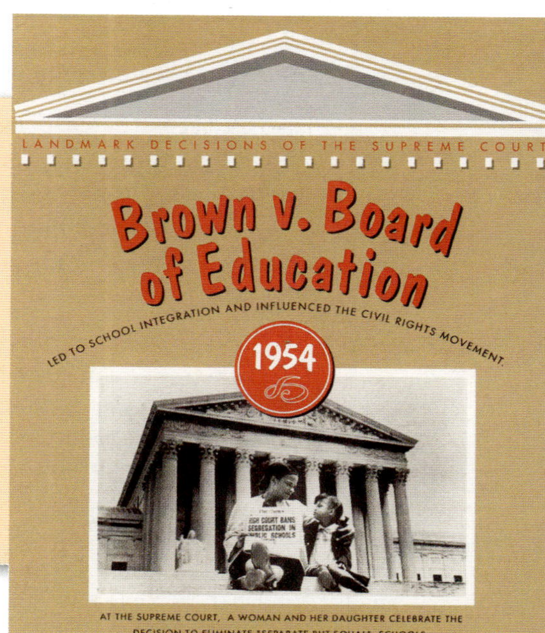

I. MEANS OF PROTEST

1 React to the photo

Sit-ins

Throughout the South, Negroes have adopted a non-violent protest technique that has been dubbed the "sit-in", to combat discrimination at lunch counters, cafeterias, libraries and beaches. The trend toward this type of protest got started on February 1, when four Negro college students refused to move from a Woolworth[1] lunch counter in Greensboro, when they were denied[2] service. The action quickly spread[3] to lunch counters in more than 50 Southern towns. This led to wade-ins[4] at all-white beaches, read-ins at libraries, and kneel-ins[5] at racially segregated churches. Many Negro students have been arrested for the protests, and the National Association for the Advancement of Colored People has stepped in to defend quite a number of them. Among the highly respected people lending their assistance to provide lessons in non-violent protest for students in Greensboro are the Rev. Dr. Martin Luther King Jr., head of the Southern Christian Leadership Conference, George Simpkins, the N.A.A.C.P. aide, and Len Holt of the Congress of Racial Equality. Sit-ins at Nashville, Tennessee, led to 76 arrests, but they have forced politicians and businessmen to deal with the Negro community and a favorable decision is believed[6] to be near.

■ *Sit-ins, cutting edge in a war on bias*, Greensboro, N.C., 1960

1. *chaîne de magasins* 2. refused 3. *s'est propagée* 4. *résistance passive, debout dans l'eau* 5. *résistance passive, agenouillés* 6. *on pense que...*

PREPARE YOUR TASK

2 Find the key information

a. Pick out a region, a State (and locate it on a map), the names of two towns and five different places.
b. Find a date.
c. Which event triggered off the movement of protest?
d. Find three numbers. What do they refer to?
e. List four different forms of resistance. Pick out one adjective characterizing them.
f. Name one famous person and one organization involved in the fight for equality.

3 Recap

Speak from your notes and include the following points:
– Sum up what you have learnt about the organization of protest (places, cause, actions taken, immediate consequences).
– Is the article optimistic or pessimistic? Why?

4 Writing workshop

Franklin E. McCain, one of the four activists of the Greensboro sit-ins, keeps a diary. Write the entry for February 1st (80 words).

2. FAMOUS LEADERS

1 Unfulfilled dreams

Listen to Martin Luther King talking in 1968. Turn to your Workbook for help. WB

2 Take it

a. Share with the class all what you know about Malcolm X.

b. Which of the following words do you expect to hear in the recording?

- action
- America
- equality
- rights
- slaves
- citizens
- freedom
- assert one's rights
- fight = struggle
- non-violence

c. Now listen to Malcolm X and turn to your Workbook for help. WB

3 Oral account

Give a two-minute account of each recording. Just use notes. Include the following points:

a. Martin Luther King

– What are Martin Luther King and his friends fighting for?
– What difficulties do they meet?
– What should they do to succeed?
– Is this speech optimistic or pessimistic? Justify.

b. Malcolm X

– Who is Malcolm X talking to? What about?
– What historical event does he refer to?
– What problem are African-Americans confronted with today? What do they want?
– What do they need to reach their goal?

c. Compare the two leaders' speeches. Are their goals similar or different? Justify your answer.

PREPARE YOUR TASK

4 Websearch

Find out more information about some famous leaders of the Civil Rights Movement either in an encyclopedia or on the Internet.
Points to include: place and date of birth, social background, education, major achievements, awards, date and circumstances of death.
Then report to the class.

- **Group 1** will work on Rosa Parks and what happened in Montgomery in 1955.
www.teacher.scholastic.com/rosa/sittingdown.htm

- **Group 2** will concentrate on Martin Luther King and what happened in Selma in 1965.
www.historycentral.com/Sixties/Selma.html

- **Group 3** will study Malcolm X and the Black Panthers.
www.malcolmx.com/about/bio.html

3. THE FREEDOM RIDERS

1 Get ready

a. What immediately strikes you when you look at this picture?

b. Before reading it, say in two or three sentences what the following text may deal with.

2 A diary page

Read the extracts A to F from the *The Freedom Writers Diary* (1999). The paragraphs have been mixed up. Reorder them in chronological order. What clues helped you?

A Hundreds of them surrounded the bus, some carried bats or metal poles, and others held vicious German shepherds[1], growling and ready to attack these unarmed people. The mob[2] was just waiting to get their hands on the riders. The Freedom Riders were barricaded on the bus. The mob, armed and hungry to attack, was just waiting for their first victim to step off that bus.

1. *bergers allemands* **2.** *foule (hostile)*

B There were seven Whites and six Blacks on the bus, most of them college students. They were called the Freedom Riders, and their goal was to change segregated interstate travel, along with everyone's life forever. The Freedom Riders had faith that what they were doing was right, and they wanted the world to know that change was necessary and that being tolerant of each other is good.

C Dear Diary,
I feel like I finally have a purpose in this class and in life. That purpose is to make a difference and stand up for a cause. Ms. G[1] showed us a video during Black History Month, about a group of Civil Rights activists, in the 1960s, who were inspired by Rosa Parks. They decided to challenge segregation in the South. Rather than boycott buses, they took their challenge a step farther. They integrated their bus and traveled from Washington, D.C., through the Deep South.

1. /mɪz/ or /məz/ Gruwell is the teacher

D I can picture myself on the road with that bus. I can visualize pulling into the bus station in Montgomery, Alabama, to discover the unsettling quietness. Even though[1] they didn't expect a warm welcome, no one was to be seen at the station, not even the attendants. All of a sudden, Ku Klux Klan[2] members were everywhere.

1. même si 2. organisation clandestine convaincue de la supériorité de la « race blanche »

E By choice, the seating arrangement on the bus was integrated: Blacks sat by Whites, and vice versa. They were breaking a law that had been established in the South. This was unheard of! Jim Zwerg, a white man, stood up from the back of the bus. He wanted to be the first person to step off, even though he knew at the other side of the door was a mob of bigots drooling for[1] a victim. What was he thinking?

1. (ici) fanatiques à l'affût de

F He felt this was his chance to fight back, nonviolently, and show his feelings to others. These strong feelings put his life at risk. Jim took that first step off the bus, and the mob pulled him into their grasp. It was as if he had been swallowed up and disappeared, like bees on honey[1]. Jim was almost beaten to death.

1. miel

3 Find the key information WB

Turn to your Workbook for help.

PREPARE YOUR TASK

4 Storytelling

Group 1

a. Who were the Freedom Riders?

b. What were they fighting for? What was their final goal?

c. What did they decide to do? What problem did they have to face?

Group 2

a. Who is the narrator?

b. Who does he side with? What clues in the text show who he sides with?

c. What is the impact of the Freedom Riders' story on him? In what way has the story changed him?

5 Translation

Translate paragraph F.

6 Testimony

You are Jim Zwerg. A school has asked you to come over and speak about your experience. Explain the reasons why you got involved in the project and the problems you were confronted with.

Video

7 Watch a video

Black Civil Rights in the USA

a. The following words are written phonetically. Read them aloud and write them.
/pə'sjuːt/ /'aʊtlɔːɪŋ/ /fɪ'lænθrəpɪsts/ /sʊ'preməsɪsts/ /ˌʌndə'maɪn/ /məʊ'mentəm/ /deθ θrets/ /ɜːdʒd/ /'tɪə gæs/

b. Watch the video and turn to your worksheet for help.

c. Prepare a two-minute oral account. Use your notes.

4. YES WE CAN

1 Observe and speak

a. What characters can you identify in the picture above? What do they have in common?
b. Give a title and find a caption for the picture.

2 Find the key information WB

a. Read the text and discuss with the class what you have understood.
PREPARE YOUR TASK → **b.** Read the passage again and turn to your Workbook for help.

Part 1

It was a creed[1] written into the founding documents that declared the destiny of a nation,
Yes we can.
It was whispered[2] by slaves and abolitionists as they blazed a trail[3] toward freedom.
Yes we can. Yes we can.
It was sung by immigrants as they struck out from distant shores[4]
And pioneers who pushed westward against an unforgiving wilderness[5].
Yes we can.
It was the call of workers who organized, women who reached for the ballot[6]
A President who chose the moon as our new frontier
And a King who took us to the mountain-top and pointed the way to the Promised Land.
Yes we can. To justice and equality. Yes we can.
Yes we can. To opportunity and prosperity. Yes we can. To opportunity and prosperity.
Yes we can heal this nation. Yes we can repair this world.
Yes we can. Yes we can. Yes we can. Yes we can. *(Si Se Puede)*

1. *credo, croyance* **2.** *murmuré* **3.** *tracèrent avec éclat un chemin* **4.** *rivages*
5. /ˈwɪldənəs/ *nature sauvage* **6.** *bulletin de vote*

Part 2

We know the battle ahead[1] will be long
But always remember that, no matter what obstacles stand in our way,
Nothing can stand in the way of the power of millions of voices calling for change.
(We want change! We want change! I want change)
We have been told we cannot do this by a chorus of cynics who will only grow louder and more dissonant.
We've been asked to pause for a reality check.
We've been warned against offering the people of this nation false hope.
But in the unlikely[2] story that is America, there has never been anything false about hope.
(We want change! I want change!)
The hopes of the little girl who goes to a public school in Dillon
Are the same as the dreams of the boy who learns on the streets of L.A.
We will remember that there is something happening in America,
That we are not as divided as our politics[3] suggest...
That we are one people, we are one nation...
And together, we will begin the next great chapter in the American story with three words that will ring from coast to coast, from sea to shining sea...
Yes. We. Can. Yes we can.

will.i.am and other artists (adapted from Barack Obama's New Hampshire primary night speech), *Yes we can*, 2008

1. *devant nous* **2.** *improbable* **3.** *(ici) vie politique*

3 Recap

Part 1

– What historical events are referred to?
– Who are the key figures mentioned? Say what role they played.
– What goals and qualities did these people have in common?
– According to you, why did Barack Obama refer to these historical events?

Part 2

– How do people feel about the present situation?
– What are the obstacles?
– What image of America is given in this song?

Fast facts

The **Bill of Rights** is the name of the first ten amendments to the United States Constitution. It is a series of limitations on the power of the United States Federal Government. It protects the natural rights of liberty and property including freedom of speech, a free press, free assembly, and free association, but also the right to bear arms.

Help!

Part 1	Part 2
immigration wave trade union: *syndicat* belief: *croyance* fight for one's rights / equality /ɪ'kwɒlɪti/ fulfil one's dream = make one's dream come true succeed in + V-ING = manage to + V overcome difficulties: *surmonter des difficultés*	determined /dɪ'tɜːmɪnd/ truthful = honest struggle = fight unite be committed to sth / V-ING: *s'engager dans / à* evolve stick together: *rester solidaires*

4 Reading aloud CD

Learn how to read Part 2 aloud with the help of the recording.

PREPARE YOUR TASK →

5 Timeline

Recap all the information you have collected here about African-American history. Include dates, events, characters and places. Draw a timeline and present it to the class.

5. CARTOONING HISTORY

THE FRONT OF THE BUS

Oral account

a. Look at the cartoons carefully.
– What events in American history do they refer to?
– What does each cartoon illustrate?
– Give each cartoon a title.

b. Give your point of view. Say which cartoon:
– better illustrates the African-American community's struggle;
– better represents the road to freedom;
– is more optimistic.

c. Report to the class and confront your views with your classmates.

Language at work

Build up your vocabulary

1 Insérez dans chaque phrase un mot formé à partir du radical entre parenthèses et de l'un de ces suffixes.

-ABLE = that can be | -LESS = without | -AL = belonging to | -FUL = full of

a. Though the situation of black people seemed ... (hope), some people decided to rebel.
b. Desegregation would have been impossible without a ... (politic) decision.
c. The attitude of the white supremacists towards the Freedom Riders was not ... (accept).
d. Martin Luther King's speech in Washington D.C. could only raise ... (respect) comments.
e. Martin Luther King could have been ... (resent) after being stoned during a protest march.
f. They kept on fighting ... (regard) of the opposition they constantly encountered.

2 À l'aide d'un dictionnaire, associez chacun des mots de la liste A. à un mot de sens voisin pris dans la liste B.

A give up • emancipate • let • challenge • march • vote • resist • force • fight • fair

B fight back • just • free • struggle • compel • yield • defy • allow • poll • demonstrate

3 Remplacez les mots soulignés par un verbe que vous choisirez dans la liste. Aidez-vous éventuellement d'un dictionnaire. Pensez à faire les changements nécessaires.

glance • march • shout • stare at • whisper

In 1957 Melba Patillo, 15, was one of the nine students who wanted to go to Central High School in Little Rock. When she arrived near the school, angry white men were speaking in a loud voice. She was so scared she walked quickly to the school to escape. She remembers people kept looking at her. She looked quickly at the bodyguard who tried to protect her. Just before getting into the classroom she said thank you very softly.

4 Les verbes ci-dessous font référence au langage du corps *(body language)*, au mouvement et à la gestuelle : *blush* • *frown* • *gasp* • *glare* • *nod*.

a. Dites ce que chacun exprime. Vous pouvez utiliser un dictionnaire.
b. Ensuite, classez-les dans la bonne catégorie : *anger* • *approval* • *embarrassment* • *shock*

5 Faux-amis MP3 9

a. Utilisez le contexte pour trouver le sens des mots soulignés. Attention, il existe en français des mots identiques ou ressemblants, mais leur sens n'est pas le même dans les deux langues. Vérifiez vos réponses à l'aide d'un dictionnaire.
– Gaining equal rights was a very long process.
– For decades Blacks demanded equal rights.
– When the Freedom Riders started their journey they knew they would be in trouble, abused and even threatened.
– Martin Luther King kept telling his audience that Blacks would eventually be equal to Whites. He actually had to wait till 1963.
b. Écoutez chacun de ces énoncés puis lisez-les à haute voix.

Language at work

Prétérit simple – prétérit en *BE + -ING*

1 Observez les énoncés suivants.

a. *The mob was just waiting to get their hands on the riders.*
b. *Hundreds of them surrounded the bus.*
c. *Jim took that first step off the bus.*
d. *When he got off the bus, they were staring at him.*
e. *The Freedom Riders were breaking a law that had been established in the South.*
f. *While the Freedom Riders were waiting at the station, they suddenly saw members of the Ku Klux Klan.*
g. *As I was watching a video about the Civil Rights Movement, I realized that I, too, wanted to stand up for a cause.*

→ Classez les formes verbales en deux colonnes : celles qui renvoient à la totalité d'un événement coupé du présent et celles qui renvoient à une action passée vue dans son déroulement.

2 Traduisez les énoncés du paragraphe 1 puis répondez aux questions suivantes.

– Quel temps utilisez-vous en français pour traduire les formes verbales au prétérit en *BE + -ING* ?
– Quel temps utilisez-vous en français pour traduire les formes verbales au prétérit simple ?

→ Qu'en déduisez-vous ? Complétez la phrase suivante : en général, on traduit le prétérit en *BE + -ING* par un ... en français et le prétérit simple par un ... ... ou un ... .

Practice

1 Mettez le verbe ou le modal entre parenthèses à la forme qui convient (à l'actif ou au passif).

a. On Thursday, December 1, 1955, Rosa Parks (board) a city bus and (sit) with three other Blacks in the fifth row, the first row that Blacks (can) occupy. A few stops later, the four front rows (fill) with Whites, and one white man (stand). According to the law, Blacks and Whites (can) not occupy the same row, so the bus driver (ask) all four of the Blacks seated in the fifth row to move. Three (obey), but Rosa Parks (refuse). She (arrest).

b. After the arrest, the black community in Montgomery (decide) to boycott the town's buses. Everyone (walk), (ride) in a friend's car or (take) a cab. The protest (be) a success, everyone realized that no one (ride) those buses. Huge crowds (gather) in churches and a leader (emerge). Loudspeakers (use) so that those who could not get in could hear what (happen). As Luther King (make) his speech, even more people (show up). It (get) dark when everyone returned to their homes at the end of the day. They (stay) off the buses until they (can) ride them with dignity. Blacks (return) to the buses on December 21, 1956, over a year after the boycott (begin).

c. On April 4th, 1968, the famous black civil rights leader, Martin Luther King, (assassinate) by a sniper. He (shoot) dead in Memphis, Tennessee, where he (go) to lead a march protesting against low wages and poor working conditions. He (take) to hospital where he (die) soon afterwards. A massive wave of violence (break) out all over the country, primarily in black urban areas. In several countries marches (hold) to honor the memory of a man who (stand) up for justice and peace.

2 Traduisez le texte suivant en choisissant la forme du prétérit qui convient.

Tandis que nous marchions vers le *Lincoln Memorial*, Martin Luther King commença son discours. C'était incroyable : des milliers de gens étaient en train de l'écouter. Ce jour-là, Martin Luther King, qui s'adressait à ses concitoyens, devint célèbre dans le monde entier.

Language at work

3 Employez le verbe donné entre parenthèses au prétérit simple ou au prétérit en *BE + -ING* (à l'actif ou au passif).

In November 1960, a tiny six-year-old black girl, Ruby Bridges, (walk) to school. She was the only African-American child to attend an elementary school in New Orleans in Louisiana. After a court (order) desegregation, she (guard) by federal marshals. As soon as they (see) her, racist demonstrators (start) throwing tomatoes at her. They also (shout) abuse at her. As she (walk) along the sidewalk, she (feel) terrified. Yet she (pretend) not to hear their insults. When she (reach) school, they still (threaten) her.
Through this painting, Norman Rockwell (want) to denounce the violence in the early years of school desegregation. He (make) people aware of the ugliness of racial discrimination and the plight black people (confront) with.

Norman Rockwell, *The Problem We All Live With*, 1964 (91cm x 147cm)

Improve your pronunciation

1 Schéma accentuel

MP3 10

À l'aide d'un dictionnaire si nécessaire, notez le schéma accentuel des mots suivants. Vérifiez ensuite à l'écoute.
Exemple : *intimidation* → □□□✔□

a. *segregation*
b. *emancipation*
c. *discrimination*
d. *constitution*
e. *rejection*
f. *exclusion*
g. *demonstration*
h. *decision*

→ Quel rôle joue la terminaison *-ion* dans la place de l'accent principal d'un mot ?

2 Suffixe

MP3 11

À l'écoute, repérez la syllabe accentuée dans chacun de ces mots :

a. *proud – proudly*
b. *curt – curtly*
c. *rude – rudely*
d. *shy – shyly*
e. *angry – angrily*
f. *naïve – naïvely*
g. *abrupt – abruptly*
h. *obedient – obediently*
i. *respect – respectfully*
j. *vicious – viciously*

→ Quelle est l'incidence de *-ly* sur la place de l'accent ?

YOUR TASK

You are a film director. Write the scenario based on the following scene.

When I was a child I knew that the white people lived somewhere but I rarely saw one in my daily routine. [...]

Everybody was poor, but nobody starved[1]. We partied on Saturday nights and praised the Lord for our babies on Sundays. We worked hard when we had to and took it easy when there was a chance. A lot of colored people tell me that they hate the South; Jim Crow and segregation made a heavy weight for their hearts. But I never felt like that. I mean, lynchings were a terrible thing, and some of those peckerwoods[2] acted so stupid that they embarrassed the hell out of you sometimes. But I still loved the little shack I shared with my mother. I'd have still been there if it wasn't for one terrible event.

That event was learning to read.

I entered school at the age of six. [...] On the first day I heard Miss Randolph read a story, and I knew that books were my destiny, not writing, or teaching or inventing spaceships, just reading and reading and reading some more. I could pick out a simple sentence based on the knowledge of a dozen words by the end of the first week. By the age of eight I was alone in the fourth classroom reading everything I could. [...]

There was a library in the white part of the town; coloreds couldn't go inside. For a while I would go there and sit out front on the bench they had, rereading old books like *The Hinkley Reader* and *Uncle Tom's Cabin*. One day the librarian, an old battle-ax[3] named Celestine Dowling, came out and asked me what I was doing.

"Readin'," I said proudly.

"Really," old Miss Dowling said.

"Yes'm," I replied.

"I don't believe you," she stated.

I didn't know what to reply to such a rude comment, so I sat tight and quiet.

"Read me a sentence," she ordered.

There is nothing worse than the snows of May, I read from a story called "Minnesota Snows." Dowling frowned and said, "Go on."

I read the first page and then the second. I read all the way through the story. I had read that book many times and so did not skip or stutter hardly at all.

When I was through, Miss Dowling said, "Come on with me."

She led me through the big double doors of the library into a large room that was at least twenty feet high, lined to the ceiling with shelves that were packed with neat rows of books. I remember my heart catching. I forgot how to breathe altogether. [...]

"This is the library," the librarian said.

I nodded and gulped.

"Close your mouth, boy."

"It's beautiful," I said finally. "I never seen nuthin' like it."

"Of course you haven't," she said. "And do you know why?"

1. *mourait de faim* 2. *« petits blancs »* 3. *(ici) mégère*

"Because I never been in here before?" I asked, not understanding the question.

"No," she said from some Olympian height[4]. "It is because this is a white library. And no matter how much you know how to read, these books are not meant for you. These books were written by white people for white people. This is literature and art and the way our country is and should be. There will be no library card for you, so you can stop sitting out in front. You have seen as much of this building as you ever will."

The impact of her words brought tears into my eyes. I was thirteen but, like I said, I've always been small. I looked up at Celestine Dowling and she seemed pleased to see me cry.

Walter Mosley, *Fearless Jones*, 2001

4. *(ici) en le prenant de haut*

PREPARATION

1 Check your understanding (class work)

Read the text and fill in the worksheet your teacher will give you.

2 How to write your scenario (group work)

1. Setting

– Find out the moment when the scene is set (e.g.: night or daytime...) and say if it is inside or outside (e.g.: in or out).

– Think of the different elements composing the setting (e.g.: room, library...) and find pictures representing them.

– "There was a library in the white part of the town; coloreds couldn't go inside." (l. 22)
How will you illustrate this sentence on the screen?

2. Cast

Imagine the character's and the narrator's identity cards. Copy the following card on your copybook and fill it in.

First name:
Last name:
Age:
Physical appearance (height, weight, eye colour, hair...):
Specific gestures:
Clothes:
Actions:

3. Stage directions

– "One day the librarian, an old battle-ax named Celestine Dowling, came out..." (l. 24)
Write stage directions, for example indicate the way the librarian walked.

– "Readin'," I said proudly.
"Really," old Miss Dowling said.
"Yes'm," I replied.
"I don't believe you," she stated (l. 26-29).

– What feelings do the highlighted words reveal? How will you show them on the screen?

– What shots or angle shots can you use to underline the characters' emotions?
→ see p. 245 for help

– "...and asked me what I was doing." (l. 25) Rewrite the text as a short dialogue.

– What type of music will you use in this scene?

4. Act it out or film it!

Reading *corner*

Holes, a film by Andrew Davis (2003)

The curse

There were no telephones, but word spread[1] quickly through the small town. By the end of the day, everyone in Green Lake had heard that the schoolteacher had kissed the onion picker.

Not one child showed up for school the next morning.

Miss Katherine sat alone in the classroom and wondered if she had lost track of the day of the week. Perhaps it was Saturday. It wouldn't have surprised her. Her brain and head had been spinning[2] ever since Sam kissed her.

She heard a noise outside the door, then suddenly a mob[3] of men and women came storming into the school building. They were led by Trout Walker.

"There she is!" Trout shouted. "The Devil Woman!"

The mob was turning over desks and ripping down[4] bulletin boards.

"She's been poisoning your children's brains with books," Trout declared.

They began piling all the books in the center of the room.

"Think about what you are doing!" cried Miss Katherine.

Someone made a grab for her[5], tearing her dress, but she managed to get out of the building. She ran to the sheriff's office.

The sheriff had his feet up on his desk and was drinking from a bottle of whiskey. "Morni', Miss Katherine," he said.

"They're destroying the schoolhouse," she said, gasping for breath. "They'll burn it to the ground if someone doesn't stop them!"

"Just calm your pretty self down a second," the sheriff said in a slow drawl "And tell me what you're talking about." He got up from his desk and walked over to her.

"Trout Walker has—"

"Now don't go saying nothing bad about Charles Walker," said the sheriff.

"We don't have much time!" urged Katherine. "You've got to stop them."

"You're sure pretty," said the sheriff.

Miss Katherine stared at him in horror.

"Kiss me," said the sheriff.

1. *la rumeur se répandit* **2.** *tournoyaient* **3.** *foule (agressive)* **4.** *arrachait* **5.** *l'attrapa*

She slapped him across the face.

He laughed. "You kissed the onion picker. Why won't you kiss me?"

She tried to slap him again, but he caught her by the hand.

She tried to wriggle free[6]. "You're drunk!" she yelled.

"I always get drunk before a hanging."

"A hanging? Who—"

"It's against the law for a Negro to kiss a white woman."

"Well, then you'll have to hang me, too," said Katherine. "Because I kissed him back."

"It ain't against the law for you to kiss him," the sheriff explained. "Just for him to kiss you."

"We're all equal under the eyes of God," she declared.

The sheriff laughed. "Then if Sam and I are equal, why won't you kiss me?" He laughed again. "I'll make you a deal. One sweet kiss, and I won't hang your boyfriend. I'll just run him out of town."

Miss Katherine jerked her hand free. As she hurried to the door, she heard the sheriff say, "The law will punish Sam. And God will punish you."

She stepped back into the street and saw smoke rising from the schoolhouse. She ran down to the lakefront, where Sam was hitching[7] Mary Lou to the onion cart.

"Thank God, I found you," she sighed, hugging him. "We've got to get out of here. Now!"

"What—"

"Someone must have seen us kissing yesterday," she said. "They set fire to the schoolhouse. The sheriff said he's going to hang you!"

Sam hesitated for a moment, as if he couldn't quite believe it. He didn't want to believe it. "C'mon, Mary Lou."

"We have to leave Mary Lou behind," said Katherine.

Sam stared at her a moment. There were tears in his eyes. "Okay."

Sam's boat was in the water, tied to a tree by a long rope. He untied it, and they waded through the water and climbed aboard. His powerful arms rowed them away from the shore.

But his powerful arms were no match for Trout Walker's motorized boat. They were little more than halfway across the lake when Miss Katherine heard the loud roar of the engine. Then she saw the ugly black smoke…

These are the facts:

The Walker boat smashed into Sam's boat. Sam was shot and killed in the water. Katherine Barlow was rescued against her wishes. When they returned to the shore, she saw Mary Lou's body lying on the ground. The donkey[8] had been shot in the head.

That all happened one hundred and ten years ago. Since then, not one drop of rain has fallen on Green Lake.

You make the decision: Whom did God punish?

Three days after Sam's death, Miss Katherine shot the sheriff while he was sitting in his chair drinking a cup of coffee. Then she carefully applied a fresh coat of red lipstick and gave him the kiss he had asked for.

For the next twenty years Kissin' Kate Barlow was one of the most feared outlaws in all the West.

Louis Sachar, *Holes*, 1998

6. *se libérer en se tortillant* **7.** *attelait* **8.** *âne*

JE M'ENTRAÎNE

1 Je fais les premiers repérages

a. De quel type de texte s'agit-il ?
b. Qui sont les différents personnages (nom, statut social, relations entre eux) ?
c. Qui est le narrateur ?
d. Où se passe l'action (pays, endroits précis) et à quel moment se déroule la scène ?

"How gloomy it is," said Laura. "But at least we can be alone here – more so than in any other place at Blackwater Park. Oh, Marian, I'm so unhappy."

Laura then began to tell me about her marriage, and her relationship with Sir Percival Glyde. She told me many things that made my heart very sad and heavy within me, as I realized how cruelly he treated her. One thing was very clear to me – Sir Percival had never loved Laura, but had married her for her money, and her money alone.

I also felt the most terrible sense of guilt. I was the person reponsible for separating Laura from Walter Hartright, the man who loved her. I had encouraged him to leave England, to go far away to a dangerous place from which he might never return. I was responsible for wasting two young lives – Laura's and Walter's – and I had done all this so that she should keep her promise to Sir Percival Glyde, a man who didn't love her and who was cruel to her.

I put my arms around Laura and held her tight. I felt her kisses as she tried to comfort me, and at last she said, "Come, Marian, it's getting late. Let's go back."

We got up and went towards the boathouse door. Suddenly Laura turned towards me, her eyes wide with alarm.

"Look!" she exclaimed.

A figure was walking along by the side of the lake, but whether of man or woman, it was impossible to tell. It moved silently and disappeared into the fog.

"I'm so frightened," whispered Laura. "Who can it be? Do you think it will follow us back to the house?"

"There's no need to be frightened," I replied. "It's probably only someone from the village out walking late. Come on, let's go."

It was difficult to find the path back to the house in the darkness. All the way back, we had a very strange feeling that someone or something was following us. At one time we thought we heard footsteps, but on turning round we couldn't see anything because of the fog. We walked so quickly that we were out of breath by the time we got back to the house.

I went immediately to the library. I was curious to know where Count Fosco had spent the evening, but he was sitting by the fire reading a book. Clearly he couldn't have been the mysterious figure down by the boathouse – he could never have got back to the house in time.

Wilkie Collins, *The Woman in White*, 1859

2 J'approfondis ma compréhension

a. Quel est le sens des mots ou expressions suivants : *guilt* (l. 15) • *held her tight* (l. 21) • *wide with alarm* (l. 24) • *whether of man or woman* (l. 26) • *path* (l. 32) • *fog* (l. 35) ?
Quels indices dans le contexte vous permettent de déduire ce sens ?
b. Utilisez la composition des mots pour comprendre : *within* (l. 10) • *boathouse* (l. 23) • *footsteps* (l. 34).
c. Attention au faux-ami : *figure* (l. 26).

3 Je réponds aux questions

a. *Who is the main character in the scene? Who is the narrator?*
How are these two characters related to each other? Quote the text to justify your answer.
b. *Who are the other important characters in this passage (full names, relationships with the main character and social status when possible)?*
c. *Where is the scene located (country, places)? When does the scene take place? Justify from the text.*
d. *How does the main character feel? Give one quotation from the text.*
e. *"I also felt the most terrible sense of guilt." (l. 15) Explain the narrator's feelings.*
f. *From line 23 down to line 35:*
– What incident happens? (one sentence)
– Compare the two characters' reactions. What do they do afterwards? (one sentence)
– What type of atmosphere is created in these lines? Include elements from the text (30 words).
g. *How does the narrator explain the incident? In your opinion, is she right or wrong (30 words)?*

4 Je m'auto-corrige

Corrigez vos réponses à l'aide de la fiche que vous trouverez sur le site compagnon et comptabilisez vos points.

JE FAIS LE BILAN

Analysez vos résultats à l'aide de cette grille d'évaluation où sont définis différents paliers de compétence en compréhension de l'écrit.

Je peux...	Paliers
... deviner le sens des mots inconnus quand je comprends le reste de la phrase.	B1
... comprendre les événements principaux dans un texte narratif.	B1
... comprendre des descriptions de sentiments exprimés dans un anglais simple.	B1
... saisir l'implicite d'un passage tiré d'un roman.	B2

ÉVALUATION

Votre professeur va vous distribuer une fiche d'évaluation de la compréhension écrite sur une des unités travaillées en cours :

Unit 4 **Dealing with the Devil** | Unit 5 **The Fourth Power** | Unit 6 **Black is beautiful**

Une fois l'évaluation terminée, votre professeur pourra déterminer à quel palier vous vous situez par rapport à la grille du Cadre Européen Commun de Référence pour les Langues.

Unit 7 FAR AND AWAY

	YOUR TASK
• Do you prefer mass tourism or outdoor activities in isolated areas? • Tourists vs. locals • Discover new ways to travel: space tourism and slum tourism	You are planning a trip to Colorado. Listen to the Tourist Information advisor and find out what is worth visiting and experiencing in and around Denver. Select your five favourite activities. → p. 117

Unit 8 UNDER CONTROL

	YOUR TASK
• What does the word Big Brother mean to you? • CCTV nation • Do new technologies threaten our privacy?	You will listen to a radio report about surveillance today. Gather as much information as possible. Then react and leave your message on the radio station voicemail. → p. 129

Unit 9 EAST WIND, WEST WIND

	YOUR TASK
• Asian influence on the USA, past and present • Learn more about the way Asian Americans were treated during WW2	You are visiting an exhibition on Asian-Americans. You stop and watch the three short videos presented. Check your understanding and post a comment on the museum forum page. → p. 143

ÉVALUATION SOMMATIVE *LISTENING* → p. 144-145

Unit 7

FAR AND AWAY

YOUR TASK AT THE END OF THIS UNIT

You are planning a trip to Colorado. Listen to the Tourist Information advisor and find out what is worth visiting and experiencing in and around Denver. Select your five favourite activities. → p. 117

TUNE IN!

Martin Parr, *Small World*, 1996

Help!

- beach towel /taʊəl/
- at the seaside
- rubber ring: *bouée*
- packed / crowded
- side by side
- barefooted: *pieds nus*
- huge = enormous
- sunbathing /sʌnbeɪðɪŋ/
- spread /spred/: *étaler*

React

a. What are your immediate reactions (atmosphere, place, people, weather, activities...)?
b. What makes you realize it is an artificial beach?
c. Does this photo make you dream? Why? Why not?
d. What image of leisure and tourism is given here?

1. FAR FROM THE MADDING CROWD

1 Discover the world

a. What elements strike you in the poster?
– landscape, colours
– tourists' size, activity

b. Find:
– where Utah is on a map of the USA;
– the name of the national park where this photo was taken.

c. Read the slogan.
– What sort of holidays is advertised?
– Imagine the activities and sports you can practise there.

d. Who is the target? Justify your answer with elements from the caption and the poster.

2 Plan your trip

a. Infosearch
Go on the Internet (www.utah.com/nationalparks) and discover five National Parks in Utah: Arches, Bryce Canyon, Zion, Monument Valley, Capitol Reef. Then choose the one that attracts you most. Select a few photos.

PREPARE YOUR TASK

b. Group work
You are planning a two-day visit to Utah with a group of friends. Discuss which park you want to visit.

PREPARE YOUR TASK

3 My destination

CD WB

Listen to five Americans talking about their favourite destinations in the USA. Turn to your Workbook for help.

Help!

Landscape	Activities	Target and goals
scenery: *paysage* rock formation stunning = amazing breathtaking: *à couper le souffle* in the wild peaceful overlook sth: *donner sur qqch*	hiking: *randonnée à pied* rock-climbing: *escalade* paragliding: *parapente* hot air balloon back-packing: *voyage sac au dos* put up a tent take a break from get away from (a hectic life)	holiday(s) (GB) = vacation (US) attract visitors urge sb to do sth be worth visiting live close /kləʊs/ to nature / outdoors unwind /ʌn'waɪnd/ = relax

2. EXTREMES

1 Get a kick out of it! WB

a. Group work: Read one of the two diary entries and find the key information.
Is the narrator's opinion on rafting positive or negative in the entry you have read? Justify your answer.

b. Confront what you have understood with the rest of the class.
Then turn to your Workbook for help.

c. Class work: Prepare an account of one of the two entries in the diary and report to the class.

Twelve passengers and three rafting guides are to navigate the rapids of the Colorado River through the Grand Canyon for thirteen days. Amy writes her diary.

July 3

I'm writing in the bathroom of our hotel room because mom is out there with everything laid out on the two double beds, FREAKING OUT[1] that she might forget something. Tonight we had our orientation meeting. Mom and I were late and we walked into the room and everybody stared at me[2]. Must have been my FAT CLUB T-shirt. Please please please don't make me go on this trip. There is nobody my age and all I'll do is eat. And it's going to be hotter than shit and I'll probably sink the boats.

Maybe if I throw myself out the window, she won't make me go.

We're supposed to get up at 5:30 tomorrow morning and the bus leaves at 6:30. I do not know what I am going to do with my mother hanging over my shoulder for two weeks. Why did she have to bring me along? I could have stayed home alone. Oh no Amy, I want some time with you, you're going off to college in another year. Oh no Amy, I wouldn't feel right. Oh no Amy, a serial killer might be able to figure out the twenty-two locks[3] on our front door.

I think I've got food-poisoning.

1. *elle flippait à l'idée de* 2. *m'a regardée fixement* 3. *serrures*

July 5 Day Two

It's the end of the second day. [...]

Okay, relax. Gotta admit, it's pretty amazing down here. I had no idea. I thought it would just be a muddy river surrounded by boring cliffs[1]. I thought it would be way too hot. I thought I would hate the rapids.

Well, it is hot, and we are surrounded by cliffs, but the water isn't muddy. It's cold and green and the cliffs are all pink and orange, with flowers growing right out of them. The rapids are awesome. Today I got to be in the paddle boat, and we did the Roaring Twenties[2], and it was like one right after the other. We got totally soaked, and now that's all I want to do, run rapids.

Elizabeth Hyde, *In the Heart of the Canyon*, 2009

1. *falaises* 2. *nom des rapides signifiant « les Années folles »*

PREPARE YOUR TASK

2 Space tourism

CD WB

a. Learn more about Dennis Tito, the first space tourist:
- nationality;
- age at the time of the travel;
- social status and price of his flight;
- motivations.

b. Two teenagers react to this interview. Listen to their conversation and sum up each person's opinion.

c. Neil Armstrong, the first man on the Moon, said "That's one small step for [a] man, one giant leap for mankind."
Do you think this is still true for Dennis Tito's experience? Why?

PREPARE YOUR TASK

3 Watch a video

Away from it all

a. Watch the trailer from the film *Surfwise*.

b. Turn to your worksheet for help.
What can you say about the family members, the places visited, the way of life on the road?

c. List the advantages and drawbacks mentioned.

4 Debate team

Choose one of these three topics. Prepare your arguments, illustrate with precise examples, then debate.

a. How would you react if you were offered to go to the North Pole or in the Australian desert? Why?

b. Your family decides on a gap year. Would you be ready to leave your friends and home behind? Why? Why not?

c. Are you attracted to extreme sports and trips or do you prefer quiet, relaxed holidays? Why? What type(s) of holiday would you choose?

Giving one's opinion
- Don't you think that...?
- I don't agree / I disagree with you.
- I don't see it that way.
- I quite share your view.
- Sorry to interrupt you, but...
- Can I just say something?
- You may be right, yet...
- Nonsense! / Rubbish!

→ see p. 248-249

Help!

Sports	Far away	For	Against
snow boarding bungee jumping: *saut à l'élastique* paragliding: *parapente* leap: *bond* kitesurfing sporty climb /klaɪm/ jump dive: *plonger*	astronaut spacesuit beyond planet Earth: *au-delà de la planète Terre* launch a shuttle: *lancer une navette* travel into outer space float into weightlessness: *flotter en apesanteur*	exciting = thrilling adventurous fearless be fond of / keen on sth / V-ING overcome: *surmonter* dare: *oser* get a kick out of sth / V-ING: *(familier) s'éclater*	risky = dangerous stressful apprehensive = anxious frightening = scary be injured: *être blessé* take risks = endanger one's life

3. A STRANGER

In the colonial India of the 1920s, Dr Aziz is ordered to go to hospital to tend to a patient. On his way back he stops at his favourite mosque.

An Englishwoman stepped out into the moonlight. Suddenly he was furiously angry and shouted: "Madam! Madam! Madam!"

"Oh! Oh!" the woman gasped[1].

"Madam, this is a mosque, you have no right here at all; you should have taken off your shoes; this is a holy[2] place for Moslems."

"I have taken them off."

"You have?"

"I left them at the entrance."

"Then I ask your pardon."

Still startled[3], the woman moved out, keeping the ablution-tank[4] between them. He called after her, "I am truly sorry for speaking."

"Yes, I was right, was I not? If I remove[5] my shoes, I am allowed?"

"Of course, but so few ladies take the trouble, especially if thinking no one is there to see."

"That makes no difference. God is here."

"Madam!"

"Please let me go."

"Oh, can I do you some service now or at any time?"

"No, thank you, really none—good night."

"May I know your name?"

She was now in the shadow of the gateway, so that he could not see her face, but she saw his, and she said with a change of voice, "Mrs Moore."

"Mrs…" Advancing, he found that she was old […] with a red face and white hair. Her voice had deceived[6] him.

"Mrs Moore, I am afraid I startled you. I shall tell my community—our friends—about you. That God is here—very good, very fine indeed. I think you are newly arrived in India."

"Yes—how did you know?"

"By the way you address me. No, but can I call you a carriage?"

"I have only come from the club. They are doing a play that I have seen in London, and it was so hot." […]

"I think you ought not to[7] walk at night alone, Mrs Moore. There are bad characters about and leopards may come across from the Marabar Hills. Snakes also."

She exclaimed; she had forgotten the snakes.

"For example, a six-spot beetle," he continued. "You pick it up, it bites, you die."

"But you walk about yourself."

"Oh, I am used to it."

"Used to snakes?"

They both laughed. "I'm a doctor," he said. "Snakes don't dare bite me." They sat down side by side in the entrance, and slipped on their evening shoes. "Please may I ask you a question now? Why do you come to India at this time of year, just as the cold weather is ending?"

"I intended to start earlier, but there was an unavoidable delay."

"It will soon be so unhealthy for you! And why ever do you come to Chandrapore?"

"To visit my son. He is the City Magistrate here." […]

She accepted his escort back to the club, and said at the gate that she wished she was a member, so that she could have asked him in.

"Indians are not allowed into the Chandrapore Club even as guests," he said simply.

E.M. Forster, *A Passage to India*, 1924

1. *dit la femme, le souffle coupé* **2.** *saint* **3.** very surprised **4.** *bassin aux ablutions*
5. take off **6.** mistaken/misled **7.** you should not

1 Find the key information WB

a. Skim through the text.
– When and where does the scene take place (country and city, historical period)?
– Who are the characters? Give their name, origin, age, occupation and social status if possible.
b. Read the text again and turn to your Workbook for help.

2 You know what?

Choose a scenario. After the meeting:
– Mrs. Moore goes back to the club and talks to her son about her encounter.
– The man talks to a friend of his about his unexpected meeting.
Include comments, reactions, feelings and emotions.

Help!

Mrs Moore	Dr Aziz
customs adventurous daring: *audacieux* open-minded be unaware of: *ne pas avoir conscience de* be eager to: *être avide de* go off the beaten track: *sortir des sentiers battus* share: *partager*	offended = insulted outraged / indignant = shocked resentful respectful ≠ disrespectful rude: *malpoli* despise / scorn: *mépriser* be used to + V-ING: *avoir l'habitude de* blame sb for + V-ING: *reprocher qqch à qqn*

3 Act out the scene CD WB

a. Define the tone for each character in the scene. Choose adjectives in the following list:
accusing • apologetic • astonished • cautious • cheerful • defensive • distrustful • reproachful • scornful • shy.

You can also use adverbs (accusingly, etc.).

b. Give details about their movements: step back, move forward, point at, walk away, etc.

c. Prepare the script.
Example:
MAN *(shouting furiously)*: Madam! Madam! Madam!
WOMAN *(surprised, stepping back)*: Oh! Oh!

d. Work on the pronunciation and the intonation with the help of your Workbook.

e. Act it out in front of the class or film it at home and show your film in class.

PREPARE YOUR TASK

4 Warning to visitors

CD WB

a. Now listen to Izzi Lokku talking about tourism in his country.
b. Can you see any relation between the recording, the photo on the right and the text.

Duane Hanson, *Tourists II*, 1988

4. TOURISM OR VOYEURISM?

Michael Cronin's job as a college admissions officer took him to India two or three times a year, so he had already seen the usual sites—temples, monuments, markets—when one day he happened across a flier[1] advertising "slum tours".

"It just resonated with me immediately," said Mr Cronin, who was staying at a posh[2] Taj Hotel in Mumbai where, he noted, a bottle of Champagne cost the equivalent of two years' salary for many Indians. "But I didn't know what to expect."

Soon, Cronin, 41, found himself skirting open sewers[3] and ducking[4] to avoid exposed electrical wires as he toured the sprawling Dharavi slum, home to more than a million. He joined a cricket game and saw the small-scale industry, from embroidery[5] to tannery, that quietly thrives[6] in the slum. "Nothing is considered garbage[7] there," he said. "Everything is used again." [...]

Slum tourism, or "poorism", as some call it, is catching on. From the favelas of Rio de Janeiro to the townships of Johannesburg to the garbage dumps of Mexico, tourists are forsaking, at least for a while, beaches and museums for crowded, dirty—and in many ways surprising—slums. [...]

Slum tourism isn't for everyone. Critics charge that ogling[8] the poorest of the poor isn't tourism at all. It's voyeurism. The tours are exploitative, these critics say, and have no place on an ethical traveler's itinerary.

■ *New York Times*, March 9, 2008

1. *prospectus* **2.** *chic* **3.** *à éviter les égouts à ciel ouvert* **4.** *à baisser la tête* **5.** *broderie* **6.** *prospère* **7.** *déchet* **8.** looking (at sb) in an offensive way

1 Find the key information

a. Find details about:
– Cronin (full name, age, job, country visited, town where he was staying, type of hotel);
– the tour (where Cronin found the information, the name of the area, the number of inhabitants).
Pick out all the words related to the living conditions and the types of jobs in the area.
Use your answers to translate the word "slum" (l. 13).

b. Find the name of the type of tourism described here and list the other areas in the world mentioned.

c. List the four reasons why some people are against this type of tourism.

Help!

Tour

in dire straits /daɪəʳ streɪts/: *dans une situation très difficile*
appalling / dreadful / awful living conditions
needy / destitute
become aware of

Feelings

objects of curiosity
ill-at-ease
picturesque: *pittoresque*
disturb
feel guilty

PREPARE YOUR TASK

2 Dharavi tour CD WB

Listen to this Mumbai tour guide and turn to your Workbook for help.
Your hotel offers the possibility on going on slum tours. Discuss with your friends and family if you want to go or not.

Language at work

Les pronoms relatifs *who, that, which* ou *Ø*

1 Observez et concluez.

a. *Dr Aziz began to shout at the woman* ***who /that*** *had entered the mosque.*
b. *Dr Aziz suddenly noticed a woman,* ***who*** *was visiting the mosque.*
c. *The woman* ***that /Ø*** *Dr Aziz had met had just arrived in India.*
d. *The people (****that /who****) he saw in the slum were needy.*

– Quel type d'antécédent trouve-t-on avant le pronom relatif *who* ? (Humain ? Non humain ?)
– Dans quel(s) énoncé(s) la proposition relative est-elle nécessaire pour indiquer précisément la personne dont il est question (proposition relative déterminative) ?
– Dans quel(s) énoncé(s) la proposition relative apporte-t-elle simplement une information supplémentaire (proposition relative non déterminative) ? Que remarquez-vous concernant la ponctuation dans ce type de proposition relative ?
– Dans quel cas peut-on employer ***Ø*** ?

2 *Which, that, Ø*

a. *He saw the small-scale industry* ***that /which*** *had developed in the slum.*
b. *He saw the small-scale industry (****that /which****) people in the slum had built.*

– Quel type d'antécédent trouve-t-on avant le pronom relatif *which* ? (Humain ? Non humain ?)
– Dans **a.**, l'emploi de ***Ø*** est impossible. Quelle est la fonction du pronom relatif dans la proposition ? Est-il sujet, complément du verbe ou complément d'un nom ?

→ Concluez :
– Lorsqu'on utilise ... , l'antécédent est obligatoirement humain, et lorsqu'on utilise ... il est obligatoirement non humain. ... et ... peuvent s'utiliser quel que soit le type d'antécédent.
– Les relatifs *that* et ***Ø*** sont utilisés dans les relatives ... , mais l'emploi de ... est impossible quand le relatif est sujet du verbe.

3 Comparez.

a. *He spoke to the woman* ***whose*** *suitcase he had found.*
b. *He spoke to the woman* ***who's*** *from Ireland.*
c. *He spoke to the woman* ***who's*** *been staying at the hotel for several days.*

Dans quel énoncé le pronom relatif est-il sujet ? complément du nom ?

→ Concluez :
– On utilise ... pour exprimer la possession dans la proposition subordonnée relative.
– Dans *who's, 's* peut être la contraction de ... ou ... .

Practice

Complétez avec *that, which, who* ou *Ø*.

"What is the type of holiday ... you have always dreamt of?"
"For people ... spend five days a week in an office, staying in a quiet place is a necessity. I want to rest and forget the hectic life ... I have all the year round. Like many people ... I know I'd like to go to Kenya to see all the wild animals ... I love. I would certainly enjoy holidays in luxurious hotels ... I can't afford at home. Many tourists ... visit Kenya remember the scenes from the film *Out of Africa,* ... they saw years ago. They can imagine Meryl Streep's romance with Robert Redford, ... is an adventurer ... she had met in Nairobi."
"My dream vacation is staying with local people ... will help me discover their customs. I feel I'm a real globetrotter ... is really curious about the countries ... I intend to visit. I also wish I could improve the language ... I learnt at school and be more fluent in English."

Language at work

Build up your vocabulary

1 Choisissez parmi les deux mots en italiques celui qui convient. Aidez-vous des articles 28 et 40 du précis grammatical.

John Brook is planning a holiday trip next month. He asks for *information* / *informations* at the nearest travel *agency* / *agencies*. He makes some *enquiry* / *enquiries* about the plane ticket. He wants to know the different prices of the *resort* / *resorts* in the capital. The lady gives him *an* / *some* advice on the various tours and what to take in his *luggage* / *luggages*. She tells him he may have to delay his trip because there *is* / *are* news of possible airport strikes.

2 Associez ces mesures américaines à leur équivalent métrique.

Length				Volume		Mass	
inch	foot	yard	mile	pint	gallon	pound	ounce

3.79 litres • 2.54 centimetres • 473.1 millilitres • 0.453 kilograms • 1.61 kilometres • 28.35 grams • 30.48 centimetres • 91.4 centimetres

Improve your listening skills

MP3 12

1 Écoutez ces conseils, extraits d'un site en faveur du tourisme équitable.

a. Relevez les groupes de souffle, les mots accentués, les liaisons consonne-voyelle éventuelles.
b. Faites attention à la prononciation des nombreux mots transparents.

One World Travel, a sustainable tourism agency

- If possible, stay with local people or in modest accommodation which does not require the expensive resource-consuming style of international hotels.
- Drink and eat local food so that more of the expenditure stays in the country.
- Get around on foot or by bicycle or local transport rather than tourist coach.
- Avoid off-road tours which could damage soil and other aspects of the natural environment.

MP3 13

2 Préparez-vous à lire la suite ci-contre à haute voix.

a. À votre avis, quels mots seront accentués ?
b. Cherchez dans un dictionnaire l'accentuation des mots de trois syllabes.
c. Vérifiez à l'écoute.

- Prepare for your trip by learning about the culture, history and customs of the people.
- Try to learn some of the language of the place you are to visit.
- Respect and try to fit in with local customs.
- Be sensitive to the intrusion when photographing people and places.
- Do not dress in ways which might offend local beliefs, especially in places of religious or spiritual significance.
- Be careful that in bargaining you are not exploiting the poverty and need of sellers.
- Respect the rights of people, when you are in the powerful position of being relatively wealthy.

YOUR TASK

You are planning a trip to Colorado. Listen to the Tourist Information advisor and find out what is worth visiting and experiencing in and around Denver. Select your five favourite activities.

LES STRATÉGIES À MOBILISER

Anticipez

a. Observez cette publicité et listez tous les mots qui vous viennent en tête dans ces champs lexicaux : *sports and leisure activities* • *places and landscapes* • *weather* • *types of holiday* • *target audience.*

b. Lisez le texte de la publicité. Classez les activités en deux catégories : *outdoor* • *indoor.*

LES ÉTAPES À SUIVRE

MP3 14

Vous allez écouter James Watson de l'office de tourisme de Denver. Une fiche va vous être distribuée.

1. Avant l'écoute, lisez attentivement les consignes.
2. Écoutez d'abord l'enregistrement en entier, sans rien écrire.
3. Lors de la deuxième écoute, commencez à remplir la fiche au fur et à mesure.
4. La troisième écoute vous permettra de vérifier et de compléter vos réponses.
5. Avant que les fiches ne soient ramassées, vous aurez quelques minutes pour vous relire.

VOTRE CHOIX

Notez les cinq activités ou destinations qui vous attirent le plus à Denver et dans ses environs. Justifiez votre sélection en parlant de vos goûts et de vos centres d'intérêt.

Unit 8

UNDER CONTROL

YOUR TASK AT THE END OF THIS UNIT

You will listen to a radio report about surveillance today. Gather as much information as possible. Then react and leave your message on the radio station voicemail.
→ p. 129

TUNE IN!

Shepard Fairey

A poster

a. When you hear "Big Brother", what comes to your mind?

b. Describe the poster: angle shot (→ see p. 245), striking elements, dominant colours...

c. Describe the atmosphere. How does it make you feel? Why?

d. What is the artist's goal?

Help!

Devices

helicopter
patrol
billboard: *panneau d'affichage*
control tower
satellite dish: *parabole*
network
broadcast: *diffuser*

Setting and atmosphere

barbed wire: *fil barbelé*
wire /ˈwaɪəʳ/: *fil électrique*
stifling /ˈstaɪflɪŋ/: *étouffant*
dehumanized
ill-at-ease: *mal à l'aise*
scary

Goals

brainwash
track down: *localiser*
spy on sb: *espionner qqn*
suspect sb of sth / V-ING
intimidate
terrorize
compel sb to do sth = oblige

1. BIG BROTHER IS WATCHING YOU

Part 1

Outside, even through the shut window-pane, the world looked cold. Down in the street little eddies[1] of wind were whirling[2] dust and torn paper into spirals, and though the sun was shining and the sky a harsh[3] blue, there seemed to be no colour in anything, except the posters that were plastered everywhere. The black moustachio'd face gazed down from every commanding corner. There was one on the house-front immediately opposite. BIG BROTHER IS WATCHING YOU, the caption said, while the dark eyes looked deep into Winston's own. [...] In the far distance a helicopter skimmed down[4] between the roofs, hovered[5] for an instant like a bluebottle[6], and darted away again with a curving flight. It was the police patrol, snooping into[7] people's windows. The patrols did not matter, however. Only the Thought Police mattered.

1. *tourbillons* **2.** *faisaient tournoyer*
3. *dur, cru* **4.** *vola en rase-mottes* **5.** *plana*
6. *mouche à viande* **7.** *regardant pour espionner*

Part 2

Behind Winston's back the voice from the telescreen was still babbling away[1] [...]. The telescreen received and transmitted simultaneously. Any sound that Winston made, above the level of a very low whisper, would be picked up by it; moreover, [...] he could be seen as well as heard. There was of course no way of knowing whether you were being watched at any given moment. How often, or on what system, the Thought Police plugged in[2] on any individual wire was guesswork. It was even conceivable that they watched everybody all the time. But at any rate they could plug in your wire whenever they wanted to. You had to live – did live, from habit that became instinct – in the assumption that every sound you made was overheard, and, except in darkness, every movement scrutinized.

George Orwell, *Nineteen Eighty-Four*, 1949

1. *(ici) continuait son blabla* **2.** *se branchait*

1 Find the key information WB

Turn to your Workbook for help.

2 What do you think?

a. What do you guess about life in that country? Justify.
b. Judging from Winston's attitude, what can you imagine about his state of mind?
c. Is the poster on the opposite page a good illustration for the text? Justify.

Help!

Human rights	Reactions
freedom of speech or thought	cautious / wary / on one's guard / on the watch for
privacy: *intimité*	frightened / scared / terrified
dictator	nightmarish: *cauchemardesque*
totalitarian regime / dictatorship	unbearable
censorship	threatening
abuse /əˈbjuːs/: *violation*	paranoid /ˈpærənɔɪd/

2. AN ORWELLIAN SOCIETY

1 Discover

a. What is the nature of the document? What elements strike you?
b. Where does the scene take place?
c. Describe the characters.

Banksy

2 Learn more about CCTV in Britain

a. Read the information about CCTV in Britain and prepare five questions you can ask your neighbour.

> Closed circuit television was introduced in the UK in the seventies and is part of the crime reduction programme.
>
> There are no officially verified estimates on the amount of CCTV cameras in the UK but the most recent and widely quoted estimate suggests that there are over 4.2 million public facing CCTV cameras now in operation across the UK (one for every fourteen people). However, this estimate should be treated with caution as it results from a survey of the number of CCTV cameras in two South London streets. The results were then multiplied to produce the estimate of CCTV cameras across the United Kingdom.
>
> ■ British Home Office, February 2009

b. Now close your books and test each other on how well you remember what is said.

"I pledge allegiance to the flag of the United States of America, and to the Republic for which it stands, one nation under God, indivisible, with liberty and justice for all."

3 Go further

a. Read the Pledge of Allegiance to the flag of the United States and find the play on words in the mural opposite.

b. What image of the country is given in Banksy's painting? Does the message apply only to London?

4 Conclude

From what you have learnt in these two pages, say what Banksy's aim was when painting the mural in London.

REPARE OUR TASK

5 News about CCTV in Britain CD WB

Listen and turn to your Workbook for help.

REPARE OUR TASK

6 Listen and draw CD

You are going to hear the description of another work by Banksy. Try to draw it as you listen. Put the different elements in the correct place and compare your drawing with the real one.

7 Watch a video

Westminster Council vs. Banksy

a. Watch the video and turn to your worksheet for help.

b. Recap:
– What do people in favour of removal say?
– What do people supporting Banksy say?
– What is the effect of the publicity on Banksy? What do you think?

Help!

Setting	Technique	Interpretation
surveillance /sɜːˈveɪləns/ concrete: *béton* camera /ˈkæmərə/ closed circuit /ˈkləʊzd ˈsɜːkɪt/ enforce the law	graffiti mural trompe-l'œil technique optical illusion perspective painting roller (for painting)	private life / privacy lack of: *manque de* challenge / defy ridicule / make fun of stand up to: *résister à* denounce / expose criticize sb for + V-ING

3. CAMERAS IN SCHOOLS

1 Get ready

a. Observe the picture. What strikes you?
b. Judging from the picture and the title, what is the article going to deal with?

SOMEONE TO WATCH OVER YOU

Part 1

In March this year, Sam Goodman, 18, walked out of his politics lesson to protest against four CCTV cameras that had been installed overnight in the classroom. He was joined by all but one of his classmates. Goodman says his school, an Essex comprehensive[1], told the class that the cameras had not been switched on yet, and that when they were, they'd be used for teacher training purposes only.

A few weeks later, Goodman says students discovered that the recording system was in a cupboard in the classroom and that the microphones were in fact on. Goodman and his friends promptly switched them off. [...]

1. secondary school in Britain

Part 2

Hundreds of primary and secondary schools across the country intend to install CCTV cameras in classrooms over the next five years to root out bad teachers and check up on naughty pupils, *Education Guardian* has learned.

The revelation comes after a comprehensive in a deprived South London neighbourhood, Stockwell Park High School, said late last month that it had installed 100 cameras – two in each of its classrooms and 40 in its canteen, corridors and playgrounds.

The company behind Stockwell Park's surveillance network is Hertfordshire-based Classwatch. [...] Classwatch's managing director, Angus Drever, says 94 schools in the UK already use its high-definition cameras in their classrooms at a cost of £1,345 a year for the lease[1] of two cameras in a classroom, including maintenance.

Footage[2] captured on the cameras is password-protected, can be stored for a month, and is usually the responsibility of a school's governors[3].

Drever says the cameras can be used by teachers to show "good practice" to colleagues and give feedback. [...]

Classwatch's website claims the cameras can also help to produce "dramatic improvements in behaviour", improve concentration and productivity, and protect staff, pupils and a school's assets[4] against vandals and thieves. [...]

Chris Keates, general secretary of the Nasuwt teaching union, says: "We do not support the use of cameras in this way and see no professional, security or educational benefits to such systems."

■ *The Guardian*, August 4, 2009

1. *location* **2.** *(indénombrable) les documents vidéo* **3.** *membres d'un conseil d'établissement* **4.** *(ici) biens*

2 Find the key information

Part 1

a. What country is mentioned?

b. Observe the word "overnight" (l. 4). How is it built? Deduce its meaning.

c. What events do the following words and phrases refer to?
In March • overnight • not ... yet • a few weeks later

d. How can you explain the expression "all but one" (l. 5)? Only one student left the class • Only one student stayed in the class. Use elements from the text to justify your choice.

e. One word is not repeated after "were" (l. 10). Which one? Put the sentence in direct speech.

f. Copy this grid on a sheet of paper; fill it in, and use the information found in part 1 to recap.

Incidents	People involved	People's reactions
What? Where? When?		

Part 2

a. Pick out all the numbers and say what they correspond to.

b. How do the following groups of people see the use of CCTV cameras in schools: the school administration • Classwatch • the teachers' union?
Classify their arguments in two columns: **for** or **against**.

3 Recap

What is the article about? Give your reactions to what you have read.

4 Watch out!

a. React to the photo on the right.
– Where are the students?
– What are they doing?
– What could they be tempted to do?
– Anticipate what the recording will be about and what words you will hear.

REPARE OUR TASK

b. Listen to this news bulletin. CD
– Try to remember as many stressed words as possible and write them down.
– Classify the keywords in a grid:

people concerned

origin of the problems

problems mentioned

– What measure is proposed to tackle the problem?
– How do the different people concerned feel about the measure?

Useful word

invigilator: a person who watches candidates during an exam

REPARE OUR TASK

5 Argue your case!

Your school-board plans to fit cameras inside the building to monitor students. List your arguments and debate the project in class.

4. PRIVACY AT RISK

Strip search: camera that sees through clothes from 80ft away

A camera that can see through people's clothing at distances of up to 80ft[1] has been developed to help detect weapons, drugs and explosives.

The camera could be deployed in railway stations, shopping centres and other public spaces.

Although it can see objects under clothes, its designers say the images do not show anatomical details. However, it is likely to[2] increase fears that Britain has become a surveillance society.

The new technology, known as the T5000 system, has attracted interest from police forces, train companies and airport operators as well as government agencies. [...]

The system can be linked to a computer so that it can automatically scan anyone passing and alert its human operator to anything suspicious. [...]

The technology works by detecting and measuring terahertz waves, or T-waves for short. [...]

The waves from any given material also carry a distinctive signature, offering the potential to distinguish Semtex[3] from modelling clay[4] and cocaine from sugar.

■ *The Sunday Times*, March 9, 2008

1. 80 feet = about 25 metres **2.** *a des chances de* **3.** an explosive **4.** *argile*

1 Group 1: Find the key information

a. You know the word "striptease". How can you explain "strip search" in the title?

b. Read the first seven lines of the article.
– Pick out all the words you understand and classify them in a grid:

characteristics of the camera

use

potential users

– Quote an advantage and a disadvantage of the camera.
– Fill in the following sentence with words from the text.
The article is about a new camera that can ... . clothes as far as ... meters away, without revealing ... .

c. Read the rest of the article: What is this part about? Choose from the list below:

- the way the camera works
- its possibilities
- its limits
- its dangers

d. Is the article:

biased

informative

neutral

controversial

critical

Explain.

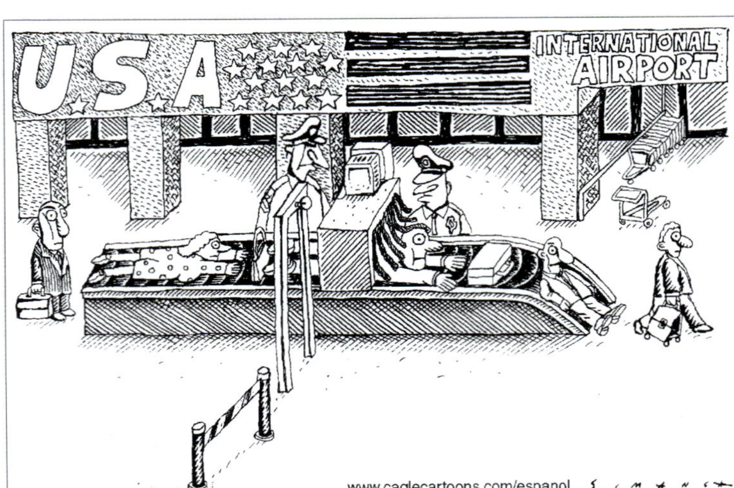

FACEBOOK CAN RUIN YOUR LIFE. AND SO CAN MYSPACE, BEBO...

In [...] a New Jersey federal court, a case is being heard that nominally affects two families but should also make millions of Britons think twice about something they do every day: put highly personal information on Facebook, MySpace or Bebo. [...]

In the US, a sex assault victim seeking[1] compensation faces the prospect[2] of her MySpace and Facebook pages being produced in court. In Texas, a driver whose car was involved in a fatal accident found his MySpace postings ("I'm not an alcoholic, I'm a drunkaholic") part of the prosecution's case[3]. From Los Angeles to Lowestoft, thousands of social network site users have lost their jobs – or failed to clinch[4] new ones – because of their pages' contents. Police, colleges and schools are monitoring[5] MySpace and Facebook pages for what they deem[6] to be "inappropriate" content. [...]

What these and other cases show is that employers and authorities are now monitoring what people imagined were private websites – and using the contents against them. [...]

Social network sites have brought unexpected pleasure to millions. But if present trends continue and users fail to wise up[7], the sites could soon be bringing them some equally unexpected shocks.

■ *The Independent*, February 10, 2008

1. *qui cherche à obtenir* **2.** *possibilité* **3.** *accusation* **4.** *(ici) décrocher* **5.** *surveillent* **6.** consider **7.** *s'assagir*

2 Group 2: Understand the article

a. Read the text once. With the help of the words you recognize, say how much you have understood.

b. Find the names of one country, two States, one nationality and one famous city.

c. Pick out all the words related to justice.
– How many cases are mentioned?
– What were the crimes committed?

d. List the words connected with the information people give on social networks.
Observe the word "drunkaholic": How is it formed? Guess its meaning.

e. Pick out the words referring to the possible use of the information given.

Help!

Risks

compromising
harmful: *nuisible*
harass /ˈhærəs/ sb: *harceler qqn*
accuse sb of
charge sb with: *condamner qqn à*
go to court: *aller en justice*
try sb: *juger qqn*
invade
infringe upon sb's rights: *empiéter sur les droits de qqn*
threaten /ˈθretn/: *menacer*

Advice

be cautious: *être prudent*
warn sb about
foresee the consequences: *prévoir les conséquences*

Video

3 Watch a video

Who's at the door?

Sum up what happens.
What is the aim of this video?
Explain why you find it funny or not.
Turn to your worksheet for help.

Language at work

Le passif

1 Observez et déduisez.

a. *In a dictatorship, people* ***are*** *constantly spied upon.*
b. *Every move you made* ***was observed****.*
c. *Many drivers* ***have*** *already* ***been caught*** *by speed cameras.*

– Observez les formes verbales en gras.
→ Le passif se forme à l'aide de ... (au temps et à la forme requis) + ...
– Quel est le sujet grammatical des formes verbales en gras ?
– Dans ces énoncés, met-on l'accent davantage sur l'auteur de l'action ou sur le résultat ?
– Dans l'énoncé **a.** où se place la préposition ?
– Traduisez les trois énoncés.

2 Comparez.

a. *In Orwell's novel, people* ***are brainwashed*** *by the Thought Police.*
b. *He* ***has*** *just* ***been refused*** *a job because of his blog.*

– Dans quel énoncé l'agent (auteur de l'action) est-il mentionné et par quel élément est-il introduit ?
– Traduisez les deux énoncés et concluez : quand l'agent n'est pas mentionné, la forme passive se traduit souvent en français par ... .

3 Forme simple ou BE + V-ING ?

a. *Smile, you* ***are being filmed****!*
b. *In Britain, wherever you go, you* ***are filmed****.*
c. *They did not behave differently when they knew they* ***were being filmed****.*

– Les formes verbales en gras sont-elles au présent ou au prétérit ?
– Comment sont construites les formes verbales dans les énoncés ci-dessus ? Classez-les en forme simple et forme en BE + V-ING.
– La forme en BE + V-ING est-elle utilisée pour parler d'une action vue dans son déroulement, d'une action habituelle ou d'une vérité générale ?

Practice

1 Transposez les phrases suivantes à la voix passive en prenant pour sujet l'élément souligné. Respectez la forme verbale utilisée dans la phrase initiale et mettez le complément d'agent si c'est possible.

a. The school headmaster punished the students after viewing the CCTV recordings.
b. With see-through cameras, security guards detect explosives through clothes.
c. Surveillance devices break into people's lives.
d. In some places they have fitted loudspeakers on the cameras to talk to people.
e. They issue a message when somebody commits an offence.

2 Réécrivez ces énoncés en utilisant la voix passive.

In Britain an increasing number of CCTV cameras spy upon passers-by. Yet statistics have not proved the efficiency of the system against terrorism. And the extension of surveillance to other places worries more and more citizens. They feel that the system threatens the right to privacy. Civil rights associations criticize authorities for this extensive use of CCTV cameras.

3 **Traduisez ces phrases.**

a. Il a été photographié dans les rues de Londres.
b. On peut utiliser la technologie pour protéger la vie privée.
c. La présence de caméras de surveillance est aussi approuvée *(approve of)* par une partie de la population.
d. Grâce aux caméras, on a découvert hier une bombe devant un magasin.
e. Il a été très surpris quand il a compris qu'on le filmait.

4 **React on your blog.**

You are shocked by the number of CCTV cameras you see around you, and you write a short article on your blog. Use the drawings opposite, and make people aware of what can happen to them on a typical day in Britain.

Build up your vocabulary

1 **Associez un mot de la première liste avec un mot de la seconde de façon à former des mots composés. Puis traduisez-les, au besoin à l'aide d'un dictionnaire.**

surveillance • strip • airport • cell • network • train • shopping • laser • railway • police • security • telephone • tapping • tracking • control • speed

room • tapping • camera • printer • search • station • operator • patrol • device • centre • equipment • company • guard • site • phone

2 **Trouvez dans la liste B l'équivalent des mots anglais donnés dans la liste A.**

A tracking device • track down • report • database • mugging • crime • bug • break the law • prevent (from) • deter (from) • safe

B base de données • agression • suivre à la trace • empêcher de • micro caché • sûr • appareil de détection • enfreindre la loi • délit • signaler • dissuader de

Language at work

Improve your listening skills

1 Recopiez cet extrait d'émission radiophonique sur papier libre.

"And in *the* case *of* CCTV, everybody should wake up and see what's becoming *of* the country before it's too late. Now here in Slough *for* example, I *was* standing outside the station not long ago waiting *for* my bus and counted the CCTV cameras within eyesight. There were eight *of them!* Do you realize that? Eight of them! Banksy is certainly right *to* denounce *the* threat they represent, believe me!"

2 Entraînez-vous à lire ce passage.

a. Marquez d'une barre (|) les groupes de sens.
b. Soulignez les mots porteurs de sens.
c. Repérez et marquez les liaisons consonne-voyelle.
d. Comment prononcez-vous les mots en italique du texte ci-dessus ? Quel est leur point commun ? Vérifiez à l'écoute.
e. Repérez l'intonation dans les énoncés exclamatifs. Est-elle montante ou descendante ? Lisez à haute voix.

3 Écoutez les phrases suivantes. Que remarquez-vous à propos des formes négatives ? Concluez et entraînez-vous à les lire à haute voix.

a. *CCTV cameras haven't helped reduce delinquency.*
b. *Strip search isn't in use in all airports yet.*
c. *Smokers shouldn't throw cigarette butts on the ground.*
d. *He doesn't tweet regularly.*
e. *You can't trust all Internet sites.*

4 Écoutez ce court enregistrement et relevez les mots accentués.

a. Selon le champ lexical auquel ils appartiennent, classez les mots relevés en deux colonnes. Donnez un titre à chacune.
b. Quels sont les deux points de vue ?
c. Reconstruisez le sens du message entendu.

5 Écoutez les réactions de Paul et Laura à ce dessin humoristique.

Relevez les différents points mentionnés et présentez-les à la classe.

YOUR TASK

You will listen to a radio report about surveillance today. Gather as much information as possible. Then react and leave your message on the radio station voicemail.

LES ÉTAPES À SUIVRE CD

1 Avant d'écouter

a. Revoyez vos notes et le vocabulaire rencontré lors de l'étude des documents de l'unité.
b. À partir du titre que vous allez entendre, anticipez les mots qui seront utilisés et imaginez le contenu de l'enregistrement.

2 Première écoute

Lors de la première écoute, ne prenez pas de notes.
a. Combien de voix avez-vous repérées ?
b. Repérez les mots porteurs de sens, les éléments lexicaux et déduisez le sens général de l'enregistrement.

3 Deuxième écoute

– Notez les chiffres et leurs référents (ce à quoi ils se rapportent), les dates, les noms de pays.
– Relevez les mots porteurs de sens et déduisez le sujet général de l'enregistrement.
– Reconstituez le sens à partir des éléments notés.

4 Utilisez vos notes

Lisez la fiche distribuée et complétez-la à l'aide des informations que vous avez recueillies.

5 Troisième écoute

Vérifiez et complétez vos réponses.

6 Vos réactions

Préparez le message que vous allez laisser sur le répondeur de l'émission en intégrant les éléments clés que vous avez compris et donnez vos réactions. Enregistrez-vous.

SPEAKING CORNER

A Give your opinion

B Read and comment

> *Twitter is a great place to tell the world what you're thinking before you've had a chance to think about it.*
> Chris Pirillo, a blogger

C Comment on this comic strip

D Tell the story

Unit 9

EAST WIND, WEST WIND

YOUR TASK AT THE END OF THIS UNIT

You are visiting an exhibition on Asian-Americans. You stop and watch the three short videos presented. Check your understanding and post a comment on the museum forum page. → p. 143

TUNE IN!

1 Test your memory

a. Look at this poster carefully for one minute, then close your book.
b. What elements can you identify?
c. What information can you remember (names of places, date, times...)?

2 Matching game

Find the elements from the poster corresponding to these definitions.
– This colour is traditionally the symbol of both happiness and good luck.
– Find another name for the Chinese New Year.
– This animal stands for hope and a peaceful and happy life. People born under this sign are said to be gentle, sensitive and have strong memory.

Help!

Festivities and decorations

gate /geɪt/
paper lantern
dragon /ˈdrægən/
fireworks: *feu d'artifice*
firecracker: *pétard*
performance
parade /pəˈreɪd/
contest
Kung fu costume
energetic
joyful = merry
wink at sb: *faire un clin d'œil à*

PREPARE YOUR TASK →

3 How the West was won CD WB

Listen to this radio programme. Professor John Wang tells us about the immigration of Asians to the USA and their early experiences. Turn to your Workbook for help.

I. SEATTLE'S INTERNATIONAL DISTRICT

1 Find the key information

a. Find the names of a city and a State in the text. Locate them on the map on the back flap of your book.
b. Pick out words or phrases about: places and directions • nationalities • time references • immigrants and immigration • Chinatown today.
c. Recap what you have learnt: where? when? who? why?

South of Seattle's downtown business core[1], adjacent to the city's initial birthplace —Pioneer Square—and next to the train station, lies the International District. Also referred to as Chinatown. [...]

Established at the turn of the twentieth century, it is one of the oldest neighborhoods[2] in the city. A major portion of the International District is on the National Register of Historic Places, primarily because it was the early settlement[3] area[4] for Chinese, Japanese, and Filipinos in Seattle. [...]

It's more than Chinatown... more than a huge Japanese American supermarket... more than a place where you hear Asian languages and music... and more than an exotic locale for movie settings.

This is the community where different Asian immigrants settled, lived, worked and established business and institutions side by side. This is the area where the East met the West, where Asians collided among themselves[5] and with the outside society. [...]

Over the years, the area evolved as the regional center for Asian American culture in Washington State. The District is now the residential area in which Asian Americans remain the majority, and where Asian American commerce and culture predominate. The area is where many new Asian immigrants still come to start their quest of the American dream.

Doug Chin, *Seattle's International District. The Making of a Pan-Asian American Community*, 2001

1. centre **2.** *quartiers* **3.** *là où se sont implantés* **4.** /ˈeəriə/ **5.** *entraient en conflit les uns contre les autres*

REPARE OUR TASK →

2 Guided tour

You are a guide working for Chinatown Discovery Tours. Tell visitors about the mural. Use what you have learnt.

Help!

Adjectives
- Chinese
- Filipino
- Vietnamese
- Korean
- Japanese
- Cambodian
- Pakistani
- Indian

Activities
- construction worker
- labo(u)rer = manual worker
- laundryman: *blanchisseur*
- cook
- shop assistant

2. HOLLYWOOD VISION

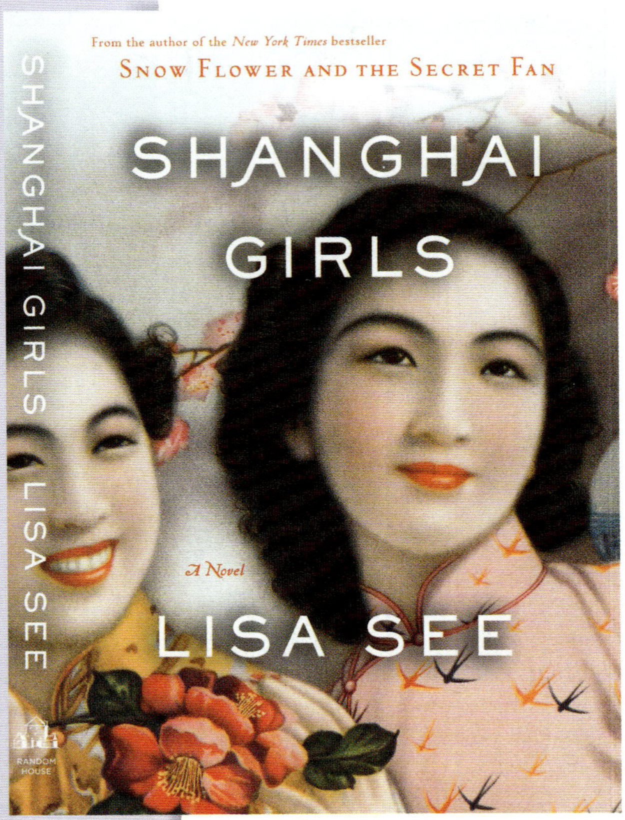

Pearl and May are two Chinese sisters living in Los Angeles. May has found a job as an extra[1] *and interpreter in a Hollywood movie.*

Part 1

I think about *The Shanghai Gesture,* which May, Sam, Vern[2] and I saw earlier this year at the Million Dollar. Josef von Sternberg, the director, had spent time in Shanghai, so we thought we might see something that would remind us of our home city, but it was just another one of those stories where a white girl was led into gambling, alcohol and who knew what else by a dragon lady. We laughed at the movie poster, which read "People live in Shanghai for many reasons... most of them bad." Toward the end of my days in Shanghai, I'd thought that was true but it still hurts to see my home city—the Paris of Asia—painted in such an evil light. We've seen this kind of thing in movie after movie, and now we're in one.

1. *figurant(e)* **2.** Sam and Vern are Pearl's and May's husbands

Part 2

"How can you do this, May? Aren't you ashamed?" I ask.

She looks genuinely[1] confused and hurt. "About what?"

"Every single Chinese in this film is portrayed as backward[2]," I answer. "We're made to giggle[3] like idiots and show our teeth. They make us pantomime because we're supposed to be stupid. Or they make us speak the worst sort of pidgin English[4]—"

"I suppose, but are you telling me this doesn't remind you of Shanghai?" She looks at me hopeful.

"That's not the point! Don't you have any pride in the Chinese people?" [...]

"Why can't you have a good time?" she asks. [...] "I admit we don't make as much as those guys over there." She points to a gaggle[5] of fake[6] rickshaw[7] pullers. "I got them a guaranteed seven fifty a day for a week, so long as they kept their heads completely shaved. Not bad—"

"Rickshaw drivers, opium smokers, and prostitutes. Is that what you want people to think we are?"

"If by people you mean *lo fan*[8], what do I care what they think?"

"Because these things are insulting—"

"To whom? They aren't slurs[9] against *us,* you and me. Besides this is just part of an evolution for us. Some people"—meaning me I suppose—"would rather be unemployed than take a job they feel is beneath them. But a job like this gives us a start, and it's up to us to go from here."

"So today those men will play rickshaw pullers and tomorrow they'll own the studio?" I ask skeptically.

Lisa See, *Shanghai Girls*, 2009

1. *sincèrement* **2.** *arriéré* **3.** *ricaner* **4.** *charabia* **5.** *troupeau* **6.** *faux* **7.** *pousse-pousse*
8. name used by Chinese for white people **9.** insults

1 Find the key information

Part 1

a. Who do the pronouns "I" and "we" refer to?
b. Pick out words and expressions linked to Shanghai.
c. List the words connected to the film industry.
d. Find out the stereotypes associated with Chinese people and China.
e. What is the characters' reaction? Quote from the text.

Part 2

a. Who do the pronouns "I", "she", "we", "they" and "this" refer to?
b. Classify the words connected with the Chinese into three columns: adjectives • jobs • actions.
c. Classify what the sisters say and the words used to describe their attitudes into two columns. What can you conclude on the way they see what is happening in the studio?
d. Sum up Pearl's opinion.
e. Explain May's point of view.

2 Recap

a. The characters (names, native country, city of adoption, activity, motivations).
b. Chinese people's roles in Hollywood movies.
c. Each girl's opinions and reactions on the way Chinese people are portrayed.

Help!

May's reactions	Pearl's reactions	Stereotypes
ambitious strong-willed: *volontaire* she doesn't care a damn about earn one's living: *gagner sa vie* work one's way up the social ladder achieve success seize /si:z/ an opportunity start from scratch: *démarrer de zéro*	shocked = outraged baffled: *déconcerté* bewildered: *perplexe* humiliated object to sth / sb / V-ING criticize / blame sth / sb for V-ING can't stand / bear sth / sb / V-ING resent sth / sb / V-ING = dislike very much	caricature stereotyped vision look down on sb despise: *mépriser* make fun of sb be biased /baɪəst/: *être partial* be prejudiced /predʒʊdɪst/ against: *avoir des préjugés contre*

REPARE OUR TASK

3 Remembering Angel Island CD WB

a. Listen and understand.
– Pick out the names of countries, of a US State and of a city.
– Pick out numbers and dates. Copy and fill in the following mindmaps:

– List words referring to people and divide them into two groups.
– Note down as many stressed words as possible, and classify them: emotions • places • goal.
b. Prepare a two-minute oral account of the document.
c. Use the information collected to write an entry in Don Lee's personal diary (150 words).

3. FRIEND OR FOE?

1 React to this film poster

a. What are your first impressions (use of colours, movements, angle shot → see p. 245)?
b. Where is Pearl Harbor? Locate it on a map.
c. What objects represent danger? Where are they?
d. What is the character doing? Imagine her feelings.
e. Pick out a date. How much do you know about this historical day?

2 Read the text WB

Say what you have understood, then turn to your Workbook for help.

Part 1

"My father can't get our money from the bank," Hatsue replied. [...] "We have a few dollars, and the rest we can't get. My parents aren't citizens."

"What will you do?"

"We don't know."

"I have twenty dollars from picking season[1]," said Ishmael. "You can have all of it—you can just have it. I'll bring it to school in the morning."

"No," said Hatsue. "Don't bring it. My father will figure out something[2] pretty soon. I could never accept your money."

Ishmael turned onto his side, toward her, and propped himself on his elbow[3]. "It's hard to believe," he said.

"It's so unreal," answered Hatsue. "It just isn't fair—it's not *fair*. How could they do this, just like that? How did we get ourselves into this?"

1. *cueillette* **2.** *trouvera une solution* **3.** *coude*

Part 2

"We didn't get ourselves in it," said Ishmael. "The Japanese *forced* us into it. And on a Sunday morning, when no one was ready. It's cheap, if you ask me. They—"

"Look at my face," interrupted Hatsue. "Look at my eyes, Ishmael. My face is the face of the people who did it—don't you see what I mean? My face—it's how the Japanese look. My parents came to San Piedro from Japan. My mother and father, they hardly[1] speak English. My family is in bad trouble now. Do you see what I mean? We're going to have trouble."

"Wait a minute," said Ishmael. "You're not Japanese. You're—"

"You heard the news. They're arresting people. They're calling a lot of people spies[2]. Last night some men stopped at the Ichiyamas' and called them names[3], Ishmael. They sat out front and honked their horn[4]. How can this be happening?" she added. "How did things get like this?"

David Guterson, *Snow Falling on Cedars*, 1994

1. *à peine* **2.** *espions* **3.** *les ont insultés* **4.** *ont klaxonné*

3 Speed check

a. Read the text and answer these questions as quickly as you can.

Part 1

– Who are the characters (first names, origin)?
– "How could they do this?" (l. 18) Who does "they" refer to? What historical event is mentioned?
– What are the consequences on Hatsue's family? Why?
– What is Ishmael's suggestion?

Part 2

– "The Japanese *forced* us into it." (l. 2) What does Ishmael mean?
– What about Hatsue's family background?
– What word is repeated several times? Why?
– What does Hatsue fear?

b. Prepare an oral account of the text. Don't forget to give your reactions.

REPARE OUR TASK

4 December 7th 1941 CD WB

Listen to Akito, a Japanese-American, recalling her family's reaction on that historical date. Turn to your Workbook for help.

5 Bombing

a. Observe the illustration opposite. Identify the characters: nationality, age, activity.

b. How is the Japanese pilot caricatured?

c. What angle shot is used?
→ see p. 245
What is its impact?
What is the picture built on (contrast, colours)?

d. What are the artist's goals?

Roger Shimomura, *Remember Pearl Harbor*, 2003 (51cm x 61cm)

6 The future ahead

Use the information collected both in the text and in the recording to write a sequel to Hatsue and Ishmael's story (150 words). Imagine what may happen to Hatsue and her family. What impact do you think the war will have on the two friends' relationship?

Help!

Ishmael and Hatsue	Historical context	Consequences
naïve ≠ realistic worried /ˈwʌrɪd/ = anxious helpless = powerless be short of money side with sb: *prendre parti pour qqn* foresee: *prévoir* fear ... might + V: *craindre que* spy on sb: *espionner qqn*	wave of aircraft: *vague d'avions* national tragedy wreckage: *épave* no warning attack attack a military base sink (sank, sunk) battleships: *couler des navires de guerre* it came as a shock	scapegoat: *bouc émissaire* second-class citizen guilty be in trouble be accused of V-ING be considered aliens /ˈeɪliənz/ be ostracized = rejected

4. CHILDREN OF THE CAMPS

Roger Shimomura, *American Infamy # 3*, 2008 (152cm x 245cm)

1 Test your memory

a. Look at this illustration carefully for one minute, then close your book.

b. How much can you remember (colours, weather, landscape, buildings, people, clothes)? Use these words: in the foreground • in the background • down below • on the platform • in the distance • through a window • binoculars.

c. What angle shot is used here? (→ see p. 245) What impression is conveyed? What are the artist's intentions?

PREPARE YOUR TASK →

2 Life in the relocation centre

a. Get ready

– The following words are written phonetically. Read them aloud, write them down and check in a dictionary if necessary.

/ˌʌnfəˈgetəbl/ /ˈsəʊldʒəʳz/ /ˈraɪfl/ /ˈpækɪŋ/ /ˈtraɪəl/ /ˈbɑːbd ˈwaɪəʳ/ /ˌriːləʊˈkeɪʃən/

– See p. 121 and find out more about *The Pledge of Allegiance to the American flag*. Then report to the class.

b. Listen to a Japanese-American actor. Turn to your Workbook for help. CD WB

c. Recap what you have learnt about Takei's childhood (age at the time, city of origin, feelings, parents' reaction, life in the camp).

3 Role play

Work in groups and act out George Takei's interview on a TV or radio talk show. Use the information you have collected.

Help!

Life in the camps	Guarding prisoners
internee: *prisonnier* deportation / relocation barracks: *caserne* cramped: *à l'étroit* be persecuted be on rations lack sth: *manquer de qqch*	barbed wire: *fil barbelé* sentry tower: *mirador* machine /məˈʃiːn/ gun search lights order sb in ≠ out round up: *rassembler*

5. MEMORIES OF THE PAST

1 Matching game

a. Observe the four illustrations: place and atmosphere, characters (appearance, actions and feelings).

b. Match each picture with its caption.

1. General DeWitt orders all Japanese or Japanese-Americans living on the Pacific coast States to get ready for evacuation.
2. Everyday life gets organized in the camp. Chores, schooling, infirmary...
3. Radio Flash: Pearl Harbor bombed! Japan's sudden attack on the USA.
4. Camp Minidoka, Hunt, Idaho; arrival at the newly-built camp.

A

B

C

D

Roger Shimomura, *An American Diary Series*, 2002-2003

2 Writing workshop

You are working for *American Heritage*, a famous history magazine. You have been asked to write an article for Asian Pacific American (APA) Heritage Month about the story of a Japanese-American boy during WW2. Use these four pictures to illustrate your text (200 words).

Language at work

For – since – ago – during

1 Lisez l'interview ci-dessous.

Classez les formes verbales en gras en quatre colonnes : prétérit (forme active et forme passive) et *present perfect* (forme simple et forme en BE + -ING).
Relevez aussi les marqueurs de temps utilisés à chaque fois.

JOURNALIST: When **did** you **leave** Taiwan?
JERRY CHEN: I **left** Taiwan forty years ago.
JOURNALIST: How old **were** you then?
J. CHEN: I **was** ten at that time. I **lived** in Taiwan for ten years before my parents settled in the US.
JOURNALIST: Where **did** you **learn** to speak English?
J. CHEN: I **was taught** English for a year, then went to High School and later to College. I must say I **found** it hard to adapt for the first five years.
JOURNALIST: What **happened** afterwards?
J. CHEN: I **set up** my own business twenty years ago.
JOURNALIST: How long **have** you **been** in California?
J. CHEN: **I've been living** in Silicon Valley since 1990. **I've been working** hard for years, since I **started** my own company. I **have achieved** my goals.

2 Repérez.

a. Quelles formes verbales indiquent :
– que l'on parle d'un événement qui a commencé dans le passé et qui dure jusqu'au moment présent ?
– que l'événement passé est coupé du présent (= on raconte l'histoire) ?
b. Quels marqueurs de temps permettent de confirmer ces deux points de vue ?

3 Traduisez ces énoncés.

– *I **was taught** English for a year.*
– *I **found** it hard to adapt for the first five years.*
– *I**'ve been working** hard for years.*
Quel est l'équivalent français de *for* dans chacune de ces phrases ?

4 Observez.

– *I**'ve been living** in Silicon Valley since 1990.*
– *I**'ve been working** hard for years / since I **started** my own company.*

Since peut introduire une ... (ou l'indication d'un moment) ou une proposition au ... .
Traduisez *since* dans chacun des énoncés.
a. Lorsque *for* a pour équivalent français ... et que l'événement est situé entièrement dans le passé, il s'utilise avec un ... .
Quand *for* a pour équivalent français ... et que l'événement dure jusqu'au présent, il s'utilise avec un ... .
b. Lorsqu'on veut indiquer le point de départ d'un événement, on se sert de ... , qui se traduit en français par... .
c. *Ago* est associé à un ... parce qu'il renvoie à ... . Il se traduit par ... .

5 Attention aux équivalents anglais de « pendant ».

a. Trouvez les questions correspondant à ces réponses.
– *My father left China during the war.*
– *My father stayed in a relocation camp for two years.*
b. *During* place l'événement à l'intérieur d'une période de temps, sans autre précision ; il répond à la question ... ? *For* indique la durée de l'événement ; il répond à la question ... ?

Language at work

Practice

1 Complétez avec *for*, *since*, *ago* ou *during*.

Angel Island museum

We sailed ... nineteen days across the Pacific Ocean until we landed in San Francisco. That was fifteen years ... . Angel Island is located in the middle of the San Francisco Bay and was used as an immigration centre ... thirty years, between 1910 and 1940. Many Asians were detained ... two weeks, many stayed ... several months or even years. ... their stay men and women were separated and lived in barracks. They went through interrogations ... hours. I was so upset about my experience that ... fifty years I refused to mention Angel Island. I only started talking about it fifteen years ... . I've had nightmares every night ... my detention.

2 Choisissez la solution qui convient.

Amy Tan (is • was • has been) born in 1950 in Auckland, California. Her parents (have migrated • migrated) to the US seventy years ago. She (gains • gained • has gained) international attention since her first novel, *The Joy Luck Club*. A few years after its publication the book (was • has been • is) translated into 25 languages. She (has known • knows • knew) Stephen King for many years now because they belong to the same rock'n'roll group.

3 Traduisez.

a. Ils sont restés enfermés dans ce camp pendant au moins deux ans.
b. Il s'est rendu compte qu'il allait devoir vendre sa boutique après son interrogatoire.
c. Pendant la guerre, certains Japonais ont été accusés d'espionnage.
d. Le cinéma américain s'intéresse aux communautés asiatiques depuis quelques années.
e. Angel Island a été transformée en musée il y a quelques années.

Build up your vocabulary

Champs lexicaux.

a. Lisez ces mots et expressions puis classez-les en quatre colonnes en fonction du champ lexical auquel ils appartiennent : exclusion • mépris • indignation • peur • désespoir. Utilisez un dictionnaire si nécessaire.

shocked • rejected • frightened • outraged • panic-stricken • appalled • terrified • ostracized • indignant • contempt • outcast • look down on • despise • (be) discriminated against • sick with fear • mad with anxiety • hopeless • desperate

b. Au sein de chaque colonne, classez ces mots en noms, adjectifs, participes passés et verbes.
c. Remplacez les groupes de mots soulignés à l'aide d'un élément de la liste ci-dessus.

After Pearl Harbor, Asian-Americans noticed they were no longer members of the community and they were treated differently. They were frightened because they felt they did not know what to do and had lost all hope. When they heard of relocation centres they were really scared and extremely worried about the future.

Language at work

Improve your listening skills

1 Anticipez.

a. Regardez les deux photos à droite et imaginez le contenu de cet enregistrement.
b. Quels mots vous attendez-vous à entendre ? Choisissez dans cette liste : *racism* • *famous* • *social network* • *geek* • *the Internet* • *talented* • *university* • *cello*.
c. Entraînez-vous à lire ces noms propres en transcriptions phonétique :
/ˈbærək/ /əʊˈbɑːmə/ /ˈkenədi/
/bræd/ /pɪt/ /ˈrɒkəfelə^r/

2 Première écoute.

MP3 19

a. Combien de voix entendez-vous ?
b. D'après le ton, diriez-vous que vous avez entendu : une interview • une dispute • une conversation amicale • un débat ?
c. Parmi ces thèmes, quels sont ceux abordés dans l'enregistrement : *successful Asians* • *hostility and racism* • *self-made men* • *Chinese immigration* • *life at university* • *a world of music ?*

3 Deuxième écoute.

Partie 1
a. Écoutez et notez sur une feuille les mots porteurs de sens.
b. Utilisez-les pour résumer ce que vous avez compris.
Partie 2
a. Écoutez et notez sur une feuille les mots porteurs de sens.
b. Utilisez vos notes pour reformuler ce que vous avez compris.

4 Présentez les personnages ci-dessus.

Pour ce faire, servez-vous de vos notes.

5 Le rythme de la phrase.

MP3 20

a. À quoi correspondent les mots en **gras** et ceux en maigre ?

Maya Lin, a **Chinese American**, was **born** in **Ohio**. Her **parents immigrated** to the **United States** from **China** in **1949** and **settled** in **Ohio** in **1958**. She **rose** to **fame** in **1981**. Just 21 years old and **still** an **architectural student** at **Yale University**, she **won** a **contest** to **design** the **Vietnam War Memorial** in **Washington, D.C.**

b. Lisez ces quatre phrases à haute voix, puis vérifiez à l'écoute.

6 L'accent de mot.

MP3 21

a. Écoutez ces mots et repérez à chaque fois la syllabe accentuée.
– *minority* • *hostility* • *university*
– *inauguration* • *discrimination* • *immigration*
– *incredible* • *horrible* • *impossible*
b. Partez de la droite du mot pour trouver le suffixe commun à chaque liste. Quelle incidence chaque suffixe a-t-il sur l'accent du mot ? → p. 246

YOUR TASK

You are visiting an exhibition on Asian-Americans. You stop and watch the three short videos presented. Check your understanding and post a comment on the museum forum page.

LES STRATÉGIES DE COMPRÉHENSION DE L'ORAL

Faites un bilan en répondant rapidement à ce questionnaire. Dans la liste suivante, repérez ce que vous faites déjà et veillez à faire ce que vous oubliez parfois.

1 Anticiper

Pensez-vous à anticiper le contenu à l'aide du titre, de la / des photo(s) mise(s) en regard ?

2 Repérer

Quels indices vous permettent de construire du sens :
– des indices sonores (bruits de fond, bruitages, cris, chants, pleurs...) ?
– la ou les musiques de la bande-son ?
– les éléments clés (nombre de personnages, voix off, lieux, activités) ?
– les dates, nombres, chiffres, marqueurs de temps ?
– les mots accentués (mots porteurs de sens) ?
– les éléments lexicaux connus ?
– les tons de voix, les intonations qui traduisent les sentiments des personnages ?

3 Établir des liens

Reliez-vous les différents indices repérés ?

4 Compenser

Vous appuyez-vous sur les images pour compenser ce que vous n'avez pas compris ?

5 Mémoriser

– Essayez-vous de mémoriser le plus d'éléments possible ?
– Avez-vous l'habitude de classer les éléments repérés (personnes, lieux, activités, sentiments...) pour pouvoir en faire une synthèse ?

LES ÉTAPES À SUIVRE

Video CD

Vous allez voir trois courtes vidéos. Une fiche va vous être distribuée.

1. Lisez d'abord les consignes. Chaque vidéo sera passée trois fois.
2. Le premier visionnage se fera en continu sans crayon.
3. Lors du deuxième visionnage, remplissez la fiche au fur et à mesure. Vous disposerez de quelques minutes pour prendre des notes et répondre aux questions posées.
4. La vidéo sera passée une troisième fois, pour vérifier et compléter vos réponses.
5. Avant de ramasser les fiches, votre professeur vous laissera quelques minutes pour vous relire.
6. Écrivez vos commentaires, expliquez ce que vous avez vu, dites ce que vous avez découvert, quelles images vous ont le plus frappé(e).

Évaluation

JE M'ENTRAÎNE

Je mets en œuvre toutes les stratégies indispensables à l'écoute d'un document sonore.

1 J'anticipe

a. Faites la liste des thèmes et des mots qui vous viennent à l'esprit en observant cette image.
b. Lisez les mots ci-dessous et leur transcription phonétique.

Help!

glacier /ˈglæsɪəʳ/
Montana /mɒnˈtænə/
Oregon /ˈɒrɪgən/
Idaho /ˈaɪdəˌhəʊ/
Mount Rainier /ˌmaʊntˈreɪnɪəʳ/
Yosemite /jəʊˈsemәti/
Canada /ˈkænədə/
acre /ˈeɪkəʳ/= about 4,000m^2

2 Je recueille les premiers indices

MP3 22

a. De quel type d'enregistrement s'agit-il (publicité radiophonique, conversation entre amis, interview, talk show, extrait de film...) ?
b. Repérez le nombre de voix et les accents.
c. Identifiez d'autres indices sonores : musique, bruits de fond, rires...
d. Repérez les noms propres (noms de pays, de personnes, de lieux célèbres).

3 J'affine ma compréhension

Écoutez l'enregistrement une seconde fois.
a. Relevez les nombres et, ici, les points cardinaux.
b. Repérez les mots porteurs de sens (ils sont plus accentués et se détachent).
c. Des mots sont-ils répétés ?
d. Classez tous les mots notés par rubrique *(history, description, activities....)*, ou sous forme de carte mentale comme ci-contre.

Listening

4 Je reconstitue le message

Dans ce document :
– que sait-on de la destination évoquée par le narrateur ?
– quelle est son opinion sur les lieux mentionnés ?

MP3 23

5 Je m'auto-évalue

Hannah Wood speaks about her holidays in Blackpool. Listen to her recording and answer the questions on the worksheet you will be given.

6 Je m'auto-corrige

Corrigez vos réponses à l'aide de la fiche que vous trouverez sur le site compagnon et comptabilisez vos points.

JE FAIS LE BILAN

Analysez vos résultats à l'aide de cette grille d'évaluation où sont définis différents paliers de compétence en compréhension de l'oral.

Je peux...	Paliers
... comprendre des phrases simples en anglais standard sur des sujets qui me sont connus, même si le message est adressé à un public large.	B1
... comprendre l'essentiel d'une émission de télévision ou de radio sur des sujets d'actualité, des thèmes familiers ou liés à mon programme, si on parle lentement et distinctement.	B1
... comprendre des détails, des informations plus complexes et / ou plus longues grâce aux marqueurs chronologiques et aux repères argumentatifs.	B2
... comprendre l'implicite en repérant les émotions et les sentiments transmis par le ton de celui / celle qui parle.	B2

ÉVALUATION

Votre professeur va vous distribuer une fiche d'évaluation de la compréhension de l'oral sur une des unités travaillées en cours :

Unit 7 Far and away CD

Unit 8 Under control CD

Unit 9 East Wind, West Wind CD

La qualité de l'anglais ne sera pas prise en compte, seule l'exactitude de la réponse le sera.
Une fois l'évaluation terminée, votre professeur pourra déterminer à quel palier vous vous situez par rapport à la grille du Cadre Européen Commun de Référence pour les Langues.

Unit 10 KING ARTHUR REVISITED

- What do you know about King Arthur, the Knights of the Round Table and their quest for the Holy Grail?
- Discover how Monty Python adapted this legend to the screen

→ YOUR TASK

You are working at Camelot Theme Park located in Lancashire. You have been asked to play a scene based on the *Holy Grail*. Use a scene from Monty Python or invent a new one!

→ p. 157

Unit 11 WHATEVER WORKS

- Choosing your job
- Dealing with your boss
- What's a workaholic?
- Discover why a woman banker was fired

→ YOUR TASK

You are applying for a summer job in an English-speaking country. You have an interview with a recruiter. The most convincing candidate will get the job.

→ p. 169

Unit 12 BORN TO SHOP?

- Confession of a shopaholic
- Have you ever heard of Black Friday and Buy Nothing Day?
- No to consumption

→ YOUR TASK

You are taking part in a debate in a TV show on the night of Buy Nothing Day: Are you for or against a day without shopping? Defend your point of view.

→ p. 183

ÉVALUATION SOMMATIVE *SPEAKING INTERACTION* → p. 186-187

Unit 10

KING ARTHUR REVISITED

YOUR TASK AT THE END OF THIS UNIT

You are working at Camelot Theme Park located in Lancashire. You have been asked to play a scene based on the *Holy Grail*. Use a scene from Monty Python or invent a new one! → p. 157

TUNE IN!

IMAGINING THE MEDIEVAL FANTASY WORLD

People have been playing fantasy-medieval roleplaying games since 1974, when the first edition of *Dungeons and Dragons* came out. In these games, each player incarnates a character such as a knight, a wizard or an elf, and they work together to vanquish evil foes[1] and complete great quests. Many similar games have come out in the last 30 years, including some on the computer, such as *World of Warcraft*, or even outdoors, as with *LARP (Live Action Role Playing)*.

1. *ennemis maléfiques*

Discuss

a. What is this document? Describe the different elements you can pick out.

b. Have you played games like this? Do you think they are interesting, or ridiculous?

c. Do you think such games can represent the medieval world as it really was?

d. Would you rather play the role of a feudal knight, such as a Knight of the Round Table, or would you prefer to play some fantasy character? Why? Confront your views with the rest of the class.

I. INFO SEARCH

1 The legend

Go on the website: editions-hatier.fr/meetingpoint

Read through the pages and find the following information on the legend of King Arthur /ˈɑːθə/.

a. King Arthur:
- When did King Arthur live?
- What role did he play?
- Find the name of Arthur's parents.
- Where was Arthur born?
- Why was Arthur taken away from his parents?
- Who took him away and who raised him?
- How old was Arthur when he ruled over Britain?
- Where did Arthur die?

b. The contest:
- Who was it organized by?
- What was its goal?
- Who won it and how?

c. Excalibur:
- What is it?
- Who gave King Arthur Excalibur?
- What was it for?

d. Camelot and the Round Table:
- What was Camelot?
- What did the Round Table symbolize?

e. Friends or foes?
- Who was Mordred?
- How was he related to Arthur?
- Name two famous knights /naɪts/.

f. Battle of Camlann:
- Why was Arthur seriously wounded?
- By whom?
- What happened to the sword?

g. Name a famous composer who based one of his operas on the life of one famous knight.

h. What values do King Arthur and the Knights of the Round Table embody or defend?
Why do they still attract people today?

2 Jumbled order WB

Reorder the different pictures in your Workbook and justify your choice.

2. THE BLACK KNIGHT

1 Get ready

a. What do you know about Monty Python? Have you seen any of their films? Which one(s)? Go on the Internet for more information and report to the class.

b. Watch and speak. Go on the Internet (www.pythonline.com/youtube_archive/black-night) and watch this scene on the Monty Python official website.
– What were your first reactions? Did you find the scene funny? Why? Why not?
– What soundtrack is used? What is the effect on the viewer?
– Sum up what happens in a few sentences.

King Arthur, accompanied by his faithful servant, Patsy, is travelling through a dark forest when he witnesses an epic battle between two armoured knights. After one of the knights dies horribly, Arthur approaches the victor, the Black Knight, and tries to recruit him.

Arthur: You fight with the strength of many men, Sir Knight. I am Arthur, King of the Britons. *(silence)* I seek[1] the finest and the bravest knights in the land to join me in my Court of Camelot. *(silence)* You have proved yourself worthy[2]; will you join me? *(silence)* You make me sad. So be it. Come, Patsy.
Black Knight: None shall[3] pass.
Arthur: What?
Black Knight: None shall pass.
Arthur: I have no quarrel with you, good Sir Knight, but I must cross this bridge.
Black Knight: Then you shall die.
Arthur: I command you as King of the Britons to stand aside!
Black Knight: I move for no man.
Arthur: So be it! *(Arthur chops the Black Knight's left arm off.)*
Arthur: Now stand aside, worthy[4] adversary.
Black Knight: 'Tis but a scratch.
Arthur: A scratch? Your arm's off!
Black Knight: No, it isn't.
Arthur: Well, what's that then?
Black Knight: I've had worse.
Arthur: You liar!
Black Knight: Come on you pansy[5]! *(Arthur chops the Black Knight's right arm off.)*
Arthur: Victory is mine! *(kneeling)* We thank thee[6] Lord, that in thy[6] merc[7]—
Black Knight: Come on then.
Arthur: What?
Black Knight: Have at you!
Arthur: You are indeed brave, Sir Knight, but the fight is mine.
Black Knight: Oh, had enough, eh?
Arthur: Look, you stupid bastard, you've got no arms left.
Black Knight: Yes I have.
Arthur: Look!
Black Knight: Just a flesh wound[8].
Arthur: Look, stop that.
Black Knight: Chicken[9]! Chicken!
Arthur: Look, I'll have your leg. Right! *(Arthur chops the Black Knight's left leg off.)*
Black Knight: Right, I'll do you[10] for that!
Arthur: You'll what?
Black Knight: Come 'ere!
Arthur: What are you going to do, bleed[11] on me?
Black Knight: I'm invincible!
Arthur: You're a loony[12].
Black Knight: Black Knights always triumph! Have at you! Come on then. *(Arthur chops the Black Knight's other leg off.)*
Black Knight: All right; we'll call it a draw[13].
Arthur: Come, Patsy.
Black Knight: Oh, oh, I see, running away then. You yellow bastards! Come back here and take what's coming to you. I'll bite your legs off!

Monty Python and the Holy Grail, 1975, Scene 4

1. I look for **2.** *(ici) valeureux* **3.** (formal) = will **4.** *(ici) noble* **5.** offensive term qualifying a man as effeminate
6. *formes, maintenant archaïques, du tutoiement* **7.** = mercy: *miséricorde* **8.** *blessure superficielle*
9. *(ici) dégonflé* **10.** (familiar) punish **11.** *saigner* **12.** *cinglé* **13.** *match nul*

2 Read and understand

a. What do the underlined pronouns refer to in the script?
"'Tis but a scratch" (l. 20) • "Well, what's that then?" (l. 23) • "... we'll call it a draw." (l. 55)

b. Read this definition of an understatement.

> A figure of speech in which a writer or speaker deliberately makes a situation seem less important or serious than it is. Contrast with hyperbole.

What lines in the text are understatements? Who uses them and why?

c. "I seek the finest and the bravest knights in the land..." (l. 3) • "You're a loony." (l. 51): Compare Arthur's attitude towards the knight at the beginning and at the end of the scene.

3 Characterization

a. Draw King Arthur's and the Black Knight's portraits. Give examples to illustrate your point.
b. Patsy is a silent character. What does he do in this scene? What explains his attitude?

4 A farce

List the elements in the scene that correspond to the following definition:

> A farce combines visual gags, exaggerated actions, and silly impossible situations intended to make the audience laugh.

Help!

The Black Knight	King Arthur	Patsy
adamant: *inflexible* impressive maimed: *mutilé* give up = abandon yield to: *céder à* defy sb = challenge sb taunt sb: *narguer qqn*	opponent / foe /fəʊ/: *adversaire, ennemi* authoritative self-confident astounded /əˈstaʊndɪd/ at: *abasourdi par* triumph over praise sb: *louer qqn* expect sb to do sth: *s'attendre à ce que qqn fasse qqch*	cowardly = chicken-hearted: *lâche* shrink back from sb / V-ING: *reculer devant* dare: *oser* dread /dred/: *redouter* avoid sb / V-ING: *éviter qqch / de*

3. OPPRESSED

1 Find the key information

a. Read the script and / or watch the video on the Monty Python official website (www.pythonline.com/youtube_archive/constitutional-peasants) and say what you have understood.

b. Read the text again and turn to your Workbook for help.

Part 1

ARTHUR: Old woman!
DENNIS: Man!
ARTHUR: Man. Sorry. What knight lives in that castle over there?
DENNIS: I'm thirty-seven.
ARTHUR: I— what?
DENNIS: I'm thirty-seven. I'm not old.
ARTHUR: Well, I can't just call you "Man".
DENNIS: Well, you could say "Dennis".
ARTHUR: Well, I didn't know you were called "Dennis".
DENNIS: Well, you didn't bother to[1] find out, did you?
ARTHUR: I did say "sorry" about the "old woman", but from behind you looked—
DENNIS: What I object to is that you automatically treat me like an inferior!
ARTHUR: Well, I am king!
DENNIS: Oh, king, eh, very nice. And how'd you get that, eh? By exploiting the workers! By 'anging[2] on to outdated imperialist dogma which perpetuates the economic and social differences in our society. If there's ever going to be any progress with the—
WOMAN: Dennis, there's some lovely filth[3] down here. Oh! How d'you do?
ARTHUR: How do you do, good lady? I am Arthur, King of the Britons. Whose castle is that?
WOMAN: King of the who?
ARTHUR: The Britons.
WOMAN: Who are the Britons?
ARTHUR: Well, we all are. We are all Britons, and I am your king.
WOMAN: I didn't know we had a king. I thought we were an autonomous collective.
DENNIS: You're fooling yourself[4]. We're living in a dictatorship: a self-perpetuating autocracy in which the working classes—
WOMAN: Oh, there you go bringing class into it again.
DENNIS: That's what it's all about. If only people would hear of—
ARTHUR: Please! Please, good people. I am in haste[5]. Who lives in that castle?
WOMAN: No one lives there.
ARTHUR: Then who is your lord?
WOMAN: We don't have a lord.
ARTHUR: What?
DENNIS: I told you. We're an anarcho-syndicalist commune. We take it in turns to act as a sort of executive officer for the week—
ARTHUR: Yes.
DENNIS: ... but all the decisions of that officer have to be ratified at a special bi-weekly meeting...
ARTHUR: Yes, I see.
DENNIS: ... by a simple majority in the case of purely internal affairs...
ARTHUR: Be quiet!
DENNIS: ... but by a two-thirds majority in the case of more major—
ARTHUR: Be quiet! I order you to be quiet!

1. *donné la peine de* **2.** = hanging (working-class people in Great Britain do not pronounce the h at the beginning of some words)
3. *(ici) fumier* **4.** *(ici) Tu te fais des illusions.* **5.** *Je dois me hâter.*

Part 2

WOMAN: Order, eh? Who does he think he is? Heh.
ARTHUR: I am your king!
WOMAN: Well, I didn't vote for you.
ARTHUR: You don't vote for kings.
WOMAN: Well, how did you become king, then?
ARTHUR: The Lady of the Lake, ... *(Angels sing.)*... her arm clad in the purest shimmering samite[1], held aloft[2] Excalibur from the bosom of the water[3] signifying by Divine Providence that I, Arthur, was to carry Excalibur. *(Singing stops.)* That is why I am your king!
DENNIS: Listen. Strange women lying in ponds distributing swords is no basis for a system of government. Supreme executive power derives from a mandate from the masses, not from some farcical aquatic ceremony.
ARTHUR: Be quiet!
DENNIS: Well, but you can't expect to wield[4] supreme executive power just 'cause some watery tart[5] threw a sword at you!
ARTHUR: Shut up!
DENNIS: I mean, if I went 'round saying I was an emperor just because some moistened bint had lobbed a scimitar at me[6], they'd put me away[7]!
ARTHUR: Shut up, will you? Shut up!
DENNIS: Ah, now we see the violence inherent in the system.
ARTHUR: Shut up!
DENNIS: Oh! Come and see the violence inherent in the system! Help! Help! I'm being repressed!
ARTHUR: Bloody peasant[8]!
DENNIS: Oh, what a give-away. Did you hear that? Did you hear that, eh? That's what I'm on about. Did you see him repressing me? You saw it, didn't you?

Monty Python and the Holy Grail, 1975, Scene 4

1. (old English) *habillée d'une robe de soie naturelle et scintillante* **2.** (littéraire) *en l'air* **3.** /ˈwɔːtəʳ/ *sorti de la profondeur des eaux* **4.** (littéraire) *exercer* **5.** *garce* **6.** *nana dégoulinante d'eau m'avait balancé une épée* **7.** *on m'enfermerait* **8.** /ˈpezənt/

2 What makes you laugh?

a. Match each word with its definition: satire /ˈsætaɪəʳ/ • nonsense.

A way of criticizing something such as a group of people or a system, in which you deliberately make them seem funny so that people will see their faults.

Subject, matter, behaviour or language that is foolish or absurd.

b. What is criticized in the scene you have studied (type of speech, language level)? How and why? Pick out elements to justify your answer. Do you find it funny? Why? Why not?

Les réponses abrégées et les *question tags* (reprises interrogatives)

1 Répondre positivement ou négativement.

a. *“I suppose you like British humour.”* *“Yes, I do. / No, I don’t.”*
b. *“You saw this film, I guess.”* *“Yes, I did. / No, I didn’t.”*
c. *“You’ve seen* The Holy Grail, *haven’t you?”* *“Yes, I have. / No, I haven’t.”*

Comment sont formées les réponses abrégées dans ces énoncés ? *Yes / No* + ... + ...
→ Au présent et au prétérit l’auxiliaire n’apparaît pas dans l’énoncé ... , il apparaît dans la ... .

2 Réponses *I think so / I don’t think so / I suppose not*, etc.

a. *“Was* The Holy Grail *filmed in Scotland?”* *“I think so.”*
b. *“Will your friend like this film?”* *“Yes, I think so. / I suppose so. / I guess so. / I expect so.”*
c. *“Will your friend lend us his DVD?”* *“No, I don’t think so.”*
d. *“Do you know who lives here?”* *“I’m afraid not.”*
e. *“You know this scene by heart?”* *“Of course not.”*

– Quels mots pourraient remplacer *so* en **a** et **b** ?
– Quels mots pourraient remplacer *no* ou *not* en **c**, **d** et **e** ?

3 Équivalents de « Moi aussi » / « Moi non plus », etc.

a. *“We found the Black Knight scene the funniest.”* *“So did we.”*
b. *“I didn’t like this sketch at all.”* *“Neither did I. Neither did my boyfriend.”*

→ On utilise *So* lorsque le premier énoncé est ... . *So* est directement suivi de ... .
→ On utilise *Neither* lorsque le premier énoncé est ... . *Neither* est suivi directement de ... .

4 Répondre par un équivalent de « Moi si » / « Pas moi ».

a. *“Nobody will fight against Arthur.”* *“I will.”*
b. *“Everybody fears the king.”* *“I don’t.”*
c. *“Everybody feared the king.”* *“Dennis didn’t.”*

MP3 24

→ Pour s’opposer à ce qui est dit on reprend l’ ... de la phrase de départ, que l’on met à la forme affirmative ou négative selon l’énoncé. On utilise ... / ... ou ... au présent et au prétérit simple.
→ Écoutez les énoncés : quel mot est accentué de façon particulière à chaque fois ?

5 *Tags* interrogatifs.

MP3 25

a. Écoutez et comparez.
– *“The serf and his wife are not impressed by the king, are they?”*
“The serf and his wife are rebellious, aren’t they?” “Yes, they are. They did not obey the king’s orders.”
– *“The knight has been seriously injured, hasn’t he?”*
“The knight has not been defeated yet, has he?” “No, he hasn’t. He is still fighting.”

→ Le *tag* permet à l’énonciateur de demander confirmation de ce qu’il vient de dire.

1. Quand l’énoncé est positif, le *tag* est ... : ... + ... + ... ?
2. Quand l’énoncé est négatif, le *tag* est ... : ... + ... ?
3. Quand le *tag* n’est pas une vraie question (on constate sans attendre de réponse), l’intonation est ... .
4. Quand le *tag* est une vraie question, l’intonation est ... .

b. *Never*
Patsy never takes any initiative, does he?
→ *Never* étant un terme négatif, le *tag* sera ... .

Language at work

Practice

1 Complétez à l'aide d'un *tag*.

a. We know very little historically about Arthur, ... ?
b. Arthur never existed, ... ?
c. If Arthur had been a real king, he would have lived around the 5th or 6th century, ... ?
d. The name Arthur comes from the Welsh, ... ?
e. In the legend, King Arthur conquered a vast empire, ... ?
f. King Arthur and the Knights of the Round Table is an epic tale, ... ?
g. Lancelot was Arthur's favourite knight, ... ?
h. The bravest knights are Lancelot and Percival, ... ?
i. Arthur was married to Guinevere, ... ?
j. Many movies on the subject have been made in the past few decades, ... ?
k. King Arthur's legends were popular in the 19th century, ... ?

2 Traduisez les réponses courtes données en français.

a. "I think *The Holy Grail* is a cult film." — *« Pas moi. »*
b. "I love black humour." — *« Moi aussi. »*
c. "I find the Pythons hilarious." — *« Pas moi. »*
d. "I have always been a fan of this British actor." — *« Moi aussi. »*
e. "John Boorman's film *Excalibur* is amazing." — *« Non, je ne pense pas ! »*
f. "No producer wanted to invest in the film *The Holy Grail*." — *« Si, les Pink Floyd. »*
g. "He doesn't see many comedies." — *« Moi non plus. »*
h. "Did you enjoy the video?" — *« Bien sûr que oui. »*
i. "Will it be easy to learn your part?" — *« Je crains que non. »*
j. "Did everybody understand what Dennis said?" — *« Non, je ne crois pas. »*

Build up your vocabulary

1 Remplacez chaque verbe souligné par un verbe suivi d'une particule adverbiale.

Faites les changements nécessaires. Utilisez un dictionnaire au besoin.

carry on • find out • give up • grow up • make up • run out of • set off • turn down

a. The whole story was <u>invented</u>.
b. He <u>spent his childhood</u> in Tintagel.
c. The Black Knight <u>rejected</u> Arthur's offer to become a knight.
d. The Black Knight will never <u>stop</u> the fight. He will <u>continue</u> fighting till he dies.
e. The king <u>had no</u> patience <u>left</u> and walked away.
f. King Arthur wanted to <u>discover</u> the location of the Holy Grail.
g. All the knights <u>started the journey</u> very early.

2 Complétez à l'aide de la préposition qui convient : *across, after, at...*

King Arthur and Patsy were riding ... the land. As it was getting dark they decided to take shelter ... a chapel. ... the following morning they arrived ... a crossroads. They took the road ... the right and they rode ... a wood. They came ... a bridge. They saw somebody ... front ... them. ... the bridge a knight stopped them. They walked ... him because Arthur wanted to talk to him. Patsy was standing ... Arthur. When Patsy realized it was quite dangerous, he hid ... a bush. Arthur tried to get closer ... the Black Knight but couldn't. Then they started crossing swords.

Language at work

Improve your speaking skills

A The Black Knight, p. 150

King Arthur, a film by Antoine Fuqua (2004)

1 Define the tone.

How do the king and the knight speak to each other? Fill in the blanks with one of these verbs: declare • warn • retort • answer • claim • assert • order.

a. "I seek the finest and the bravest knights in the land to join me in my Court of Camelot," Arthur ... .
b. "I have no quarrel with you, good Sir Knight, but I must cross this bridge," Arthur ... .
c. "Then you shall die," the Black Knight ... .
d. "Now stand aside, worthy adversary," Arthur ... .
e. "'Tis but a scratch," the Black Knight ... .

2 Intonation and feelings.

MP3 26

a. Listen to these dialogues. For each sentence say if the intonation is rising (↗), falling (↘) or if it is a fall-rise (↘↗).

ARTHUR: A scratch? Your arm's off!
BLACK KNIGHT: No, it isn't.
ARTHUR: Well, what's that then?
BLACK KNIGHT: I've had worse.
ARTHUR: You liar!

ARTHUR: You are indeed brave, Sir Knight, but the fight is mine.
BLACK KNIGHT: Oh, had enough, eh?
ARTHUR: Look, you stupid bastard, you've got no arms left.
BLACK KNIGHT: Yes I have.
ARTHUR: Look!
BLACK KNIGHT: Just a flesh wound.
ARTHUR: Look, stop that.
BLACK KNIGHT: Chicken! Chicken!

b. Then say what feeling each intonation reveals: He sounds amazed • contemptuous • defiant • brave • provocative • matter of fact = unemotional...

c. Listen to these two sentences. What words are particularly stressed? Why?
"You are indeed brave, Sir Knight, but the fight is mine."
"Look, you stupid bastard, you've got no arms left."

d. Now in pairs read these passages aloud.

3 How to pronounce. WB

Work on the pronunciation with the help of your Workbook, then read the dialogue aloud.

B Oppressed, p. 152-153

1 Train your ears and memory.

MP3 27

Listen to these words, then read them aloud:
exploit • worker • imperialist • economic • social • system • government • executive power • emperor • repress • majority • dictatorship • peasant • inferior • progress.

2 Silent letter.

MP3 28

What letters are not pronounced in the following words? knight • sword • castle

3 How to pronounce. WB

Work on the pronunciation and the stage directions with the help of your Workbook, then read the dialogue aloud.

YOUR TASK

You are working at Camelot Theme Park located in Lancashire. You have been asked to play a scene based on the *Holy Grail*. Use a scene from Monty Python or invent a new one!

TASK 1: ACT OUT

In groups you will choose one scene you have studied and stage it. Imagine the setting, invent the stage directions, learn your part and act it out in front of an audience.
– Three students can be the stage directors and give instructions to the actors.

– Take the time to do what we have planned and don't be shy.
– Look at / Face the **au**dience much more.
– Make a change in your voice for...
– When you say... you need to make b**i**gger g**e**stures, it's imp**o**rtant.
– You need to speak more sl**o**wly when you say... make a g**e**sture... to **i**ndicate... .
– You should sound more exc**i**ted / ex**a**sperated / ch**a**rming / n**e**rvous and **a**nxious.
– You need to ex**a**ggerate much more and **o**pen up your b**o**dy.

– You need a prompter *(souffleur)*.
– Somebody must be in charge of the props *(accessoires sur scène)*.
– In your own notes write down the places where you will breathe (|), the words that must be stressed, the stresses or specific phonetic symbols of the words you find difficult to pronounce, your movements in the scene, the tone you will be using, who you must be looking at (your partner, the audience).

Sir Edward Burne-Jones, *St. George and the Dragon*, 1868

TASK 2: WRITE YOUR OWN ADVENTURE OF KING ARTHUR

1. **Location:** in the wilderness • in the woods • on a battleground • in a secret chamber • in a cave, etc.
2. **Characters:** King Arthur • a Saxon invader • Patsy • a dragon at the entrance of a cave • one of the twelve Knights of the Round Table
3. **Identity card:** Give each character a name, indicate his strength, intelligence, dexterity and equipment.
4. **Events:** King Arthur meets, battles with and defeats his opponent.
5. **Choose your style:** an epic • a farce • a satire, etc.
6. **Write the scenario** and divide the roles.

Vote for the best
Decide who the winners will be: best actor / actress • best stage director • the funniest sketch (task 1) • best scenario (task 2).

Unit 11

WHATEVER WORKS

YOUR TASK AT THE END OF THIS UNIT

You are applying for a summer job in an English-speaking country. You have an interview with a recruiter. The most convincing candidate will get the job. → p. 169

TUNE IN!

1 Observe and speak

a. What are your immediate reactions when you see this picture? In your opinion, where could you see this picture? What could it be used for?

b. Would you like to go on holiday or live on this island? Why? Why not?

2 Watch a video

Video

Hamilton Island

Watch the video and explain to a friend why you have decided to apply for the job or not.

PREPARE YOUR TASK →

3 Job application

Group 1: Write the job description corresponding to the video you have just seen (150 words). WB

Group 2: Make a video in which you explain why you are the ideal candidate.

Help!

Places and activities	Goals	Personal opinion
southern hemisphere /'hemɪsfɪəʳ/ palm /pɑːm/ tree scenery: *paysage* waterskiing windsurfing scuba diving /'daɪvɪŋ/: *plongée* walking in the bush	promote /prə'məʊt/ advertise /'ædvətaɪz/ urge /ɜːdʒ/ sb to + V: *inciter fortement qqn à* persuade /pə'sweɪd/ sb to + V	exciting = thrilling stressful ≠ peaceful dull / boring remote /rɪ'məʊt/ / far away feel like + V-ING relax = unwind /ˌʌn'waɪnd/ live close to nature / outdoors

1. IT'S MY PASSION!

There are only a few more weeks left at school when I tell the good Sister I'm leaving. She is a bit taken aback[1] when I hand in my resignation, even though matters had become somewhat fraught[2] earlier in the term when the awful *Hellfire*[3] matinees had clashed with my teaching commitments[4]. She had indulged me[5] over this, much to the irritation of the other staff, and perhaps she expected some form of loyalty from me in return. [...] I'd tried to explain to her over most of the last two years that I couldn't see teaching as my life's vocation and that it was music that was my passion, but she could never understand how music could be anything more than a hobby. She had been indulging my fantasies because she liked me, or because my eccentricities amused her, or made her feel less isolated. When she finally realizes that I'm serious about giving up my job, despite the fact that there is a baby on the way, she will play her final card. Shaking her head sadly, with the exasperation of someone who can't make head nor tail[6] of an argument, she offers this:

"But you'll lose your pension[7]."

I look out the window across the playing fields at the vans and lorries heading south on the motorway and I'm silent for a while.

"I'm sorry, Sister, it's what I want to do."

Sting, *Broken Music, A Memoir*, 2003

1. surprised **2.** *quelque peu inquiétantes* **3.** name of a musical **4.** /kəˈmɪtmənts/ *engagements*
5. /ɪnˈdʌldʒd/ *(ici) elle avait pris mon parti* **6.** *ne comprend rien* **7.** *droits à la retraite*

1 Find the key information WB

a. Read the text and say what you have understood.
b. Read the passage again and turn to your Workbook for help.

2 Speak from your notes

a. Who is the narrator? Who is he talking to?
b. Where does the scene take place?
c. What has the narrator decided to do?
d. What is the other character's reaction? Does she approve of the narrator's choice of career?

PREPARE YOUR TASK

3 Reactions

Two colleagues have overheard the conversation. They discuss the pros and cons of the decision and say if they would be ready to make the same choice.

PREPARE YOUR TASK

4 Take a stand

To what extent should people interfere with other people's choices? List arguments and discuss in groups.

Help!

The narrator

resign /rɪˈzaɪn/: *démissionner*
achieve one's goals: *atteindre ses objectifs*
break the news to sb: *annoncer une nouvelle à qqn*
change one's mind: *changer d'avis*

The Sister

stunned / astonished
puzzled / perplexed
disappointed
object to sth / V-ING
disapprove of sth / V-ING

Personal opinion

square / conventional
fearless
risky
dare to do sth: *oser faire qqch*
if I were him, I would(n't)...

2. THE DEVIL

1 Get ready

a. Look at the photo and react (place, characters: age, clothes, relationships, jobs).
b. Imagine what the text is about.

"I simply do not understand what takes you so long to speak after you pick up the phone," she stated. From any other person on earth that would have sounded whiny[1], but from Miranda, it sounded appropriately cold and firm. Just like her. "In case you haven't been here long enough to notice, when I call, you respond. It's actually simple. See? I call. You respond. Do you think you can handle that Ahn-dre-ah?"

I nodded[2] like a six-year-old who'd just been reprimanded for throwing spaghetti on the ceiling[3], even though she couldn't see me. I concentrated on not calling her "ma'am", a mistake I'd made a week earlier that had almost gotten me fired[4]. "Yes, Miranda. I'm sorry," I said softly, head bowed[5]. And for that moment I *was* sorry, sorry that her words hadn't registered in my brain three-tenths of a second faster than they had, sorry that my tardiness in[6] saying "Miranda Priestly's office" had taken a fraction of a second longer than absolutely necessary. Her time was, as I was constantly reminded, much more important than my own.

Lauren Weisberger, *The Devil Wears Prada*, 2003

1. /ˈwaɪnɪ/ *pleurnichard* **2.** *je hochai la tête* **3.** /ˈsiːlɪŋ/ *plafond*
4. *avait failli me faire virer* **5.** /baʊd/ *baissée* **6.** *lenteur à*

2 Find the key information

Read the text and discuss with the class what you have understood.

a. "**I** simply do not understand what takes **you** so long to speak after you pick up the phone," **she** stated. (l. 1) Who do "I", "you" and "she" refer to? Give their full names if possible.

b. Who is the narrator?

c. What are the characters' respective roles?
What field or sector do they work in? Use the title of the novel.

d. Pick out two sentences showing how they are communicating.

e. "[...] when I call, you respond. It's actually simple. See? I call. You respond. Do you think you can handle that Ahn-dre-ah?" (l. 4)
– Who says this?
– In the second paragraph pick out one sentence explaining the problem more precisely. Rephrase it in your own words.
– Define the tone used here. Complete the sentence using "she said..." and adverbs chosen from the following list:

reproachfully | kindly | contemptuously | angrily | drily | quietly

f. Pick out all the words showing the narrator's physical attitude and tone of voice. What adjective is repeated four times? How does she react?

g. Complete the following summary (one blank = one word). Use the toolbox below.

> Miranda is ...'s boss. When facing her boss, the young assistant feels as if she were a ... . It's not surprising since Miranda is ... . She looks down on the young woman who is too ... to ... against her ... boss. She is ... to Miranda who is very ... and keeps telling her new assistant off. Miranda is so ... that the young woman can only feel ... .

3 Summarize briefly

Speak from your notes and include the following points:
a. What is the relationship between the two characters?
b. According to Miranda, what should Andrea do in order to improve her skills?

Help!

Miranda	Andrea	Interpretation
bossy = authoritarian demanding: *exigeant* disdainful = scornful: *méprisant* reproachful reprimand sb (formal) = tell sb off (informal) look down on sb / despise sb / scorn sb: *mépriser qqn*	obedient /ə'bi:dɪənt/ guilty: *coupable* efficient reliable: *fiable* shy: *timide* shameful: *honteux* submissive /səb'mɪsɪv/ retarded: *demeuré* obey sb's orders dread /dred/: *redouter*	quick to react focused: *concentré* pick up the phone be expected to + V rebel against / stand up against

4 Go further

a. Explain the last sentence in your own words.
b. Justify the title on page 160.
c. How would you react if you were in Andrea's shoes?

PREPARE YOUR TASK

5 Camera café

Andrea relates the incident to her friend and asks for advice. Act the dialogue out in front of the class.

3. WORK AROUND THE CLOCK

1

2

3

4

5

6

Fast facts

Sempé (born in 1932) is a French artist whose covers and cartoons (more than a hundred) have appeared in *The New Yorker*, a famous American magazine, for over 30 years.

1 Understand the comic strip

a. Observe cartoons n°1 and n°6. What do they have in common? What differences are there between them? What has happened in between?

b. Give a precise account of the situation in each cartoon.

2 Storytelling

a. What has happened to the main character? Sum up the main events of his life. Use the following words: first • then • later • after that • eventually = finally • although • yet • once *(une fois que)* • consequently.

PREPARE YOUR TASK → **b.** What do you think of the man's attitude towards work?

c. Do you find this cartoon funny? Why? Why not?

d. In your opinion, what is the cartoonist's message?

- He was told to + V
- The doctor insisted he must + V
- He was advised to + V
- He could not help + V-ING

Help!

Situations	Activities	Personal opinion
corporate life nervous breakdown: *dépression nerveuse* exhausted: *épuisé* depressed be under pressure relax = unwind /ˌʌnˈwaɪnd/	vegetable lettuce /ˈletɪs/ wheelbarrow: *brouette* staff: *personnel* grow sth: *faire pousser qqch* hire: *engager* run: *diriger*	workaholic /ˌwɜːkəˈhɒlɪk/ addicted to dedicated to interested in bored unbalanced: *déséquilibré* expose = denounce

4. GET A KICK OUT OF IT!

Understand the poem

Read these lines. Close your book. What words can you remember?

a. Form: The poem is composed of ... stanzas of ... lines each.

b. In the poem find the equivalents in English of: *il est inutile de* • *à moins que* • *printemps*.

c. What is the message of the poem? What is the link with the comic strip?

d. Learn the poem by heart. Then recite it in front of the class. CD

There is no point in work
Unless it absorbs you
Like an absorbing game.

If it doesn't absorb you
If it's never fun
don't do it.

When a man goes out into his work
he is alive like a tree in spring,
he is living, not merely working.

D.H. Lawrence, *The Complete Poems*, 1957

5. FIRED

1 Get ready WB

Brush up your vocabulary on clothes, the human body and law. Turn to your Workbook for help.

NEW YORK BANKER CLAIMS SHE WAS FIRED FOR BEING ATTRACTIVE

Citibank[1] denies sex discrimination claim it sacked worker because her appearance "too distracting" for male colleagues.

Debrahlee Lorenzana likes to dress sharp when she goes to work – she is a fan of Burberry and Hermes and has five closets full of well-fitting[2] dresses and skirt suits. What the New York banker hadn't anticipated was that in some workplaces looking good can earn you the sack.

Lorenzana claims in a sex discrimination lawsuit filed with[3] the Manhattan supreme court that her employer, Citibank, dismissed her, in part because her figure and her clothes were "too distracting" for her male colleagues and supervisors to bear. She claims that soon after she joined as a banking adviser in September 2008 she was subjected to a stream of comments about her appearance.

Documents lodged with the court complain[4] that two of her immediate bosses told her to stop wearing turtleneck tops, pencil skirts, fitted business suits or any other form of tailored attire[5]. When she protested that other women in the office wore the same kind of clothes as her, they allegedly replied that those other women could "wear what they like, as their general unattractiveness rendered moot their sartorial choices[6]." [...]

Further humiliation followed, her lawyers contest, because she was relatively tall (5ft 6), and had a "curvaceous figure[7]". She was told not to wear high-heeled business shoes, as this purportedly "drew attention to her body in a manner that was upsetting to her easily distracted male managers".

"I couldn't believe what I was hearing," Lorenzana told the *Village Voice*. "I said, 'You gotta be kidding me!' I was like, 'Too distracting? For who? For you? My clients don't seem to have any problem.'"

From April 2009 she made a series of complaints of sexism to the bank's human resources department. In July she was transferred to a different Citibank branch which she claims was a retaliatory[8] action as the new job held less prospects for her, and a month later she was dismissed, less than a year after she joined the firm.

Citibank had given her a number of formal warnings based it said on her performance, including failure to meet a quota for the number of new business accounts. But in her lawsuit, Lorenzana accuses the bank of taking revenge on her for complaining about her sexist treatment. The lawsuit will be decided by an arbitrator.

■ *The Guardian*, June 4, 2010

1. a major US financial services company **2.** *exactement à sa taille* **3.** *dans une plainte pour discrimination sexuelle déposée auprès de* **4.** *(ici) font état du fait* **5.** vêtements sur mesure **6.** *(style pompeux) annulait la pertinence de leurs choix vestimentaires* **7.** *silhouette tout en courbes* **8.** *de représailles*

2 Find the key information WB

a. Read the text and say what you have understood.
b. Read the text again and turn to your Workbook for help.

3 Speak from your notes

Group 1: Debrahlee Lorenzana and her different actions

a. Draw Debrahlee Lorenzana's portrait:
possible age • job • physical appearance • personal prospects.
b. Draw a timeline about her different actions against Citibank.

Group 2: The colleagues and supervisors

a. What did the colleagues and supervisors complain about and why?
Select in the list the adjectives that best describe their attitude:

> supportive • friendly • jealous • helpful • sexist • submissive • authoritarian • hypocritical • apprehensive • revengeful • scared • mean • competitive • hostile

b. List the different sanctions she had to face.

Help!

Debrahlee Lorenzana

independent
sexy / hot
glamorous / gorgeous
sophisticated
outraged: *scandalisé*

dress sharp / dress smartly / dress up
be discriminated against
take one's revenge on sb
sue sb: *poursuivre qqn en justice*
lodge a complaint: *déposer une plainte*

Her colleagues and supervisors

lame excuse = not a valid excuse
discriminatory practice
provocative

be focused on: *se concentrer sur*
obey sb: *obéir à qqn*
submit
prevent sb from + V-ING: *empêcher qqn de faire qqch*
blame sb for + V-ING

PREPARE YOUR TASK

4 The trial

Debrahlee Lorenzana has gone to court.

a. Choose a role and get ready to act it out: Debrahlee Lorenzana's lawyer • a member of Women's Lib • a prosecutor • a colleague • Debrahlee Lorenzana's boss.
Find arguments for or against her case.

b. Choose one of these four topics:

- A workplace is not just a male-dominated world.
- A workplace is not a fashion podium.
- Workers are free to do as they wish.
- Workers have to comply with their bosses' will.

c. Select arguments:

- authority (submission to superiors, rules)
- freedom (dress code)
- sexism (equality between men and women, differences)
- revenge
- attitude (work • leisure • concentration)
- competition / jealousy between workers

d. Find a precise example for every argument you have.

TIPS!
Use the vocabulary given on pages 248-249.

Language at work

Prétérit simple ou *present perfect* ?

1 Classez.

a. Dans le paragraphe suivant, relevez les formes verbales au prétérit et celles au *present perfect* ainsi que les compléments de temps utilisés. Classez-les dans un tableau de ce type.

Matthew graduated from High School a year ago. Soon after Graduation Day he decided to travel all around the world and work at the same time to earn enough money to live. Since he left home he has been to many countries and has changed jobs every three months. Over the past few months he has worked as a baby sitter, a waiter in a café, a sales assistant in a bookshop. Last Christmas he was Santa Claus in an Australian shopping mall. He is now very happy because he has achieved one of his dreams.

	Formes verbales	Compléments de temps
Prétérit		
Present perfect		

b. Observez et comparez.
– Quelles propositions renvoient à un passé complètement coupé du présent ?
– Quelles propositions expriment le bilan dans le présent de faits passés ?

c. Traduisez les compléments de temps relevés dans le paragraphe.

d. *He has worked for a year. He is more mature.*
– Identifiez la forme verbale utilisée dans chaque proposition, puis coordonnez ces deux propositions à l'aide d'un ou plusieurs des mots de liaison pris dans cette liste :
before • *consequently* • *already* • *as a result* • *that's why.*
– Quel est le point commun entre les mots de liaison choisis ?

2 Déduisez.

→ On utilise le ... (forme : ... + ...) pour parler du résultat présent d'un événement passé.
→ On utilise le ... pour évoquer un fait passé sans le relier au moment présent.

Practice

1 Formez des énoncés au *present perfect* à la forme interrogative (?) ou négative (-).

a. ever • regret • Sting • his decision to • give up • his job as a schoolteacher (?)
b. Miranda • give the opportunity • Andrea • defend • herself • not yet (-)
c. Sting • miss • his past life • never (-)
d. how much • money • earn • Andrea • so far (?)
e. be interviewed • Debrahlee • a lot • since she was fired (?)
f. Andrea • be able to • protest • never (-)
g. in this job • be • you • how long (?)
h. you • have • already • a job • abroad (?)

2 Mettez le verbe entre parenthèses au prétérit ou au *present perfect*.

a. In my previous job I (take on) new responsibilities, which was very rewarding.
b. He (be) on sick leave for two weeks. It must be serious.
c. So far their boss (not • promote) them. They are getting impatient.
d. As they (have) no qualifications, they found it difficult to find a job in this sector.
e. The office manager (cancel) all the meetings last week.
f. Steve (send) an application form last month and (not • have) any answer yet.

3 **Traduisez ces phrases.**

a. Le mari de la directrice des ressources humaines *(The HRD = human resources director)* vient d'appeler sa femme. La secrétaire vient de lui dire que son mari est paniqué.
b. Il est à la maison depuis qu'un de ses enfants est revenu de l'hôpital.
c. Ces dernières années, sa femme a géré la situation seule.
d. Jusqu'ici il ne s'est jamais occupé du bébé seul.
e. Il n'a pas encore donné à manger à ses enfants car il a trop de choses à faire.
f. Il n'a jamais cuisiné car sa femme prépare tout à chaque fois.

"Your husband is on line two. He says it's an emergency. He wants to know how to work the microwave."

Build up your vocabulary

1 **Trouvez les mots dérivés ou composés à partir des mots racines fournis. Utilisez un dictionnaire si nécessaire.**

a. *apply :* un demandeur d'emploi • un formulaire
b. *rely :* fiable • autonome
c. *work :* travail d'équipe • horaires de travail • conditions de travail • surchargé de travail
d. *computer :* qui sait utiliser l'informatique • informaticien • créateur de sites • graphiste

2 **Complétez avec les prépositions qui conviennent. Vérifiez à l'aide d'un dictionnaire.**

a. Andrea, the young assistant, is really dedicated ... her new job.
b. He is keen ... playing chess because this game helps him concentrate.
c. This new employee has always been very good ... fund-raising for charities.
d. All the members of my team are fond ... using this new software.
e. You have to be very patient and interested ... children if you want to babysit.
f. Above all my partner is attracted ... the advertising project for this sports brand.
g. This senior accountant is experienced ... problem solving.
h. What are you specialized ...?

3 **À l'aide d'un dictionnaire, traduisez ces énoncés.**

a. Il vient juste d'être licencié. (Trouvez cinq verbes différents, du plus familier au moins familier.)
b. Elle n'est plus au chômage. (Trouvez deux adjectifs différents.)

4 **À l'aide de l'entrée *time* dans un dictionnaire, trouvez les équivalents anglais de :**

a. travailler à plein temps
b. travailler à temps partiel
c. faire des heures supplémentaires
d. emploi du temps
e. être à l'heure
f. rendre un projet à temps

Improve your pronunciation

1 Accentuation à l'intérieur de l'énoncé.

MP3 29

Écoutez les énoncés suivants.

a. Les adverbes soulignés sont-ils accentués ou non accentués ?

– *"I simply do not understand what takes you so long to speak after you pick up the phone."*
– *"It's actually simple."*
– *"It had taken a fraction of a second longer than absolutely necessary."*
– *"Her time was, as I was constantly reminded, much more important than my own."*

→ **Concluez :** en anglais les adverbes sont ... .

b. Repérez les liaisons consonne-voyelle dans chacune des répliques.

→ **Concluez :** lorsque le premier mot se termine par une ... ou un « e » muet et que le second mot commence par une ... , il faut lier les deux mots sans pause.

c. Réécoutez le passage en vous concentrant sur les mots en **bleu**. Qu'ont-ils en commun ?

– *"I simply do not understand what takes you so long* ***to*** *speak after you pick up the phone."*
– *"It* ***had*** *taken* ***a*** *fraction* ***of a*** *second longer* ***than*** *absolutely necessary."*
– *"Her time was, as I* ***was*** *constantly reminded, much more important* ***than*** *my own."*

→ **Concluez :** ces auxiliaires, articles, conjonctions et prépositions ne sont pas ... . Leur voyelle se réduit au son /.../.

d. Réécoutez les énoncés et entraînez-vous à les lire à haute voix. Imitez le modèle donné. Travaillez en binômes.

2 Intonation montante ou descendante ?

MP3 30

a. Écoutez l'échange entre ces deux personnages.

– Repérez les intonations utilisées dans chaque énoncé.
– Quelle attitude exprime chacune d'elle :
reproche • mépris • regret • surprise • ordre • curiosité ?

b. Repérez l'intonation utilisée dans chacun des groupes intonatifs.

– *"You're quite ambitious, aren't you?"*
– *"I am. Girls don't always obey."*
– *"Will you be up to the job, young lady?"*
– *"Certainly. My parents say I'm determined, energetic and bossy."*
– *"You know you'll have to work hard, don't you?"*
– *"Of course, I do."*

c. Classez ces phrases selon les différents types d'énoncés :
affirmation / certitude • demande de confirmation • question ouverte.

→ **Concluez :**
– on utilise en général une intonation descendante quand il s'agit d'une ... ;
– on utilise en général une intonation montante quand il s'agit d'une ... .

YOUR TASK

You are applying for a summer job in an English-speaking country. You have an interview with a recruiter. The most convincing candidate will get the job.

PREPARE YOUR INTERVIEW

1 Work in pairs, choose your part (recruiter or applicant) and select a position among the following:

sales assistant | au-pair | lifeguard | summer camp instructor | office boy / girl | waiter / waitress

2 Use the following grid.

Recruiter	Applicant
– Job description and required skills. – Meeting and greeting the candidate. – Questions on: candidate's studies, training *(formation)*, computer and language skills, work experience and hobbies. – Answers to the candidate's specific questions about the job (tasks involved, working hours, salary, days off, benefits and perks, etc.). ⚠ Listen to the applicant, take his / her remarks into account.	– Interest in the job you are applying for. – Skills for the job. – Language level you are going to use (formal English). – Information about your education (formation), specific skills (computer and language skills...), work experience and hobbies. – Details about the job itself (tasks involved, working hours, salary, days off, etc.). ⚠ Sound convincing.

TIPS FOR A SUCCESSFUL INTERVIEW

- Don't read. Talk. Use notes only.
- Make eye contact with the person you are speaking to.
- Speak loud and clear.
- Sit up and don't fidget *(gigoter)*.
- If you hesitate, use gap fillers (→ see p. 249).
- If you do not understand a question, kindly ask the person to repeat.

WHO IS THE BEST RECRUITER AND THE BEST CANDIDATE?

The rest of the class will listen to the different interviews and decide on the winners.

"...and I'm proficient in two languages — English and text messaging."

Seven years later

During her seven years on the street, she had somehow forgotten her given name. There, people called her lady, or hey you. Others completely bypassed such formalities. That was okay, she never did care for people to know her business.

The streets hadn't always been her home. She grew up in a house the way most people did, with a mother, father, and an older sister. Later, she received an Associates Degree from a secretarial school and it hung on the wall in her own home. She lived in Chicago in a nice condo[1], not too far from Lake Michigan. Things were good then, and her boyfriend even asked her to marry him. Of course, she said yes and they planned a June wedding.

That was before her life fell apart. No, her life didn't fall apart. Someone tore it to shreds[2]. Someone she dedicated twelve years to as an executive secretary. A man she had trusted completely, a man with connections to every big shot[3] in the city—including the mob[4]. She had not known about the mob or a great many other things until that final year.

Strangers began coming to the office and anonymous letters arrived. When she opened them, she was shocked. People threatened to kill her boss for the terrible things he had done. She decided not to show him, but instead kept a folder in her locked desk drawer. She also decided to do a little investigating on her own. Before long, she found out things that made her wonder how she could have been so blind. One word described him, crook[5]. An attorney who advertised his commitment to help the poor and downtrodden[6] and he stole from almost every one of them.

Not sure what to do, she finally confronted him. She took the folder from her drawer into his office and threw it on his desk. "You're stealing from these people."

He laughed. He looked at her and laughed. "That's right, honey, that's how you make those big condominium payments every month." She stared. Was he the same man she had worked for all those years? She told him she could not be a part of it and that she would go to the police. He found that even funnier. "You go ahead, go to the cops, for all the good it will do you." Then his face grew stern. "You tell anyone anything, and as long as I'm alive you'll never have a job in this city."

She left the office and went to the police. He had been right about their reaction and he made good on his threat[7]. He not only fired her, but also slowly began to dismantle her life. He had somehow been able to have the two largest papers run a completely bogus[8] story about her selling drugs from her home. With his power and influence, he convinced the condo organization to repossess it and throw her out. Another newspaper picked up the article but added another charge. They said she often entertained male visitors there to supplement her income. She was grateful her parents were not alive to see it, but her fiancé and her sister read the paper. Though they said they knew it could not be true, her boyfriend took an extended vacation, and her sister suggested she not come over. She worried about her kids.

He had someone follow her, and that person thwarted[9] every action she took. She answered a number of ads, but no one would even give her an initial interview. Living in hotels was expensive and she could no longer afford a room. Without an income, her wardrobe began to deteriorate. Within a few months, she found herself living on the street. She thought it would be temporary, that she would find work and be

1. *appartement dans un immeuble en copropriété* **2.** *mit en pièces* **3.** *toutes les grosses huiles* **4.** *pègre* **5.** *escroc* **6.** *les pauvres et les opprimés* **7.** *menace* **8.** *fausse* **9.** *contrecarrait*

able to afford an apartment. She stayed at a women's shelter for a while, but most of the other women were in much worse shape and she gave up her bed.

For seven years, she wandered around the city streets. She climbed the steep sharp rises under viaducts, hauling[10] her belongings and cardboard to make a noisy, exhaust fumed shelter[11] for the night. The climb created thick calluses on her hands and delivering babies under those viaducts created thicker calluses on her heart. The hardships began to wear on her[12].

She imagined herself crossing back and forth between indefinable realities. There were days that she thought she might have been a pigeon. They were her only companions. The world she knew pushed her away and she had little strength to put up a fight.

Then she saw him, and as though it were yesterday, remembered his words—"as long as I'm alive you'll never have a job in this city."

He looked right at her and had no idea who she was. "Got a quarter, mister?" She asked, holding out a hand he would have only recognized if it were soft and pink with long red fingernails. He pulled a dollar from his pocket and threw it in her direction. She laughed and knew it sounded insane, but that was what she felt—completely insane. Now, she had a purpose[13]. [...]

Honor among Pigeons, Jean Sheldon, www.jeansheldon.com

10. *hissant* **11.** *refuge au milieu des gaz d'échappement* **12.** *les difficultés commençaient à l'user* **13.** goal

Unit 12

BORN TO SHOP?

YOUR TASK AT THE END OF THIS UNIT

You are taking part in a debate in a TV show on the night of Buy Nothing Day: Are you for or against a day without shopping?
Defend your point of view. → p. 183

TUNE IN!

Barbara Kruger, *Untitled*, 1987

1 Get ready

a. What immediately strikes you in the photomontage?
– What colours are used? What for? What impact do they have on the viewer?
– The card: What does it remind you of? What strikes you?
– What does the slogan mean to you at first glance?
Check the meaning of "therefore" in a dictionary if necessary.

b. Imagine the shopping habits of the person who is showing the card.

c. What are the artist's goals?

I have to have it!

"Hi," I say, trying to stay calm. "You're… you're having a sale."

"Yes." The blond girl smiles. "Bit unusual for us."

My gaze sweeps[1] the room. I can see rows of scarves, neatly folded, with dark green "50 per cent off" signs above them. Printed velvet[2], beaded silk[3], embroidered[4] cashmere, all with the discreet "Denny and George" signature. They're everywhere. I don't know where to start. I think I'm having a panic attack.

"You always liked this one, I think," says the nice blond girl, taking out a shimmering[5] grey-blue scarf from the pile in front of her.

Oh God, yes. I remember this one. It's made of silky velvet overprinted in a paler blue and dotted with iridescent beads[6]. As I stare at[7] it, I can feel little invisible strings, silently tugging me[8] towards it. I have to touch it. I have to wear it. It's the most beautiful thing I've ever seen. The girl looks at the label. "Reduced from £340 to £120." She comes and drapes the scarf around my neck and I stare at my reflection. There is no question. I have to have this scarf. I *have* to have it. It makes my eyes look bigger, it makes my haircut look more expensive, it makes me look like a different person. I'll be able to wear it with everything. People will refer to me as the Girl in the Denny and George scarf.

"I'd snap it up, if I were you." The girl smiles at me. "There's only one of these left."

Involuntarily, I clutch at it.

"I'll have it," I gasp. "I'll have it".

Sophie Kinsella, *Confessions of a Shopaholic*, 2000

1. *balaie* **2.** *velours* **3.** *soie incrustée de perles* **4.** *brodé* **5.** *chatoyant*
6. *perles* **7.** *regarde fixement* **8.** *(ici) qui me tirent*

2 Find the key information WB

Turn to your Workbook for help.

3 Go further

a. Choose the adjectives that best apply to the shop assistant and justify your choices:

helpful | indifferent | rude /ruːd/ | tempting | clever

b. What does the narrator finally decide?

c. What does the repetition of "have to" (l. 20) and the use of italics suggest?

d. Draw a parallel with the photomontage opposite.

PREPARE YOUR TASK

4 Conduct a survey

Prepare a list of ten questions you will ask your classmates about their shopping habits: When? How much? What? How often? Alone or with somebody?...

Help!

Selling and buying

shopper / customer: *client*
shop assistant (GB) = sales clerk /klɜːʳk/ (US)
shopping centre (GB) = mall /mɔːl/ (US)
purchase /ˈpɜːtʃɪs/ = buy

Influence

attractive = appealing / tempting
urge sb to + V: *inciter fortement qqn à*
make sb do sth
talk sb into + V-ING: *convaincre qqn de*
attract sb = appeal to

Reactions

addicted to
fascinated by
resist temptation ≠ yield to temptation
refrain from + V-ING: *s'abstenir de*
can't help + V-ING: *ne pas pouvoir s'empêcher de*

I. BLACK FRIDAY

1 Info search

Go on the Internet to learn about Black Friday (What? When? Why? Who? Where?).
Give a two-minute oral account.

2 Get ready!

Rule #1: To find the best deals, you have to be the first person in line, no matter what.

Rule #2: Everyone, including the soccer moms, becomes incredibly vicious and frenzied[1]; so be prepared to hold your own, and don't back down.

Rule #3: Know what you're shopping for, get in, get it, and get out.

■ www.runforbargains.com

1. *frénétique*

a. Understand the rules: Which definition best corresponds to the following words and phrases?

– "No matter what": whatever the implications • whatever you may buy • whatever the weather
– "Soccer moms": mums who are soccer fans • middle-class mums driving their kids around to various activities • professional football players' mums
– "Vicious": violent and dangerous • immoral • perverted
– "Back down": put back on the shelf • go back home • accept defeat

b. Which of the following adjectives best apply to Black Friday fans? Defend your point of view. Use a dictionary if necessary.

ruthless • organized • clever • insane • civilized • uncontrollable • greedy • mad • determined

c. What ideas do the adjectives above convey?
Choose from this list: the more the merrier • survival of the fittest • consumer paradise • law of the jungle • rat race • seize the day.

PREPARE YOUR TASK →

3 Act out

You are the woman in the foreground. You explain to the other jogger why you are training so hard. (Use the Black Friday rules for help.)

– If...
– You'd better + V
– You'd better not + V
– You have to...
– As soon as you enter the shop, you will / should...

TRAMPLED TO DEATH

An employee at Wal-Mart was killed yesterday when "out-of-control" shoppers broke down the doors at a sale at the discount giant's store in Long Island, New York. [...] Customers shouted angrily and kept shopping when store officials said they were closing because of the death, police and witnesses said. The store, in Valley Stream on Long Island, closed for several hours before reopening. Nassau county police said about 2,000 people were gathered outside the store doors at the mall about 20 miles east of Manhattan. The impatient crowd knocked the man [...] to the ground as he opened the doors, leaving a metal portion of the frame crumpled like an accordion.

Shoppers stepped over Damour as he lay on the ground and streamed into[1] the store. When told to leave, they complained that they had been in line since Thursday morning for the Black Friday sale that traditionally follows the Thanksgiving holiday. [...] Shoppers around the US line up early outside stores on Black Friday, an annual bargain-hunting ritual that marks the day after Thanksgiving.

■ www.guardian.co.uk, November 29, 2008

1. *déferlèrent*

4 Find the key information

a. What is Wal-Mart? Justify by quoting from the text above.

b. Copy this grid on a sheet of paper; fill it in and use the information found in the article to recap.

Incident	Victim	People involved	Cause	After the accident
What? / Where?	Job? / Name?			

c. What image of customers is given in these two pages? Choose adjectives from the following list and explain your choices:

greedy — sensible — heartless — frantic — selfless — thoughtful
superficial — selfish — inhumane — pitiless — ruthless — mean

PREPARE YOUR TASK

5 Letter to the editor

You have just read this article. You react and post a mail on the newspaper website (100 words).

- What a...! / How..! → see p. 38
- I wish I had / hadn't + *participe passé*
- I would never have thought / believed / imagined...
- People should have + *participe passé*

Help!

Sales	Attitudes
item /ˈaɪtəm/ = article	indifferent to sb / sth
go to the sales: *faire les soldes*	selfish: *égoïste*
get a good deal: *faire une bonne affaire*	greedy: *avide*
hunt for bargains: *chercher des bonnes affaires*	merciless = ruthless
purchase /pɜːtʃɪs/ = buy	mean: *mesquin / méchant*
rush to the stores: *se précipiter dans les magasins*	mad with excitement
queue (up) (GB) = stand in line (US)	be frantic = be in a frenzy: *être frénétique*

2. NO TO CONSUMPTION

Part 1

Atlanta Restaurant. […] Chris and Carine join their parents Walt and Billie at the table. Billie gets up and gives Chris a big hug.

BILLIE: You scared the daylights out of me[1], jumping on to that stage, oh my God.

Chris gives Carine a look. Walt extends his hand to Chris.

WALT: Congratulations, son.

They all sit and pick up menus.

[…] Atlanta Restaurant, later. The food is on the table. Chris is devouring a steak.

CHRIS: My grades are gonna be good enough, I think, to get into Harvard Law.

WALT: That's a big deal. What do you have left in your college fund?

CHRIS: It's an inheritance[2], dad. I've only been spending it as a college fund. Exactly twenty-four thousand five hundred dollars and sixty-eight cents.

BILLIE: That's very specific[3].

CHRIS: I had to go to the bank this morning.

WALT: Well, we'll certainly contribute the balance[4] for Harvard.

CHRIS: Yeah. I've got to figure out[5] what I'm going to do. I got a lot of things to pack and organize here first.

BILLIE: I'm so glad you're getting out of that place you're living. It was so much nicer when you lived on campus.

WALT: You'll come to Annandale before you disappear on us[6], won't you?

CHRIS *(reluctantly)*: Sure, I will.

Carine's not so sure.

BILLIE: You promise?

CHRIS *(whining)*: Mom.

1. *tu m'as fait une peur bleue* **2.** *héritage* **3.** precise
4. *(ici) le complément financier* **5.** *(ici) trouver*
6. *nous faire le coup de disparaître*

Part 2

BILLIE: Well, your father and I want to make a present to you.

WALT: We want to get you out of that junker[1].

CHRIS: What's a junker? *(Walt points outside to the Datsun.)* The Datsun?

WALT: Yes. We want to get you a new car.

CHRIS *(appalled)*: A new car? Why the hell would I want a new car? The Datsun runs great. *(Mocking the Cadillac)* Do you think I want some fancy boat? Or are you worried about what the neighbors might think?

BILLIE: We weren't going to get you a Cadillac, Chris. Just a nice new car that's safe to drive. You don't know when that thing's just going to suddenly blow up[2].

CHRIS: Blow up? Blow up?! Are you guys crazy? It's a great car. I don't need a new car. I don't want a new car. I don't want anything. Thing, thing, thing.

Under the table, Carine jabs Chris's leg. Chris returning to polite conversation.

CHRIS: But, thanks anyway.

WALT: Everything's gotta be difficult.

CHRIS: I said thank you. I just don't want anything.

The group returns to some superficial calm.

CARINE: I wouldn't say no to a new car.

Into the Wild, directed by Sean Penn, 2007

1. *épave* **2.** explode

1 Find the key information

Part 1

a. Who are the characters? Give their names and say how they are related.
b. Pick out all the words referring to: the celebration • Chris's future plans • money or college fees *(frais universitaires)*. Classify them in three columns.

Part 2

a. Find all the words related to the present (gift).
b. List the reasons given by Chris's parents.
c. Pick out all the words referring to Chris's and Carine's reactions.
d. Copy the following grid and organize your notes. Sum up this part.

The present	Reasons given by Chris's parents	Chris's reactions	Carine's reactions

2 Recap

a. Who are the characters? What are they celebrating?
b. What do they disagree about?
c. How does the atmosphere evolve in the passage?
d. Who intervenes at the end, and why?

3 Chris's values

a. Look at the cover of the book. What does the photo tell you about Chris's values?
b. Compare Chris's values to his parents'.

PREPARE YOUR TASK →

4 Take a stand

In groups of three or four discuss how you would react if you were in Chris's situation or a similar one (→ see p. 248-249).

Video

5 Watch a video

Into the Wild **(two extracts)**

Watch two scenes from the film.
Say what you have understood.
Turn to your worksheet for help.

PREPARE YOUR TASK →

6 Act out CD WB

Work in groups on the pronunciation with the help of your Workbook, then read the dialogue aloud.

Help!

Attitudes to money	Chris's parents	Chris
materialistic extravagant ≠ thrifty: *économe* superfluous (expense): *(dépenses) superflues* he / she doesn't care (a damn) about it's no use + V-ING	wealthy / well-off anxious concerned / worried about dumbfounded: *sidéré* tense = strained	angry / furious with sb = mad at sb refuse point blank / categorically lose one's temper: *se mettre en colère* conform to rebel against

3. ACT NOW

1 Anticipate

a. Observe the illustration below. What strikes you? What is denounced here?
b. Judging from what you see, what do you think the articles are going to deal with?

2 Find the key information WB

Turn to your Workbook for help.

A HOW TO DO WITHOUT ALMOST EVERYTHING

Part 1

For 11 months, Libby Pearson [...] has stopped buying anything but essentials in the hope of helping the environment and ending her dependence on shopping as entertainment. She has, however, allowed herself one irresistible purchase: Archie. In May, having endured five months of denying herself[1] all but toiletries[2], food and drink as one the UK's few "compacters" – former consumers trying to recycle a lot more and buy a lot less – Pearson [...] found herself facing a moral dilemma when her pet rabbit, Oscar, died. "I suppose I could have gone foraging for[3] a new one, but I found it hard to live without a house rabbit," she said. And so it was that Archie became her first and – to date – only breach of[4] her strict code of conduct.

1. *se refuser* **2.** *tout sauf des produits d'hygiène et de beauté*
3. looking for **4.** *(ici) entorse à*

Part 2

The compacters' movement [...] was started two years ago by a group of friends in San Francisco who wanted to "go beyond recycling in trying to counteract the negative global environmental and socio-economic impacts of US consumer culture". Although compacting is popular in the US, it is still in its infancy[1] here: The European compact, to which Pearson belongs, has just 103 online members. "I maybe didn't realise what a big decision it would be," she said. "But then I looked around and wondered if I really needed two wardrobes of clothes I never wore and all those shoes. Then I started to think about landfills[2] and all that."

1. early development **2.** *décharges*

Part 3

Despite the sacrifices, Pearson says that compacting has enriched her life. "I used to watch the seasons change by looking at the different jumpers in the shops, but now I go for a walk in the forest and look at the leaves."
She will also be very well prepared for today's Buy Nothing Day (BND), a global protest event now in its 15th year.
The concept is simple. For 24 hours, BND organisers ask people to keep their change in their pockets and their plastic[1] in their wallets. The timing is intended to damage the retail trade[2] as the Christmas shopping season begins in earnest and help shoppers "detox from consumerism[3]".

■ *The Guardian*, November 24, 2007

1. credit card **2.** *commerce de détail*
3. an increasing consumption of goods

B E-waste

Electronic waste, or e-waste, is the fastest growing part of our municipal waste stream[1]. We have a rather un-earth-friendly habit of replacing electronics like cell phones, computers and televisions before we really need to, sending millions of these chemical-laden[2] items to landfills[3] and so-called "recycling centers" where they really end up getting dumped[4] in countries like China. Cell phones have a rather abysmal[5] recycling rate, with only about 1% ending up at recycling facilities like this one where they are processed to recover[6] metals that are then used to make more electronics.

■ www.webecoist.com

1. flow 2. *chargés de produits chimiques* 3. *décharges* 4. thrown away 5. *abominable* 6. *récupérer*

Chris Jordan, *Circuit Boards # 2*, 2005

3 Speak from your notes

Text A

a. Libby Pearson's experience:
– What does it consist in?
– What has changed in her way of shopping? Why?
– How easy or difficult is it for her to stick to her principles?

b. What movement does Libby Pearson belong to? What do you learn about it here?

c. What is Buy Nothing Day? Where and when was it born? What does it consist in?

Text B

a. What problem does the article focus on? What are its causes and consequences?

b. Why is the issue so important? What are the long-term risks?

– If we keep wasting / depleting the Earth...
– It's high time we + preterite...
– Unless we... = If we don't...

PREPARE YOUR TASK

4 What about you?

a. List the ten things you could do instead of shopping.
b. Are there things that you could not stop buying? Explain why to your neighbour.

5 Writing workshop

Write the message printed on the flyer which a Buy Nothing Day activist could be handing out in the street (80 words).

Help!

Issues	Campaign for	Campaign against
overconsumption debt /det/ waste (*nom indénombrable singulier*): *déchets* short-term ≠ long-term vision scourge /skɜːdʒ/: *fléau* harm: *nuire à* become aware of: *prendre conscience de*	advocate sth: *prôner qqch* support: *soutenir* stand up to take drastic measures cope with a problem find alternatives to raise public awareness	oppose blame sb / sth for V-ING object to sth / demonstrate against do without sth: *se passer de* deter sb from + V-ING / talk sb out of + V-ING: *dissuader qqn de*

Language at work

L'accroissement parallèle

1 Observez.

a. ***The less*** *time you spend in shopping centres,* ***the more*** *time you have to do other things.*
b. ***The more*** *often you go shopping,* ***the more*** *you buy.*
c. ***The bigger*** *the discount,* ***the greater*** *the savings.*
d. ***The less*** *expensive the product,* ***the more*** *tempted you are to buy it.*

– Quelle forme les quatre énoncés ont-ils en commun : le comparatif ou le superlatif ?
– Quels sont les autres éléments communs à ces énoncés ?
– Combien d'éléments sont mis en parallèle ?
– Dans les groupes de mots en gras, la comparaison porte-t-elle sur un adjectif, un adverbe, un nom ou un verbe ? Classez-les dans les rubriques suivantes.

Comparaison portant sur un adjectif	Comparaison portant sur un adverbe	Comparaison portant sur un nom	Comparaison portant sur un verbe

– Traduisez les énoncés en français. Quelles différences observez-vous ?

2 Déduisez.

Pour traduire « plus... / plus... », « moins... / moins... », « plus... / moins... », etc., on utilise en anglais le ... . Attention ! L'élément sur lequel porte la comparaison est toujours placé ... et on utilise ... devant chacun des éléments mis en parallèle.

Practice

Présentez ce document.

Utilisez la construction ci-dessus et aidez-vous de ces mots :
– *difficult* • *selfish* • *big* • *concerned* • *responsible*
– *rubbish* • *landfills* • *Earth*
– *buy* • *waste* • *produce* • *get rid of* • *consume* • *pollute*

Souhait et regret

1 Classez ces énoncés.

Les énoncés suivants indiquent que certains faits ont lieu / ont eu lieu, ou au contraire qu'ils n'ont pas lieu / n'ont pas eu lieu. Classez-les en deux colonnes (« a lieu ou a eu lieu » et « n'a pas lieu ou n'a pas eu lieu »).

a. *I wish I* ***had*** *a new handbag.*
b. *I wish I* ***hadn't spent*** *so much money yesterday.*
c. *I wish I* ***earned*** *more money.*
d. *I wish people* ***cared*** *more for the environment.*
e. *He wishes he* ***had adopted*** *a different lifestyle earlier.*
f. *I wish governments* ***would recognize*** *the extent of the damage.*

2 **Identifiez les formes verbales en gras.**

Comment sont-elles formées ?

3 **Traduisez ces énoncés en utilisant le verbe « regretter ».**

Quelles différences remarquez-vous entre le français et l'anglais ?

4 **Déduisez.**

→ Pour exprimer un souhait ou un regret qui porte sur un fait présent on utilise … .
→ Pour exprimer un regret portant sur un fait passé on se sert de … .

Practice

1 **Traduisez en utilisant le verbe *wish*.**

a. Il regrette que sa mère ne lui achète pas de vêtements de marque.
b. Elle regrette qu'il ait dépensé autant d'argent.
c. Il regrette que j'aie passé ma journée au centre commercial.
d. Elle regrette de ne pas avoir d'amies pour aller faire les courses avec elles.

2 **Imaginez la conversation entre le mari et sa femme.**

Exprimez les souhaits et regrets de chacun.

Improve your pronunciation

1 **Accent de mot.**

a. À l'aide d'un dictionnaire, vérifiez l'accentuation des mots suivants :
– *advert* • *advertise* • *advertisement* • *advertiser* • *advertising*
– *consume* • *consumer* • *consuming*
b. Classez-les dans un tableau selon qu'ils sont accentués sur la première ou la deuxième syllabe.

2 **Lisez silencieusement ce texte.** MP3 31

Once upon *a* **time**, *we* **used** *to* **buy what** *we* **needed**. **Now** *that we* **have all** *we* **need**, *we* **buy** *for* **other reasons**: *To* **impress each other**, *to* **fill** *a* **void**, *to* **kill time**. **Buy Nothing Day** *is a* **simple idea**: **Try not** *to* **shop** *for a* **day**, *and* **see how** *your* **view** *of our* **world changes**.
You*'ll* **realize how much shopping uses up** *your* **free time**. *For* **24 hours** *you'll* **get** *your* **life back** *and* **that'***s a* **big achievement**! **Buy Nothing Day** *is an* **opportunity** *for* **you** *to* **make** *a* **commitment** *to* **consume less**, **recycle more and challenge corporations** *to* **clean up** *and be* **fair**. **Anyone** *can* **take part provided** *they* **spend** *a* **day without spending**!

a. À l'aide de l'enregistrement, repérez à quoi correspondent les mots en gras et ceux qui sont en italique.
b. Quelles liaisons consonne-voyelle avez-vous entendues ?
c. Lisez maintenant ce texte à haute voix en essayant d'être aussi convaincant(e) que possible.

Language at work

Build up your vocabulary

1 ***Do* ou *make* ?**

Complétez ces phrases à l'aide de *do* ou *make*. Procédez aux changements nécessaires.

If we want to protect our planet we should ... changes. Drastic decisions must be ... . Let's ... our best to consume less. Overconsumption has ... a lot of damage already. When we shop, we should all ... sensible choices. Before Christmas, let's all ... an experiment: Let's reduce our spending and our waste. If we all ... an effort, we will certainly ... progress. We can't go on ... the same mistakes. For future generations let's ... something now!

2 **Mots composés.**

a. À partir du mot *consume* et en utilisant un dictionnaire si nécessaire, trouvez l'équivalent anglais de : société de consommation • produits de consommation • magazine de consommateurs • consommation de masse.
b. Faites la même chose avec le mot *shop* : vendeur / vendeuse • vitrine.
c. Faites la même chose avec le mot *shopping* : lèche-vitrines • liste de courses • caddie • centre commercial • sac à provisions.

→ Quel est l'élément principal dans chacun des mots formés ?

3 **Traduisez ces phrases à l'aide du vocabulaire vu dans l'unité.**

a. Des mouvements de protestation s'organisent pour lutter contre la surconsommation et le gaspillage.
b. Le recyclage est une façon de limiter l'impact environnemental de nos habitudes de consommation.
c. Il est important de prendre conscience des risques liés au gaspillage.

4 **Écoutez un vendeur et un client dans un magasin.** MP3 32

Quelles questions pose le vendeur ? Écrivez-les sur papier libre.

5 **Vous voulez acheter un vêtement dans un grand magasin en Angleterre.**

Avec votre voisin, imaginez la scène. Aidez-vous des mots ci-dessous.

PLACES: women's department • men's department • fitting / changing room • cash desk • escalator • on the ground floor *(rez-de-chaussée)* = first floor (US)

ITEMS: dress • skirt • shirt • jeans • pair of trousers • shorts • sweater /ˈswetəʳ/ • blouse /blaʊz/ • jacket • coat

MISCELLANEOUS *(divers)*: bargain /ˈbɑːʳɡɪn/ • return an item • change one's mind • make up one's mind • get a refund • receipt /rɪˈsiːt/

TRYING ON CLOTHES: size • fit *(être à la bonne taille)* • loose /luːs/ ≠ tight *(serré)*

YOUR TASK

You are taking part in a debate in a TV show on the night of Buy Nothing Day: Are you for or against a day without shopping? Defend your point of view.

STEP BY STEP

1 Choose a role

Work alone for a few minutes. Find five convincing arguments and precise examples. Go through your notes on this unit and pick out vocabulary and ideas that may prove useful.

- For **i**nstance / ex**a**mple...
- As I told you...
- In **o**ther words...
- In part**i**cular...

- Why not...?
- Inst**ea**d of + V-ING
- Wouldn't it be a b**e**tter id**ea** to...

- I'm well aw**a**re that... but...
- Do you r**ea**lly mean to say...?

- I wish they / you...
- The more... / the less...

 OR 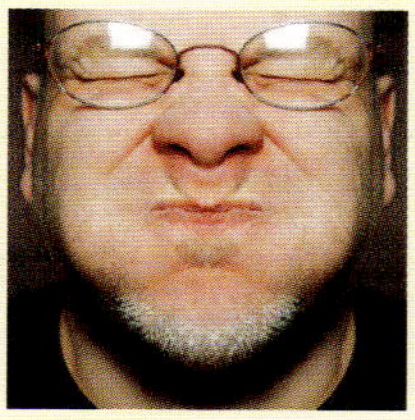	You are a busy working mum or dad who just wanted to do her shopping for the week and was stopped by Buy Nothing Day activists.
 OR 	You are a shopaholic. You love shopping or hunting for bargains. You feel you have the right to spend your money as you wish.
	You are a Buy Nothing Day activist. You are convinced that people spend too much and that it can be harmful to the environment.
	You feel that people buy too much but you are not sure Buy Nothing Day can change things.

2 Check your vocabulary

Go to p. 248-249 in your book and make sure you remember all the useful expressions for a debate.

3 Get ready to speak

Write keywords only. Check their pronunciation. Don't forget to stress the most important words to sound more convincing.

4 Debate with three other people

The rest of the class will listen to you and take notes. Then listen to the other groups.

SPEAKING CORNER

A Read and react

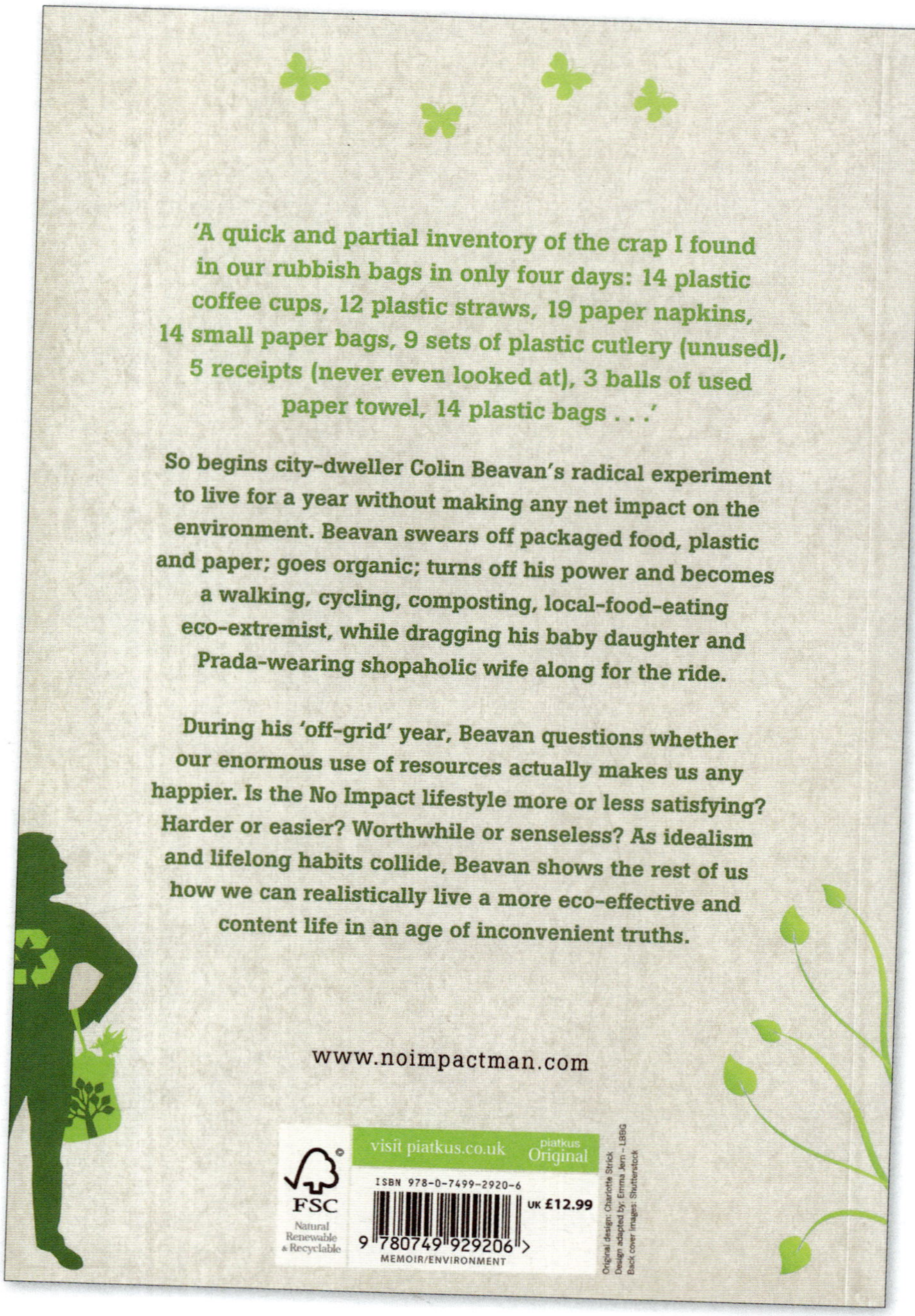

'A quick and partial inventory of the crap I found in our rubbish bags in only four days: 14 plastic coffee cups, 12 plastic straws, 19 paper napkins, 14 small paper bags, 9 sets of plastic cutlery (unused), 5 receipts (never even looked at), 3 balls of used paper towel, 14 plastic bags . . .'

So begins city-dweller Colin Beavan's radical experiment to live for a year without making any net impact on the environment. Beavan swears off packaged food, plastic and paper; goes organic; turns off his power and becomes a walking, cycling, composting, local-food-eating eco-extremist, while dragging his baby daughter and Prada-wearing shopaholic wife along for the ride.

During his 'off-grid' year, Beavan questions whether our enormous use of resources actually makes us any happier. Is the No Impact lifestyle more or less satisfying? Harder or easier? Worthwhile or senseless? As idealism and lifelong habits collide, Beavan shows the rest of us how we can realistically live a more eco-effective and content life in an age of inconvenient truths.

www.noimpactman.com

FSC
Natural Renewable & Recyclable

visit piatkus.co.uk
piatkus Original

ISBN 978-0-7499-2920-6

UK £12.99

9 780749 929206

MEMOIR/ENVIRONMENT

Original design: Charlotte Strick
Design adapted by: Emma Jern – LBBG
Back cover images: Shutterstock

B Podcast

MP3 33

Listen to Caroline and Andrew reacting to the book *No Impact Man* by Colin Beavan.

C Observe and react

Banksy, *Show me the Monet*

D Do you agree?

I cannot afford to waste my time making money.
Louis Agassiz, American geologist, teacher and naturalist (1807-1873)

Money can't buy happiness.
Popular wisdom

A large income is the best recipe for happiness I ever heard of.
Jane Austen, *Mansfield Park* (1814)

JE M'ENTRAÎNE

MP3 34

1 J'écoute ce débat

Would you be ready, if necessary, to go and work in another country?

"Nowadays there aren't so many jobs available and people have to go abroad to find a job. I think mobility of labour is a necessity."

"I believe it's more comfortable to stay in your native country."

"Maybe, but it can be boring too. I'm convinced it is a great opportunity to do an interesting job. It's more enriching than visiting the country just as a tourist."

"That may be true, but I wouldn't like to leave my family and friends behind. I would feel homesick all the time. I would miss my parents and friends terribly."

"Sure, but when you spend a long period of time somewhere you make new friends. And adapting to a new country is a real challenge."

"Don't you think the language is another difficulty?"

"Of course, but you speak English and you could choose to go to an English-speaking country. That would be easier. Don't you want to discover the world and learn about new cultures?"

"Of course I do. But I would only go abroad for a short period. As far as I'm concerned I would never settle there for good."

"I don't see it that way! If I could, I'd jump on this opportunity immediately."

Je classe ensuite les arguments en deux colonnes : « pour » et « contre ».

MP3 35

2 J'écoute ce dialogue

– Identifiez la **situation** (ce que la fille a décidé de faire).
– Repérez les **arguments** utilisés par chaque personnage.
– Notez sur papier libre les **tournures** utilisées pour :
  - exprimer son **accord** et / ou son **désaccord** ;
  - demander des **explications** ;
  - manifester sa **surprise** ou son **agacement** ;
  - marquer son hésitation avec des ***gap fillers***.

MP3 36

3 J'améliore ma prononciation

Je répète ces répliques à haute voix en suivant le modèle donné.
Veillez à respecter :
– la réduction des syllabes non accentuées ;
– les liaisons consonne-voyelle ;
– les intonations. Pour donner l'impression d'être sûr(e) de vous, utilisez des intonations descendantes. Une intonation montante implique généralement doute et incertitude ;
– les mots mis particulièrement en relief.

4 J'imagine un dialogue

Par groupes de deux, imaginez le dialogue entre un jeune garçon qui veut jouer de la guitare toute la journée et sa mère qui désire qu'il fasse ses devoirs.
– Mobilisez le lexique et les structures que vous connaissez (mots clés uniquement).
– Trouvez trois arguments pour chaque personnage.
– Comment allez-vous donner votre opinion, exprimez votre désaccord ? Donnez trois expressions.
– Exprimez votre surprise, votre agacement ou votre colère. Donnez deux expressions.

5 Je m'auto-corrige

MP3 37

Écoutez l'enregistrement correspondant à cette évaluation et comparez votre production à celle enregistrée par des anglophones.

JE FAIS LE BILAN

Analysez vos résultats à l'aide de cette grille d'évaluation où sont définis différents paliers de compétence en production orale en interaction.

Je peux…	Paliers
… discuter de divers sujets en exprimant mes sentiments. … interroger quelqu'un pour connaître son opinion et exprimer mon opinion poliment. … couper la parole à quelqu'un poliment si je n'ai pas compris ce qu'il disait ou pour exprimer mon désaccord.	B1
… reformuler mes propos si mon interlocuteur ne me comprend pas. … réagir pour exprimer mon désaccord.	B1
… être à l'origine d'une discussion (aborder un sujet qui m'intéresse). … participer activement à une conversation (sans avoir préparé mon intervention).	B1
… commencer, soutenir et terminer une conversation tout en invitant mes interlocuteurs à (re)prendre la parole. … exprimer mes idées et mes opinions avec précision, les défendre en donnant des explications, des arguments et faire des commentaires. … participer activement à une conversation d'une certaine longueur sur un thème d'actualité.	B2

ÉVALUATION

Votre professeur va vous demander d'inventer un dialogue à partir de la situation figurant sur votre fiche. Plusieurs jeux de rôles seront proposés sur chacune des unités travaillées en cours :

Unit 10 King Arthur revisited — Unit 11 Whatever Works — Unit 12 Born to shop?

→ **Temps de préparation individuel :** de 5 à 10 minutes
Vous n'aurez droit qu'à des notes.
→ **Temps de parole :** de 2 à 3 minutes
Une fois l'évaluation terminée, votre professeur pourra déterminer à quel palier vous vous situez par rapport à la grille du Cadre Européen Commun de Référence pour les Langues.

Ready, Willing and Able, a film by Ray Enright (1937)

Unit 13 EVERLASTING YOUTH

- Is the myth of Narcissus still alive?
- For or against plastic surgery?
- Read extracts from *The Picture of Dorian Gray*

→ YOUR TASK

The movie adaptation of *Dorian Gray* has just been released. Choose the person you want to interview: the film director, or the actors playing either Dorian Gray or Henry Wotton. Write the interview.

→ p. 197

Unit 14 GUNS OR ROSES?

- Why join the army?
- Discover anti war songs
- Listen to army veterans
- Study a song about war

→ YOUR TASK

You are a war reporter writing an article on the life of soldiers in combat. Your text will be based on the photos provided.

→ p. 208

Unit 15 THE LAND OF OZ

- Discover Australia, its environment, first inhabitants and settlers
- Learn more about the Aborigines' mythology and culture: the Dreamtime, Aboriginal art
- What happened to the Stolen Generation?

→ YOUR TASK

You have just spent three weeks in Australia. You post an entry on your blog to tell your friends about your experience there. Include photos and comments.

→ p. 223

ÉVALUATION SOMMATIVE *WRITING* → p. 226-227

Unit 13

EVERLASTING YOUTH

YOUR TASK AT THE END OF THIS UNIT

The movie adaptation of *Dorian Gray* has just been released. Choose the person you want to interview: the film director, or the actors playing either Dorian Gray or Henry Wotton. Write the interview (180 words). → p. 197

TUNE IN!

John William Waterhouse, *Echo and Narcissus*, 1903

1 The myth of Narcissus

a. Read the story of Narcissus either on the Internet or in an encyclopedia. Then report to the class and include the following points:

– Narcissus's physical appearance and the influence it has on his character;
– Who fell in love with him and how he reacted;
– Who decided to punish him;
– What led him to his death;
– What he left behind.

b. Define the adjective "narcissistic".

c. Observe this painting and say why it is an illustration of the myth of Narcissus.

PREPARE YOUR TASK →

2 A virtual exhibition

Go on the Internet to discover other paintings of Narcissus by Caravaggio and Dali. Which of the three (Waterhouse, Caravaggio or Dali) do you prefer? Why?

Help!

Setting

the woods
pool of water
stream: *ruisseau*
narcissus / daffodil

Narcissus

laurel wreath /riːθ/: *couronne de lauriers*
perfect features: *traits parfaits*
well-shaped
vain: *vaniteux*
self-centred: *égocentrique*
be amazed at / by one's beauty
be mesmerized / hypnotized by
see one's own reflection

1. MORE FOR MYSELF

1 Get ready

a. React to this cartoon.
What are the patients promised?
b. Is the ad realistic?
c. What are the cartoonist's goals?

2 Find the key information

Read the article below.
Compare Gail Clough and her mother (age, job, nationality, activities, lifestyle, hobbies, values).

COSMETIC SURGERY FAN EXPLAINS WHY SHE'S SPENT £50K TRYING TO STAY YOUNG

GAIL CLOUGH IS 45 BUT SHE'S ALREADY HAD ALMOST £50,000 WORTH OF COSMETIC SURGERY IN A BID[1] TO HOLD BACK THE YEARS. HERE SHE EXPLAINS WHY SHE'S DETERMINED NEVER TO LOOK OLD.

Gail Clough is sure of one thing – she never wants to get old.

Though she's only 45 she has already had 15 cosmetic surgery procedures totalling almost £50,000 and, in her bid to stay young and attractive, is determined to have lots more.

While many women her age might be staying in every night to look after kids or cook the family meal, Gail is out DJing at clubs, rarely getting in before 6 a.m.

She spends holidays at music festivals or partying in Ibiza and says she wants the looks to match her youthful lifestyle.

"I hope I'm still clubbing when I'm 65. You could call me the female Peter Pan because I never want to grow old," says Gail, who was brought up in Manchester. "I remember my mum at my age and she looked dreadful. She worked in a chip shop and was huge. She was too busy cooking, cleaning and looking after us to think about herself. She never wore make-up or did her hair, and bought her clothes from jumble sales[2]. I always used to think to myself, 'I don't want this life'. It was a hard, thankless existence and I wanted more for myself. Call it vanity, but I like to look good."

Gail's mission to distance herself from her upbringing[3] led to a passion for age-erasing plastic surgery.

She moved to Dubai and set up a plastic surgery holiday business, flying Brits out for cosmetic procedures.

■ www.mirror.co.uk, June 15, 2010

1. *tentative* **2.** *ventes de charité* **3.** education

3 Go further

a. What do you think about Gail's life and ambitions?
b. Would you like to have such a life? Why or why not?
c. In groups, discuss the pros and cons of Gail's lifestyle.

EPARE OUR TASK

4 Write a flyer

You want to advertise Gail's plastic surgery business. Include the following information: where, advantages, price, services offered... (at least 60 words).

2. "MY SOUL FOR THAT"

Dorian Gray, a film by Oliver Parker (2009)

Part 1

Dorian made no answer, but passed listlessly in front of his picture and turned towards the painting. When he saw it he drew back, and his cheeks flushed for a moment with pleasure. A look of joy came into his eyes, as if he had recognized himself for the first time. He stood there motionless and in wonder, dimly conscious that Hallward was speaking to him, but not catching the meaning of his words. The sense of his own beauty came on him like a revelation. He had never felt it before. Basil Hallward's compliments had seemed to him to be merely the charming exaggeration of friendship. He had listened to them, laughed at them, forgotten them. They had not influenced his nature. Then had come Lord Henry Wotton with his strange panegyric[1] on youth, his terrible warning of its brevity. That had stirred him at the time, and now, as he stood gazing at the shadow of his own loveliness, the full reality of the description flashed across him. Yes, there would be a day when his face would be wrinkled and wizened[2], his eyes dim[3] and colourless, the grace of his figure broken and deformed. The scarlet[4] would pass away from his lips and the gold steal from his hair. The life that was to make his soul would mar[5] his body. He would become dreadful, hideous, and uncouth[6].

Oscar Wilde, *The Picture of Dorian Gray* (chapter 2), 1891

1. /ˌpænɪˈdʒɪrɪk/ **2.** *ridé et ratatiné* **3.** *ternes* **4.** bright red **5.** *causerait la ruine de* **6.** /ˈʌnkuːθ/ *mal dégrossi*

1 Read and understand

a. List all the characters present and mentioned in the passage.

b. Can you infer who Dorian is: the painter • somebody who is looking at the painting • somebody who is looking at the painting of himself?

c. "When he saw it he drew back" (l. 4). What do "he" and "it" refer to?
Who do "his" (l. 5), "his" (l. 7), "him" and "he" (l. 14) and "his" (l. 18) refer to?

d. List all the words and phrases related to the body (head, eye, shape...).

e. Find the words derived from the following roots *(racines)*: mere *(simple)* • friend • young • warn • brief • lovely • colour.

f. In the text, find the word corresponding to the following definition: a speech or piece of writing that praises somebody or something a lot *(discours très élogieux)*.

2 Speak from your notes

a. What will be the physical marks of time?
b. What is Dorian Gray's vision of old age?
c. Use your answers to questions **d.** and **e.** to compare the three characters' reactions to the picture.

Help!

appearance
cult of beauty

obsessed with
haunted by
worried about

fear + might + BV

PREPARE YOUR TASK

3 Go further

Draw a parallel between Dorian Gray and Narcissus.

Part 2

As he thought of it, a sharp pang of pain[1] struck through him like a knife and made each delicate fiber of his nature quiver[2]. His eyes deepened into amethyst, and across them came a mist of tears[3]. He felt as if a hand of ice had been laid upon his heart.

"Don't you like it?" cried Hallward at last, stung a little by the lad[4]'s silence, not understanding what it meant.

"Of course he likes it," said Lord Henry. "Who wouldn't like it? It is one of the greatest things in modern art. I will give you anything you like to ask for it. I must have it."

"It is not my property, Harry."

"Whose property is it?"

"Dorian's, of course," answered the painter.

"He is a very lucky fellow[5]."

"How sad it is!" murmured Dorian Gray with his eyes still fixed upon his own portrait. "How sad it is! I shall grow old, and horrible, and dreadful. But this picture will remain[6] always young. It will never be older than this particular day of June... If it were only the other way! If it were I who was to be always young, and the picture that was to grow old! For that—for that—I would give everything! Yes, there is nothing in the whole world I would not give! I would give my soul for that!"

Oscar Wilde, *The Picture of Dorian Gray* (chapter 2), 1891

1. *douleur foudroyante* 2. *frémir* 3. *ils s'embuèrent de larmes* 4. young man 5. *type / bonhomme* 6. stay

4 Main facts

a. What do the underlined pronouns refer to in the text? "As he thought of it..." (l. 1) • "... what it meant" (l. 9) • "Of course he likes it," (l.10) • "How sad it is!" (l. 20) • "It will never be older..." (l. 22).

b. Find the infinitive and the translation of the following verbs in the preterite:
struck (l. 2) • laid (l. 6) • stung (l. 8) • meant (l. 9).

c. Organize your notes. Classify in two columns the keywords related to: pain or emotion • age. Use your answers to understand Dorian's feelings when he discovers the painting.

d. What would Dorian be ready to do? Why?

REPARE OUR TASK

5 A different perspective

Basil Hallward writes to a friend and narrates the discovery of the painting (100-120 words).
Prepare your draft:
– You are Basil Hallward. Write a first-person narrative.
– Describe the scene (date, place, setting). List the different characters present. Mention their reactions to the painting. Focus on Dorian's reactions and feelings. Make your own comments.
– Mind your verb forms: simple preterite to relate the story, BE + -ING preterite to describe what you saw.
– Vary the verbs you use: when I looked at him, I wondered if... • he declared / asserted that... • he complained that... • he replied... • he added... • he moaned that... .

6 Read more

To have a better idea of the plot read a few chapters: chapters 1, 2, 4, 6, 7, 12, 13 and 20.

3. THE DISCOVERY

The Picture of Dorian Gray, a film by Albert Lewin (1945)

He looked round and saw the knife that had stabbed Basil Hallward. He had cleaned it many times, till there was no stain left upon it. It was bright, and glistened[1]. As it had killed the painter, so it would kill the painter's work, and all that that meant. It would kill the past, and when that was dead, he would be free. It would kill this monstrous soul-life, and without its hideous warnings, he would be at peace. He seized the thing, and stabbed the picture with it.

There was a cry heard, and a crash. The cry was so horrible in its agony that the frightened servants woke and crept[2] out of their rooms. Two gentlemen, who were passing in the square below, stopped and looked up at the great house. They walked on till they met a policeman and brought him back. The man rang the bell several times, but there was no answer. Except for a light in one of the top windows, the house was all dark. After a time, he went away and stood in an adjoining portico and watched.

"Whose house is that, constable[3]?" asked the elder of the two gentlemen.

"Mr Dorian Gray's, sir," answered the policeman.

They looked at each other, as they walked away, and sneered[4]. One of them was Sir Henry Ashton's uncle.

Inside, in the servants' part of the house, the half-clad[5] domestics were talking in low whispers to each other. Old Mrs Leaf was crying and wringing her hands. Francis was as pale as death. [...]

When they entered, they found hanging upon the wall a splendid portrait of their master as they had last seen him, in all the wonder of his exquisite youth and beauty. Lying on the floor was a dead man, in evening dress, with a knife in his heart. He was withered, wrinkled, and loathsome[6] of visage. It was not till they had examined the rings that they recognized who it was.

Oscar Wilde, *The Picture of Dorian Gray* (chapter 20), 1891

1. *luisait d'un reflet métallique* **2.** walked slowly and quietly **3.** policeman **4.** *ricanèrent* **5.** half-dressed **6.** *repoussant*

1 Find the key information WB

Read the text and say what you have understood. Then turn to your Workbook for help.

2 Storytelling

Speak from your notes and include the following points:
- What has Dorian just done? Why?
- What does he do afterwards? Why?
- What was heard?
- What did the servants discover?

PREPARE YOUR TASK

3 Cries and whispers

Domestics were talking in low whispers to each other. (l. 28) Imagine the conversation. One of the servants mentions Dorian Gray's life and personality, tells the others the story of the painting, and tries to explain Dorian Gray's death (150 words).

Language at work

L'expression du conditionnel

1 Observez et comparez.

a. *If she **had** more money, she would probably develop her business in other countries as well.*
b. *If she **had felt** less insecure, she would never have been afraid of growing old.*

– Dans ces deux énoncés, comparez les formes verbales en gras. Ensuite comparez les formes verbales soulignées.
– Laquelle des deux subordonnées en *If* exprime un regret, c'est-à-dire que quelque chose ne s'est pas réalisé dans le passé ?
– Laquelle des deux subordonnées en *If* exprime une hypothèse irréelle portant sur un fait présent ?

→ **Déduisez :**

Hypothèse irréelle portant sur un fait présent	*If* + ...	... + ...
Hypothèse irréelle portant sur un fait passé	*If* + ... + ...	... + ... + ...

2 Traduisez les énoncés a. et b.

Practice

1 Selon ce qu'elles sous-entendent, reliez les phrases de la colonne A à celles de la colonne B.

A	B
1. If appearances were not so important, plastic surgeons wouldn't make so much money.	a. I know how important it is for you and anyway you don't need to.
2. If you had put on weight, you would have gone on a diet.	b. I don't want to get fatter.
3. If it had been possible, she would have changed the colour of her eyes.	c. Unfortunately, people depend more and more on their physical appearance.
4. If everlasting youth existed, people would feel miserable.	d. But she can't do so.
5. If I put on weight, I would go on a diet.	e. Fortunately, medical researchers are not very likely to find the miracle drug before long.

2 *If...*

Rédigez un paragraphe sur cette illustration en utilisant des subordonnées en *if* et les mots ci-dessous.

noms : *prey* • *feathers* (plumes) • *claws* (serres) • *beak* • *might* (puissance) • *stereotypes*

adjectifs : *powerful* • *fragile* • *aggressive* • *shy* • *weak* • *concerned with* • *fascinated* • *self-confident*

verbes : *rule* • *respect* • *assert one's rights* • *dare* • *yield* (céder) • *give up* • *take risks* • *show off* • *impress*

Language at work

3 **Reformulez ces phrases.**

Example: Dorian was obsessed with youth and was not happy.
→ If he hadn't been obsessed with youth, Dorian would have been happier.
a. Dorian met Lord Wotton and his life was different.
b. The painting grew old and ugly since Dorian committed sins.
c. Sibyl Vane committed suicide because Dorian broke his engagement to her.
d. As Dorian became anxious and fearful he destroyed the painting.

Build up your vocabulary

1 **Adjectifs composés.**

Pour décrire une personne, on peut utiliser des adjectifs composés. Voici une liste de mots dans le désordre. Fabriquez autant d'adjectifs composés que possible en combinant un mot de la liste **a.** avec un mot de la liste **b.** Utilisez un dictionnaire si nécessaire. Exemple : ***young-looking***

a. cold well *young* absent medium black middle self bad easy cool dark broad blue

b. going tempered blooded haired shouldered sized hearted dressed *looking* confident headed green minded eyed aged

2 **Complétez chaque blanc avec un mot pris dans la liste ci-dessous. Faites les changements nécessaires.**

beauty parlour • cosmetic surgery • diet • dye • get rid of • glamorous • be operated on • stay • undergo • unlike • wrinkles • youth

Gail Clough is determined to ... young, to ... ... her ..., to be attractive and to look ... . She is haunted by ... and as a result she has already spent a lot of money on ... . She ... a complete facelift and ... ... several times. ... her mother, she has her hair ... and takes care of herself. She goes to a ... ... regularly, watches her ... and does a lot of sport.

Improve your pronunciation

1 **Cherchez ces mots dans un dictionnaire.** MP3 38

cruel • *curt* • *envious* • *honest* • *jealous* • *obstinate* • *sadistic* • *stubborn* • *trustworthy* • *weird*

À l'aide de la transcription en signes phonétiques que vous trouverez à côté du mot, prononcez-les à haute voix. Vérifiez à l'écoute. Puis prononcez-les à nouveau à haute voix, en vous corrigeant si nécessaire.

2 **Comment se prononce le groupe de voyelles *-ea-* dans ces mots ?** MP3 39

Classez-les dans la colonne correspondante. Vérifiez à l'écoute.
already • *meal* • *dreadful* • *clean* • *pleasure* • *meaning* • *dead* • *peace* • *death* • *hear* • *heard* • *heart* • *great*

/e/	/iː/	/ɪə/	/ɜː/	/ɑː/	/eɪ/

3 **Lisez ces phrases à haute voix. Puis vérifiez à l'écoute.** MP3 40

a. Lying on the ground was a dead man with a knife in his heart.
b. I shall grow old, and horrible, and dreadful.
c. It is one of the greatest things in modern art.

YOUR TASK

The movie adaptation of *Dorian Gray* has just been released. Choose the person you want to interview: the film director, or the actors playing either Dorian Gray or Henry Wotton. Write the interview (180 words).

Video

BEFORE WRITING...

1 **Watch the trailer of *Dorian Gray* (2009) by Oliver Parker.**

2 **Key questions to ask:**
– reasons for this choice;
– portrait of Dorian Gray (physical and moral), his vision of time;
– if Dorian Gray lived today;
– Dorian Gray: an echo of a myth?
– Dorian Gray: a likeable character?
– difficulties met during the shooting.

3 **Find a short and punchy title.**
Read this one for example:

MEN RISK
HEALTH FOR
A BOOST OF YOUTH

Don't forget to write a subheading *(sous-titre)* summing up the contents of your article. → see p. 74-75

4 **Choose a photo or a painting to illustrate your article. Write a caption.**

5 **Give the name of the newspaper you work for, your name and the date of the issue.**
For example: Cameron Houston and Jill Stark, *The Daily Mirror*, July 10, 2010

AFTER WRITING...

Proofread your article:
– word order in questions;
– no "s" at the end of adjectives;
– want sb to do sth;
– every + singular;
– people + plural
– which or who?

Unit 14

GUNS OR ROSES?

YOUR TASK AT THE END OF THIS UNIT

You are a war reporter writing an article on the life of soldiers in combat. Your text will be based on the photos provided. → p. 208

TUNE IN!

React to this poster

a. What elements strike you? Which country published this poster? How do you know?
b. When do you think this ad was published? Justify your answer.
c. Who is the woman looking at? What is her attitude? (angle shot used → see p. 245)
d. Who is the target?
e. What are the goals of the advertisers?
f. Do you think this ad was effective? Why or why not?

I. WHAT CAN YOU DO FOR YOUR COUNTRY?

1 Winston Churchill's speeches CD WB

a. Listen and understand. Turn to your Workbook for help.

b. Recap

► **May 13th 1940**
– What sort of war does he predict?
– Who is the enemy?
– What is the ultimate goal?

► **June 4th 1940**
– Where are the battlefields?
– What is the mission?
– What does his tone reveal?

2 The Soldier's Creed

a. Read the text, then close your book.
b. What elements do you remember (first line, last line, verbs, adverbs)?
c. Who is speaking?
d. Which words are repeated several times?
e. What image of the American soldier is given here?

PREPARE YOUR TASK

3 Oral account

Choose one of the three posters (p. 198 and 199) and give a two-minute oral account (origin, target, message, goals, impact on the viewer...).

Video

4 Watch a video

Military recruiting up

Watch this report then turn to your worksheet for help.

Help!

In the forces	Qualities	Actions
private /'praɪvɪt/ = simple soldier medic = military nurse or doctor army combat uniform battle / combat dress beret /'bereɪ/ (GB) /be'reɪ/ (US) rank insignia /ɪn'sɪgnɪə/ join the army	determined strong-willed tough /tʌf/: *dur, tenace* fearless / daring dedicated: *dévoué* courageous ≠ cowardly	do one's duty sacrifice oneself give up one's life surrender deter sb from V-ING: *dissuader qqn de* fight to the end

2. A MATTER OF CHOICE

1 Group work

a. Read one text (A or B) and discuss in groups if the point of view is positive or negative. Pick out all the words and phrases that can help you.

A A girl's prospects

There was another reason why her heart leaped at the prospect of war. It would surely mean the end of the narrow, suffocating life she lived with her parents. She was bored, cramped and frustrated by their unvarying rituals and their pointless social life. She longed to[1] escape and have a life of her own, but it seemed impossible: She was under age[2], she had no money, and there was no kind of work that she was fit for. But, she thought eagerly[3], surely everything would be different in wartime.

She had read with fascination how in the last war women had put on trousers and gone to work in factories. Nowadays there were female branches of the army, navy and air force. Margaret dreamed of volunteering for the Auxiliary Territorial Service, the women's army. One of the few practical skills[4] she possessed was that she could drive. Father's chauffeur, Digby, had taught her on the Rolls; and Ian, the boy who died, had let her ride his motorcycle. She could even handle a motorboat, for Father kept a small yacht at Nice. The A.T.S. needed ambulance drivers and dispatch riders[5]. She saw herself in uniform, wearing a helmet, astride[6] a motorcycle, carrying urgent reports from one battlefield to another at top speed, with a photograph of Ian in the breast pocket of her khaki shirt. She felt sure she could be brave, given the chance.

Ken Follett, *Night over Water*, 1991

1. *aspirait à* **2.** *mineure* **3.** *avec enthousiasme* **4.** *compétences*
5. *agents de liaison à moto* **6.** *à califourchon sur*

PREPARE YOUR TASK

b. Each group writes a short account of the text (about 100 words). WB
Include the points listed for each text. Turn to your Workbook if you need help.

Text A

a. Give details about the narrator:
– Age, skills, her life and family;
– Her relationship with her parents.

b. Give details about women in the army:
– List jobs they could do;
– Name the women's branch of the British Army.

c. Future prospects:
– How does the narrator imagine her future life (actions, clothes, qualities)?
– What sort of life is she trying to escape?

Help!

honour (GB) = honor (US) /ˈɒnə^r/
discipline
volunteer
patriotic
join the army / enlist
be drafted: *être enrôlé*
look forward to V-ING
be willing to
contribute to V-ING
be worth sb's sacrifice: *valoir le sacrifice de qqn*

B More than words

During WWI, the hero, Joe Bonham, is lying on a hospital bed suffering from severe injuries.

There's nothing noble about dying. Not even if you die for honor. Not even if you die the greatest hero the world ever saw. Not even if you're so great your name will never be forgotten and who's that great? The most important thing is your life little guy. You're worth nothing dead except for speeches. Don't let them kid you[1] anymore. Pay no attention when they tap you on the shoulder and say come along we've got to fight for liberty or whatever their word is there's always a word.

Just say mister I'm sorry I got no time to die I'm too busy and then turn and run like hell[2]. If they say coward[3] why don't pay any attention because it's your job to live not to die. If they talk about dying principles that are bigger than life you say mister you're a liar. Nothing is bigger than life. There's nothing noble in death. What's noble about lying on the ground and rotting[4]? What's noble about never seeing the sunshine again? What's noble about having your legs and arms blown off? What's noble about being an idiot? What's noble about being blind and deaf and dumb[5]? What's noble about being dead? Because when you're dead mister, it's all over. It's the end. You're less than a dog less than a rat less than a bee or an ant less than a white maggot[6] crawling around on a dungheap[7]. You're dead mister and you died for nothing.

You're dead mister.

Dead.

Dalton Trumbo, *Johnny Got his Gun*, 1939

1. *ne les laisse pas t'avoir* **2.** *décampe à toute vitesse* **3.** *lâche* **4.** *pourrir* **5.** *muet* **6.** *ver* **7.** *tas de fumier*

Text B

a. The characters:
- Imagine who the narrator is.
- Who do you think he is advising?

b. The narrator's values:
- Which is the most important?
- What does he advise doing to preserve it?
- What values or ideas does he oppose?
- What is death associated with?

Help!

cannon fodder: *chair à canon*
useless / meaningless
gruesome / horrid
bloodthirsty: *assoiffé de sang*
value life over sacrifice
denounce = expose
be sick of / fed up with sth / V-ING
can't stand / bear sth / V-ING
resent sb V-ING: *ne pas admettre que*
dread: *redouter*

2 Act it out!

You are with a group of friends and one of them decides to volunteer for active service in the army. Either you support him (or her) or make him (or her) change his (or her) mind.

3. PROTEST SONGS

1 Group work

a. Go on the Internet and listen to the following songs, then read the lyrics.

Group 1
- *We Shall Overcome*, Joan Baez
- *Blowin' in the Wind*, Bob Dylan
- *The Unknown Soldier*, The Doors

Group 2
- *Machine Gun*, Jimi Hendrix
- *Billy, Don't Be a Hero*, Paper Lace
- *Where Have all the Flowers Gone?*, Pete Seeger

Group 3
- *Born in the USA*, Bruce Springsteen
- *War*, Bob Marley
- *For What it's Worth*, Buffalo Springfield

b. Work on the lyrics.
- Try and define what the songs in each group have in common.
- Find the point of view in each of them.
- Who is the target?
- What does each song describe / denounce?
- Do you find the song effective? Why? Why not?

2 Top of the Pops

Choose the protest song you like best and prepare an oral account (historical context, message of the song, goal). Explain the reasons for your choice. You can also make a slide presentation (PowerPoint).

PREPARE YOUR TASK

3 Poet's corner

Write a poem or the lyrics of a song, either supporting military action or protesting against the war (about 20 lines).

Help!

Artists	Goals
activist opponent: *adversaire* committed: *engagé* involved in: *impliqué dans* side with: *prendre le parti de* hold sb responsible for advocate: *prôner*	protest against sth object to V-ING blame / criticize sb for sth / V-ING accuse sb of sth / V-ING put an end to withdraw (troops): *retirer* denounce / expose: *dénoncer* stand up against / rebel

4. I AM A VETERAN

1 Get ready

a. React to the document.
– This monument is in Washington, D.C. What is it?
– Observe the man (age, clothes, attitude, feelings).

b. What are the artist's goals?

c. Read this testimony and answer the questions.
– Who do "I", "he", "we" refer to?
– Can you explain "the welcome we deserved"?

> The first week back, I was the best man[1] in a wedding, and I had a Vietnam War veteran come up to me, and he handed me $50 and said, "Take your wife out to dinner. I appreciate what you did. We didn't get the welcome we deserved[2] when we got back, and I don't want that to happen to you; I want you to go out and enjoy yourself."
>
> Navy Corpsman Jim Weller, Hospital Corpsman, Jan.-Nov. 2004
>
> ■ *The Washington Post*, May 14, 2006
>
> 1. *témoin de mariage* 2. *méritions*

2 Staten Island Veteran Center

CD WB

Listen to these interviews with Vietnam and Iraq veterans comparing the way they were considered back home. Turn to your Workbook for help.

3 Recap

a. Which wars are mentioned in these interviews: WWII, Afghanistan, Iraq, Rwanda, Vietnam?
b. Find out about the consequences of war and classify them into two groups: gratitude • trauma.
c. How are veterans treated by civilians?
d. Compare the present and the past.

EPARE OUR TASK

4 Newspaper clip

Write an article for a newspaper about the interview at Staten Island Veteran Center (120 words).

Fast facts

American involvement in Vietnam (1961-1973)

- It was a Cold War military conflict between communist North Vietnam and the government of South Vietnam, supported by the United States.
- It was an unpopular war among students and young people who could be drafted and sent to Vietnam.
- After the war, veterans were often ignored and felt guilty when they came back home because they embodied failure.
- The Washington War Memorial was built in 1983. There are 58,022 names of fallen soldiers.

5. NO BRAVERY

James Blunt

Before being a popular English singer and song-writer, Blunt was an officer in the Life Guards, a cavalry regiment of the British Army, and served under NATO in Kosovo during the conflict in 1999. He was shocked at the atrocities of the war he witnessed and has tried to help the victims ever since.

There are children standing here,
Arms outstretched into the sky[1],
Tears drying on their face.
He has been here.
Brothers lie in shallow[2] graves[3].
Fathers lost without a trace.
A nation blind to their disgrace[4],
Since he's been here.

And I see no bravery,
No bravery in your eyes anymore.
Only sadness.

Houses burnt beyond repair.
The smell of death is in the air.
A woman weeping in despair says,
He has been here.
Tracer[5] lighting up the sky.
It's another family's turn to die.
A child afraid to even cry out says,
He has been here.

And I see no bravery,
No bravery in your eyes anymore.
Only sadness.

There are children standing here,
Arms outstretched into the sky,
But no one asks the question why,
He has been here.
Old men kneel and accept their fate.
Wives and daughters cut and raped[6].
A generation drenched[7] in hate.
Says, he has been here.

And I see no bravery,
No bravery in your eyes anymore.
Only sadness.

James Blunt, *No Bravery*, 2006

1. *tendus vers le ciel* **2.** *peu profondes* **3.** *tombes* **4.** *honte, déshonneur* **5.** *balle / obus traçant* **6.** *violées* **7.** *imprégnée*

1 Understand the song and find key information

Skim through (read rapidly) the song. What lines are repeated?

Stanza 1

a. Who or what do the underlined words refer to?
– "There are children standing here." (l.1)
– "Tears drying on their face." (l.3)
– "A nation blind to their disgrace," (l.7)
Regarding the sentence: "He has been here", who do you think "he" refer to?
a Serbian politician • a soldier • the army • a journalist

b. Pick out all the elements related to despair and death.

c. "Since he's been here." (l. 8):
– Who is speaking? What verbal form is used here?
– Write the full verbal form.
– What does this verbal form insist on?
the consequences of the soldiers' attack on civilians • the story of the soldiers' arrival

Chorus

a. What words are repeated? What words are opposed?

b. Who do the underlined word refer to?
"No bravery in your eyes anymore."

c. Explain in your own words what has changed and why.

Stanza 2

a. Classify each line of this stanza into four columns:
destruction • victims • armament • feelings.

b. "He has been here." (l. 15) Replace "be" in this line. What other verbs could you use to explain what "he" has done?

c. What does the narrator focus on in this stanza?

Stanza 3

Classify each line of this stanza into three corresponding groups:
resignation • horrors of war • consequences.

2 Go further

a. Sum up James Blunt's message in the song.
b. Do you find such a song effective? Why? Why not?

PREPARE YOUR TASK

3 Write a magazine article

Write an article about James Blunt's war experience for a teenagers' magazine (120 words).

Help!

Damage	Casualties	Horror
wreckage: *décombres* rubble: *décombres* debris *(indénombrable au singulier)* ashes: *cendres* destroy / damage / demolish burn down burn to ashes be covered in dust	body / corpse slaughter /ˈslɔːtəʳ/: *massacre* death toll /təʊl/: *nombre de morts* shelter: *abri* sufferings bloodshed: *effusion de sang* call for help run for safety	wound: *blessure (par arme)* be wounded /ˈwuːndɪd/ be tortured be raped: *être violé* shout / scream suffer from mourn /mɔːn/ sb: *pleurer qqn* despair

Language at work

L'expression du futur dans les subordonnées de temps

Observez.

a. *He will go back home as soon as he can.*
b. *He will marry his fiancée when he goes back home.*

– Ces énoncés renvoient-ils à des situations présentes ou futures ?
– Quelle forme verbale utilise-t-on après *when* ou *as soon as* dans ces subordonnées ?
– Traduisez les énoncés. Quelle différence remarquez-vous entre le français et l'anglais ?

→ **Déduisez :** en anglais, pour exprimer le futur on n'utilise pas le modal ... dans les subordonnées de temps renvoyant au futur, on utilise ... .

Les équivalents anglais de « pour »

Observez les mots et expressions en gras dans ce poème.

> We interrupt this war **to** find our future.
> We interrupt this war **for** soldiers **to** hug their children, **for** family reunions,
> **for** more time to find a lasting peace **for** our world [...]
> We interrupt this war **so that** we might feed the hungry, save the whales
> and find a cure **for** cancer and AIDS. [...]
> We interrupt this war **in order to** hear a message from our Number One Sponsor:
> "THOU SHALT NOT KILL"
>
> Cappy Hall Rearick, *We Interrupt this War*, 2003

– Combien de sujets grammaticaux y a-t-il lignes 1 et 6 ?
– Combien de sujets grammaticaux y a-t-il dans *We interrupt this war for soldiers to hug their children* ou *We interrupt this war so that we might feed the hungry* ? Relevez le(s) sujet(s).

→ **Déduisez.**

– Lorsqu'il introduit un verbe à l'infinitif, « pour » a pour équivalent anglais ... + base verbale ou ... ... + base verbale. L'énoncé ne comporte alors qu'un seul sujet grammatical.
– « Pour que » peut avoir deux équivalents :
  • *so that* (ou *so*) + sujet + modal (*can / could* ou *will / would,* ou dans un style recherché *may / might*) + BV.
  • *for* + ... + ...
– Lorsqu'il introduit un nom (ou un pronom), « pour » a pour équivalent ... .

Practice

1 Mettez les verbes entre parenthèses au futur en *will* ou au présent.

Air raid warning, 1939: As soon as you (hear) the warning, you must stop what you are doing. You (run) to the nearest air raid shelter. You (stay) there until the air raid (be) over. Don't move until you (hear) a continuous sound from the siren. The All Clear Signal (mean) you are safe again. You (then/be) allowed to go back home.

2 Traduisez.

a. Quand il rentrera, sa famille et ses amis seront heureux.
b. Dès qu'ils le reverront, ils seront très émus.
c. Pourra-t-il tout oublier quand la guerre sera terminée ?
d. Elle ne sait pas si elle le reconnaîtra quand il reviendra.
e. Dès qu'elle aura des nouvelles, elle sera soulagée.

Language at work

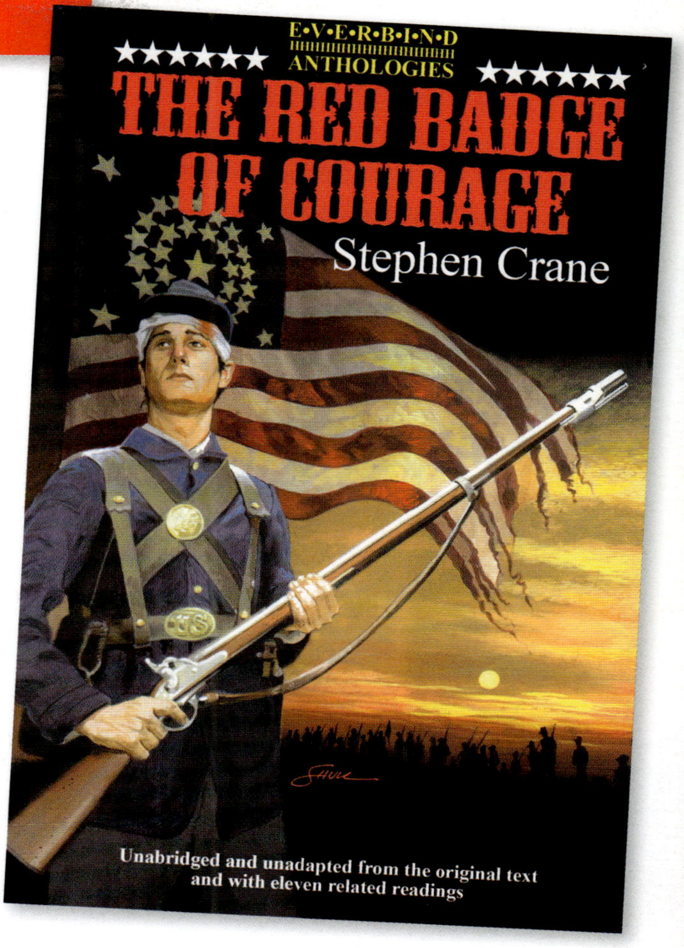

3 Après la bataille.

À partir de cette couverture de roman, imaginez :
a. ce que le soldat va faire ;
b. quels souvenirs il aura de ce moment plus tard.

Help!

in a state of shock
pluck up courage
join the rest of the troops
flee = run away
be haunted by
recover
be traumatized

4 Traduisez ce texte.

Il s'est engagé pour la gloire et dans le but d'avoir des médailles, mais au front, il a vite appris à se battre pour survivre. Il a eu peur pour sa vie mais il est resté auprès de ses camarades blessés pour ne pas être considéré comme un lâche.

Build up your vocabulary

1 Associez chacun des mots de la liste a à un mot de sens voisin de la liste b.

Utilisez un dictionnaire si nécessaire.

a call up • cowardly • daring • save • damage • weep • injured • deter

b discourage • destroy • chicken-hearted • wounded • cry • enlist • bold • rescue

2 Associez les mots et expressions (à gauche) à leur définition (à droite).

- cannon fodder
- down-hearted
- numb with fear
- let someone down
- at a loss

- unable to do anything when facing danger
- have no idea what to do and where to go
- pessimistic and depressed
- people sent to the front in deadly battles
- not help someone at a time when they need you most

3 Classez ces verbes en deux catégories : mouvements des soldats • solidarité.

Utilisez un dictionnaire si nécessaire.

stand by • lie on the ground • backtrack • care for sb • help to the wounded • come to sb's rescue • dodge enemy fire • creep • take cover • save

YOUR TASK

**You are a war reporter writing an article on the life of soldiers in combat.
Your text will be based on the photos provided (200 words).**

LES ÉTAPES À SUIVRE

1 Observez les images ci-contre.

Repérez pour chacune d'elles les lieux, moments, personnages, actions et détails importants.

2 Inventez une identité pour chacun des protagonistes.

Trouvez un nom, un prénom, des traits de personnalité, un rôle. Imaginez aussi la hiérarchie (qui est le chef, qui obéit) et enfin les rapports entretenus avec le soldat blessé.

3 Élaborez un scénario.

– Imaginez les événements antérieurs et le dénouement.
– Citez éventuellement les phrases marquantes prononcées par les soldats.

LES STRATÉGIES POUR LA RÉDACTION

1 Travaillez votre brouillon.

a. Utilisez des marqueurs chronologiques.
first... • then... • after a while... • later / a few minutes later... • little by little... • suddenly / all of a sudden... • then... • eventually / finally...

b. Ayez recours à des mots de liaison.
when • as • as soon as • while • after • until • that's why • because

c. Veillez aux temps du récit.

> – Le prétérit simple s'emploie pour faire un récit.
> – Le prétérit BE + V-ING s'emploie pour faire un « arrêt sur image », une description.
> – Le *past perfect* s'emploie pour évoquer une action passée qui précède une autre action déjà située dans le passé.

2 Soyez précis.

a. Ajoutez des verbes d'action.
<u>*Examples:*</u> *He rushed to help his friend.*
He leaned over him.
He shouted, screamed, whispered.

b. Incluez des adjectifs qui traduisent la peur et le désarroi.

c. Décrivez les réactions des personnages.

3 Complexifiez vos énoncés.

Utilisez des pronoms relatifs *(who, which, that, when, where)*.
<u>*Example:*</u> *The soldier was shot. He shouted for help.*
→ *The soldier who had been shot shouted for help.*

Help!

horrified / aghast
shocked
speechless
worried / concerned
stunned: *abasourdi*
helpless
desperate /ˈdespərɪt/
down-hearted: *démoralisé*
cowardly: *lâche*
supportive

Stills from *The Thin Red Line*, a film by Terrence Malick (1998).

SPEAKING CORNER

A Comment on this painting

Paul Nash, *Spring in the Trenches* (during WWI)

B Do you agree?

“*Mankind must put an end to war, or war will put an end to mankind.*
John Fitzgerald Kennedy (1917-1963)”

“*Never think that war, no matter how necessary, nor how justified, is not a crime.*
Ernest Hemingway (1899-1961)”

“*The pen is mightier than the sword.*
Popular wisdom”

C Observe and react

Shepard Fairey

D Podcast

MP3 41

Listen to Jenny Klyne, an American woman whose son is a soldier serving in Afghanistan.

Unit 15

THE LAND OF OZ

YOUR TASK AT THE END OF THIS UNIT

You have just spent three weeks in Australia. You post an entry on your blog to tell your friends about your experience there. Include photos and comments. → p. 223

TUNE IN!

Observe and compare

a. Observe this postcard, then read the fast facts below.
b. Compare Australia to all the countries and continents and justify the catchphrase.

Fast facts

About Australia

- The 6th biggest country in the world
- Population: 21.75 million
- Indigenous people: about 2% of the population
- Capital city: Canberra
- Main cities: Sydney, Melbourne, Brisbane, Perth, Adelaide

Help!

How to express comparison

(much) bigger... than
twice / three / four... times as big / large as: *deux / trois / quatre... fois plus grand que*
as... as
it's the first / second / third / fourth / fifth / sixth largest country in the world /wɜːld/
compared to
contrary to
tiny: *minuscule* ≠ huge: *immense*
(densely) populated ≠ uninhabited

I. A UNIQUE ENVIRONMENT

1 A journey to Australia

a. What vision of Australia is given here?
b. List the positive and the negative points.

It is the home of the largest living thing on earth, the Great Barrier Reef[1], and of the most famous and striking monolith, Ayers Rock (or Uluru to use its now-official, more respectful Aboriginal name). It has more things that will kill you than anywhere else. Of the world's ten most poisonous snakes, all are Australian. […] If you are not stung[2] or pronged to death in some unexpected manner, you may be fatally chomped by sharks or crocodiles, or carried helplessly out to sea by irresistible currents, or left to stagger to an unhappy death in the baking outback[3]. It's a tough[4] place.

In short, there was no place in the world like it. There still isn't. Eighty percent of all that lives in Australia, plant and animal, exists nowhere else. More than this, it exists in an abundance that seems incompatible with the harshness[5] of the environment.

Bill Bryson, *Down Under*, 2000

1. *Grande Barrière de corail* **2.** *piqué*
3. rural and isolated areas of Australia **4.** /tʌf/ *rude* **5.** *rigueur*

'The thing that Bryson most loves about Australia – its "effortlessly dry, direct way of viewing the world" – is, in fact, his own. They're a perfect fit'

NEW YORK TIMES BOOK REVIEW

It is the driest, flattest, hottest, most infertile and climatically aggressive of all the inhabited continents and still Australia teems with life – a large portion of it quite deadly. In fact, Australia has more things that can kill you in a very nasty way than anywhere else.

Ignoring such dangers – and yet curiously obsessed by them – Bill Bryson journeyed to Australia and promptly fell in love with the country. And who can blame him? The people are cheerful, extrovert, quick-witted and unfailingly obliging: their cities are safe and clean and nearly always built on water; the food is excellent; the beer is cold and the sun nearly always shines. Life doesn't get much better than this…

'Bryson is the perfect travelling companion…when it comes to travel's peculiars the man still has no peers'

THE TIMES

'He arrives at his destination, finds a hotel, checks in, meanders around the neighbourhood, visits any museums or public monuments he happens to encounter, has a couple of drinks, eavesdrops on a conversation or two, then goes to bed. A year later, people on three continents are hospitalised as a result of ruptures caused by laughing so hard at his account of the experience'

THE AGE, MELBOURNE

2 Info search

a. Either in an encyclopedia or on the Internet, find information about the Whites' arrival and the first Australians.
– Who first sailed along the coast of Australia? When?
– What was Australia used as?
– Who were the first settlers?
– When is Australia Day celebrated and why?
– What made Australia prosperous?
– What does the year 1901 correspond to?
– Why is today's Australian society multicultural?

b. Report to the class.

PREPARE YOUR TASK → **c.** Write your own article about the Whites' arrival and the first settlers.

Uluru (Northern Territory).

2. THE FIRST AUSTRALIANS

1 Past and present WB

Read and understand the articles with the help of your Workbook.

A BEFORE THE WHITES' ARRIVAL

The Aborigines[1] developed an enduring attachment to the land and an intricate understanding of their natural surroundings.

The Aborigines lived a semi-nomadic existence. They crafted tools, implements[2] and weapons for use in hunting, fishing, trapping and foraging[3]. They weren't random meanderers[4], but followed set patterns[5] of travel according to the seasons and availability of food, water and shelter.

Under white Australian domination during the first half of the 20th century, the Aborigines were compelled to[6] forsake[7] their heritage and assimilate. Tribes were removed from traditional territories and confined to reservation-like tracts. Customs, ceremonies and languages were lost.

The 1970's public awareness and acknowledgement of the appalling injustices suffered by the Aborigines spurred[8] a reconciliation process, although it remains a work in progress.

■ www.australiatodaymag.com

1. /ˌæbəˈrɪdʒɪniz/ 2. *outils, ustensiles*
3. *fouiller le sol à la recherche de nourriture*
4. *(ici) ils n'erraient pas au hasard* 5. *(ici) itinéraires fixés*
6. obliged to 7. (literary) abandon 8. *(ici) déclenchèrent*

B Australia despairs of easing Arboriginal suffering

Children six times more likely to[1] be the victims of neglect, adults seven times more likely to be murdered, women 34 times more likely to need hospital treatment after being abused at home and men 13 times more likely to serve time in prison. On and on it went – the government's latest lack-of-progress report on the welfare[2] of Australia's 500,000 Aborigines. "It's unacceptable, and it requires decisive action," Prime Minister Kevin Rudd said when releasing the report showing no improvement. [...]

Almost a quarter of male prisoners, a third of female prisoners and half of all detained juveniles are Aborigines. Infant mortality, even suicide, is double the rate for other Australians. The report released last week showed no advance in reading and writing skills[3] with 60 per cent of indigenous children failing to finish high school.

1. *ayant plus de chances de / plus susceptibles de* 2. *bien-être* 3. *compétences*

Ted Wilkes from Perth's Curtin University said he also despairs of government attempts to better the welfare of his fellow Aborigines – particularly programmes to keep them away from alcohol and drugs and keep them out of prison. [...]
Everyone agrees things are dire[4], that something must be done. [...]
Aboriginal elder Joy White, speaking in Darwin, said [...] "All our people are dying, and it's through alcohol and drugs," she said. "And we are struggling, our people, because we don't have the same rights as any individual living in Australia. We have no name whatsoever[5]."

■ *Earth Times*, July 8, 2009

4. *(ici) terribles* **5.** *(ici) du tout*

2 Recap

Group 1: After reading article A, comment on the photo with the help of the text.

Group 2: Read article B and describe the situation of indigenous people today. What problems are they confronted with? Has the situation improved over the years?

3 A cartoonist's vision of Australia

Look at these two cartoons. With the help of what you have learnt on pages 213 and 214:
– Identify the different characters. When do these scenes take place?
– List the different elements. What do they represent or symbolize?
– What are the cartoonist's goals?
– Give each cartoon a title.
– Which one is funnier? Why?

Help!
settler: *colon*
(sharp / striking) contrast
ironic
compel / oblige sb to do sth
land
impose sth on sb
deprive sb of sth: *priver qqn de qqch*
dispossess sb of sth

Help!
lack of: *manque de*
prospects: *perspectives d'avenir*
backward areas /ˈeəriəz/
awful / dreadful / appalling /əˈpɔːlɪŋ/
be confronted with
be in dire straits: *être en très grande difficulté*
denounce / expose

3. THE JOURNEY INTO THE DREAMTIME

1 Memory game

Read this introduction, then close your book and say which words you remember.

The Dreamtime: definition

The Aboriginal traditional way to educate about Aboriginal history, culture and law was storytelling, using a combination of art forms such as painting, singing, music and dancing to illustrate the ancient "Dreamtime stories". During the Dreaming, ancestral spirits came to earth and created the landforms, the animals and plants. Because the "Stories of the Dreaming" have been handed down through the generations, they are not owned by individuals. They belong to a group or nation, and the storytellers of that nation are appointed by the elders[1], with an obligation to pass the stories along, ensuring that young people build and retain a sense of who they are.

1. *les anciens*

2 A lost culture WB

Read the text below and answer the questions.

a. What was the impact of the white settlers on the Aborigines' culture?
b. What is the Aborigines' relationship with the land?

WE ARE ALL ONE

These elders speak limited English. But even so, their words, spoken softly in short sentences, have a poetic directness. Neidjie has said, for example, "First [white] people come to us, they started and run our life... quick. They bring drink. First they should ask about fish, cave, Dreaming, but... they rush in. They make school, ... teach. Now Aborigine lose... everything."
To understand the Gagudju[1] is to understand their Dreamtime – to us a very complex concept, to the Gagudju a simple one that explains the cohesion and interdependence of all living things.
"Dreaming" and "Dreamtime" are direct translations from Aboriginal words but, in fact, have little to do with dreams as we know them. Dreamtime refers to the beginnings of life and its continuation into the future. [...]
"Aboriginals have a special connection with everything that is natural... We see all things natural as part of us. All the things on earth we see as part human." [...]
In all these things, Neidjie stressed, all living things are as one. He said, "Earth our mother, eagle our cousin. Tree, he is pumping our blood. Grass is growing. And we are all one." He added that when the ancestral beings had completed their creation, they told the people: "Now we have done these things, you make sure they remain like this for all time. You must not change anything."
Thus the people were charged with the custodianship[2] of the land and all living things. It is what the Gagudju call "looking after the country." The Dreamtime is the cohesive force that keeps man and his environment in harmony. It has done so for perhaps 2,000 generations.

■ *The National Geographic*, February, 1988

1. *peuple aborigène dont la langue est aujourd'hui disparue* 2. *conservation*

3 Cultural heritage

Read the text below and answer the questions.
a. What do Aborigines paint on now?
b. What geometrical forms are used?

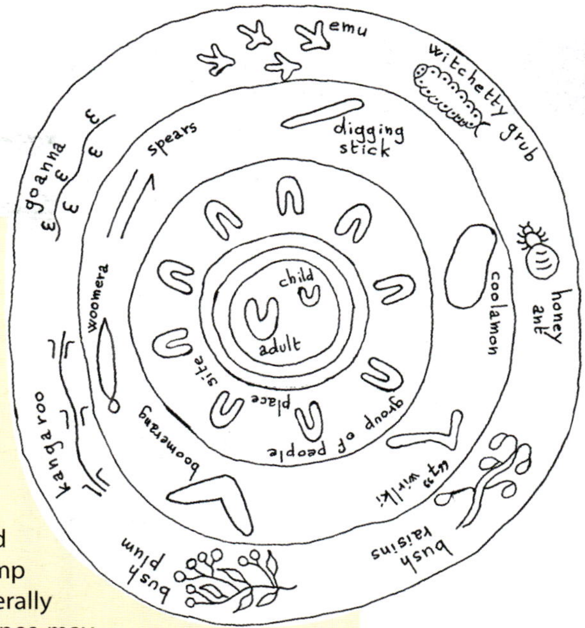

ABORIGINAL ART

It is still in the tradition to represent many of the desert Dreaming stories, and the sand paintings have been replaced by paintings on canvas[1] and new styles like dot[2] paintings, and X-rays styles are the most popular modern art styles based on traditional Dreamings and totemic representations. Symbols used within paintings include concentric circles, curved lines and straight[3] lines. Concentric circles usually represent camp sites, waterholes or places of significance. Curved lines generally represent rain or water travelling underground. Straight lines may be indicative of travelling and when these lines join concentric circles it may show the pathway travelled by the ancestors. A small "U" shaped figure may represent a person and depending on the iconography next to the person determines whether it is male or female.Tracks[4], whether human or animal, are often shown as they appear on the ground. Lizards and snakes are frequently seen from a topographical view – as one would see them from above.
Dotted motifs and design work have become the trademark of the contemporary Aboriginal art movement.

■ www.aboriginalart.com

1. *toile* **2.** *point* **3.** *droites* **4.** *pistes*

4 Art revival CD WB

Listen to Andrew McRae speaking about Arboriginal art.

5 A traditional instrument CD

– Can you recognize this instrument?
– Do you like the sound of it?
– What do you know about it?

PREPARE YOUR TASK

6 Follow the guide

a. You are a museum guide. You explain to tourists what Aboriginal art is:
– What is the Dreamtime?
– What are Dreamtime stories about?
– What role do they play in Aboriginal culture?
The documents you have studied will give the key information.

b. Write a small leaflet for the visitors who did not take the guided tour.

4. THE STOLEN GENERATION

1 A true story

a. Read the text on this back cover.

Rabbit-Proof Fence
by DORIS PILKINGTON

THE REMARKABLE TRUE STORY OF THREE YOUNG GIRLS WHO CROSS THE HARSH AUSTRALIAN DESERT ON FOOT TO RETURN HOME.

Following an Australian government edict in 1931, black Aboriginal children and children of mixed marriages were gathered up by Whites and taken to settlements to be assimilated. In this book, award-winning author Doris Pilkington traces the captivating story of her mother Molly and of three young girls uprooted from her community in South Western Australia.

b. Here are six extracts from the novel. They have been jumbled. Read each of them.

A Molly and Gracie sat silently on the horse, tears streaming down their cheeks as Constable Riggs turned the big bay stallion[1], and led the way back to the depot. A high pitched wail[2] broke out. The cries of agonised mothers and the women, and the deep sobs[3] of grandfathers, uncles and cousins filled the air. Molly and Gracie looked back just once before they disappeared through the river gums[4]. Behind them, those remaining in the camp found strong sharp objects and gashed themselves and inflicted wounds to their heads and bodies as an expression of their sorrow.

The two frightened and miserable girls began to cry, silently at first, then uncontrollably.

1. *étalon* 2. *gémissement*
3. *sanglots* 4. *gommiers (arbres)*

B When they saw the camp site they almost ran but they didn't have the energy. They knew exactly where to find their aunt's camp as they had both been there before. Their aunt greeted them in the traditional manner by crying with them and for those who had passed away since their last meeting.

"Where did you girls come from? Where have you been?" she asked. Their aunt and other relations couldn't believe what the girls told them. They were amazed and intrigued by their story.

"You poor silly girls, you could have died in the bush somewhere and no one would have known." She began to cry loudly.

C Instead of a residential school, the Aboriginal children were placed in an overcrowded dormitory. The inmates[1], not students, slept on cyclone beds with government-issue blankets. There were no sheets or pillow slips[2] except on special occasions when there was an inspection by prominent officials. Then they were removed as soon as the visitors left the settlement and stored away until the next visit. On the windows there were no colourful curtains[3], just wire[4] screens and iron bars.

1. *pensionnaires* 2. *ni draps, ni taies d'oreiller* 3. *rideaux* 4. *fil de fer*

D As soon as the other girls left the dormitory, Molly beckoned the two sisters to come closer to her, then she whispered urgently. "We're not going to school, so grab your bags. We're not staying here." Daisy and Gracie were stunned and stood staring at her.

"What did you say?" asked Gracie.

"I said, we're not staying here at the settlement, because we're going home to Jilagong."

Gracie and Daisy weren't sure they had heard correctly or not.

"Move quickly," Molly ordered her sisters. She wanted to be miles away before their absence was discovered; time was of the essence.

Her two youngsters faced each other, both looking very scared and confused. Daisy turned to Molly and said nervously, "We're frightened, Dgudu. How are we going to find our way back home to Jilagong? It's a long way from home."

Molly leaned against the wall and said confidently. "I know it's a long way to go, but it's easy. We'll find the rabbit-proof fence[1] and follow that all the way home."

"We're gunna walk all the way?" asked Daisy. "Yeah," replied Molly, getting really impatient now. "So don't waste time."

1. a boundary between certain Australian States, marked by a fence through which rabbits are unable to pass

E One day about midday, when the sun was high in the azure sky, Daisy and Gracie heard an excited shriek[1] from Molly who, as usual, was walking ahead of them.

"Here it is. I've found it. Come and look," she yelled as she laughed and waved her arms.

"What is it?" asked Gracie. "What are you shouting for?"

"I've found the rabbit-proof fence. See," she said, pointing to the fence. "This will take us all the way home to Jilagong."

1. *cri perçant*

F Molly, Daisy and Gracie were very much at home in this part of the country. They evaded capture by practising survival skills inherited from their nomadic ancestors.

"My legs are sore, Dgudu," cried Gracie. "I can't walk."

"My legs hurt too," chimed in Daisy.

"Mine are sore, too," said Molly. "But we can't hang around here all day, we gotta walk on further."

"I'll carry Daisy first, have a rest then it will be your turn, Gracie," said Mollie.

"Alright," both agreed.

The progress was slow and laborious but they persisted.

c. Re-organize the different parts in chronological order.
Which clues helped you?

PREPARE YOUR TASK **d.** Sum up the story (80 words).

e. Justify the title of the book and the title at the top of page 218.

f. React to the story you have just read.

2 Closing the gap

CD WB

a. Listen to the speech delivered in Parliament by Prime Minister Kevin Rudd on February 13, 2008 and turn to your Workbook for help.

b. Listen to the testimony of an Aboriginal woman.

PREPARE YOUR TASK **c.** An Aboriginal woman writes a letter to the Prime Minister in answer to his speech (150 words).

La détermination du nom : *the* ou Ø (article zéro)

1 Observez et comparez.

a. *Sharks can be dangerous.*
b. *Don't go swimming on that beach: You might be attacked by sharks.*
c. *The sharks that attacked them were very dangerous.*
d. *Curved lines represent water travelling underground.*
e. *The music they heard was by ACDC.*

Quels mots ou groupes de mots soulignés désignent :
(1) un groupe d'éléments dont on parle « en général » ;
(2) un groupe d'éléments bien définis ;
(3) un groupe d'éléments non définis ;
(4) une « masse » indénombrable non définie ;
(5) une « masse » indénombrable bien définie.

→ **Concluez :**
– on utilise le nom seul (= ø + nom), pour désigner quelque chose qui n'est pas ... , ou dont on parle ... ;
– on utilise *the* + nom pour désigner quelque chose qui est ... .

Traduisez en français les énoncés ci-dessus. Dans quels cas est-il impossible d'utiliser *the* comme équivalent de « le / la / les » ?

2 Observez.

a. *Australia was first used by the British as a prison.*
b. *Measures must be taken to protect the poor and the homeless.*

– Quelle est la nature des éléments qui constituent les groupes soulignés ?
– Ces groupes ont-ils un sens singulier ou pluriel ?
– Pourquoi, à votre avis, ne portent-ils pas la marque du pluriel ?

→ **Concluez :** on emploie *the* devant des ... pour désigner des catégories de personnes.

3 Lisez cet énoncé.

Australia is the sixth largest nation after Russia, Canada, China, the United States of America and Brazil.

→ **Concluez :** les noms de pays au singulier s'emploient sans ... . Les noms de pays au pluriel sont précédés de ... .

4 Comparez.

a. *Captain Cook landed in Australia in 1770.*
b. *Queen Elizabeth II is the official Head of State.*
c. *Prime Minister Kevin Rudd delivered a famous speech in 2008.*

Traduisez ces énoncés en français.

→ **Concluez :** en anglais, les noms propres s'emploient sans ... même lorsqu'ils sont précédés d'un titre, contrairement au français.

5 L'article *a/an*

Jim Burns is a truck driver. He drives his road train[1] across the country, doing about 90,000 miles a year, at a maximum speed of 100km an hour. He is proud of his low fuel consumption, which is about 8mpg (= 8 miles per gallon, which is about 29.4 litres per hundred kilometers).

1. camion suivi de plusieurs remorques

– Dans certains cas, *a /an* peut être remplacé par *per* (= « par », dans un style formel). Dans quelles expressions du texte est-ce le cas ?
– Dans quelle expression *a /an* est-il utilisé pour indiquer le métier de quelqu'un ?

Language at work

Practice

The Aboriginal flag

1 Complétez avec *the* ou Ø lorsque c'est nécessaire.

a. ... Ayers Rock is ... British name of ... biggest monolith on ... Earth. ... Aboriginal name of ... rock is Uluru.
b. ... Aborigines acquired ... right to vote in 1967.
c. ... Australia was colonized by ... British and ... Queen Elizabeth II is now ... Head of State because ... Australia is still part of ... Commonwealth. ... head of government is ... Prime Minister.
d. ... Aboriginal flag is divided horizontally into halves. ... top half is black and the lower half red. There is a yellow disk in ... centre of ... flag.
What do ... three colours in ... flag symbolize? ... black represents ... Aboriginal people of ... Australia. ... red represents ... red earth, ... red ochre used in ceremonies, and Aboriginal people's spiritual relationship with ... land. The yellow disk represents ... Sun, ... giver of ... life.

2 Complétez avec *a/an* ou *the* ou Ø lorsque c'est nécessaire. Attention à rétablir les majuscules le cas échéant.

The Twelve Apostles (State of Victoria).

a. 85 percent of the population live in ... urban areas. Immigration is ... important feature of ... Australian society.
b. ... meat and ... wool are Australia's major exports.
c. About one third of the country lies in ... tropics. Australia has ... coastline of 36,735km.
d. ... Australians glue themselves to ... surfboards, ... kayaks and ... boats and stay in ... surf for hours (days even!). They also flee to ... immense Barrier Reef and spend ... days under ... water defending themselves from ... sharks and ... dolphins. Visit Australia if you like ... wide open skies, ... dramatic landscapes, ... outdoor activities, ... fine wines and ... friendly locals.
e. ... Aboriginal people throughout most of ... Australia believe that in ... beginning of time, in the Dreaming, there were no visible landmarks; ... world was flat. As time progressed, ... creatures emerged from ... ground and had ... power to change from their animal to their human form.

3 Répondez en utilisant les éléments entre parenthèses pour construire un énoncé complet.

a. How often do they go swimming? (about twice • week)
b. What do they intend to do in favour of the Aborigines? (fight / infant mortality – improve / education – fight against / desertification – develop / irrigation programmes)
c. How many miles a gallon does his car get? (over 30 miles • gallon)
d. What does she do for a living? (is • trilingual tourist guide)
e. How much does this Australian wine cost? ($9 • bottle)
f. What speed are we going? (90 miles • hour)

Language at work

Improve your writing skills

1 **Associez chacun des mots de la liste a. à un mot de sens voisin pris dans la liste b. Utilisez un dictionnaire si nécessaire.**

a. far • spectacular • surprising • fun • beautiful • sunny • visiting places • marvellous • advice • amazing • big

b. incredible • impressive • sightseeing • dramatic • sun-drenched • tips • fascinating • gorgeous • remote • entertaining • stunning

2 **Classez ces mots en deux colonnes en fonction du champ lexical auquel ils appartiennent : *actions* ou *impressions*.**

unbelievable • discover • visit • amazing • tour • walk about • stunning • experience • fascinate • explore • try • taste

3 **Complétez ce texte à l'aide d'un des mots de la liste ci-dessous. Faites les changements grammaticaux nécessaires.**

close to • dispossessed of • driven off • drought /draʊt/ *(sécheresse)* • hunting • plague • reservations • savages • scarce *(peu abondant / rare)* • self-sufficient

For centuries, the Aborigines lived by [1]. They lived very [2] Nature, knew how to survive in a hostile environment. They had adapted remarkably well to the [3] and a dry environment. They knew how to use [4] resources. They were independent, [5], contented and free. They were [6] their land by the white settlers. They were [7] their land by mining companies. They were considered primitive [8] who had to be saved. They were isolated in [9]. Alcoholism became a [10].

4 **Complétez cette carte postale à l'aide des mots ou expressions pris dans la liste ci-dessous.**

are worth • breathtaking • cosmopolitan • fabulous • famous • lively • a lovely time • place • sightseeing • touristy

Hi everyone,

Australia is a [1] country. We had [2] everywhere. We've done a lot of [3] in Sydney which is a very [4] and [5] city. We had a look around some indigenous galleries. They [6] a visit, I love the paintings we saw because they are quite abstract and look very modern. We then discovered the amazing beaches along the coral Barrier Reef. The landscapes are [7]. We will soon fly to Darwin to see Uluru. I've always dreamt of seeing this [8] [9] even if it's a bit [10]. I'll tell you everything as soon as I get back.

Love to you all,

XXX Jennifer

YOUR TASK

You have just spent three weeks in Australia. You post an entry on your blog to tell your friends about your experience there. Include photos and comments.

LES ÉTAPES À SUIVRE

1 Construisez votre itinéraire.

Faites la liste de tous les endroits que vous avez visités. Choisissez plusieurs photos qui vous semblent représentatives du pays. Complétez vos connaissances sur Internet ou à l'aide d'une encyclopédie.

2 Sélectionnez les aspects sur lesquels vous voulez insister :

nature et environnement • population • histoire • art • activités • rencontres.

3 Mobilisez les connaissances acquises au cours de l'unité.

Relevez toutes les informations nécessaires à la rédaction de la page de votre blog.

4 Traitez les points suivants :

– ce que vous avez appris sur les Aborigènes (mythes, rapports à la nature, *Stolen Generation*) ;
– rencontres et découvertes ;
– remarques sur les écarts entre les Aborigènes et le reste de la population ;
– opinions personnelles.

LES CONSEILS POUR LA RÉDACTION

1 Attention aux formes verbales.

Rappel :
– le prétérit simple s'emploie pour le récit ;
– le prétérit *BE* + V-*ING* s'emploie pour faire un « arrêt sur image » à l'intérieur d'une action ;
– le *past perfect* s'emploie pour évoquer une action passée qui précède une autre action déjà située dans le passé ou pour effectuer un bilan par rapport à un point de repère passé.

2 Évitez ces quatre mots : *good, bad, big, interesting.*

– *~~good~~: great • pleasant • delightful*
– *~~bad~~: harmful • dangerous • awful • dreadful • appalling • terrible*
– *~~big~~: huge • impressive • large • enormous • gigantic*
– *~~interesting~~: attractive • exciting • fascinating • entertaining • thrilling*

A Koobor the Koala: The Drought Maker

Long ago in the Dreamtime lived an orphaned Koala-boy called Koobor who was constantly ill-treated and neglected by his relatives. Consequently he had learnt to live on the leaves of the gum tree[1] but was never given sufficient water to quench his thirst.

One morning when his relatives set out to gather food, they had forgotten to hide their water buckets so for once in his life, Koobor had enough water to drink. Koobor realised that he must store some water for himself so he collected all the water buckets and hung them on a low branch. He then climbed into the branches and chanted a special song that caused the tree to grow quickly to be the tallest tree in the forest.

That evening when Koobor's people returned from their hunt, they were tired and thirsty and soon became very angry when they saw their water buckets hanging from the highest tree next to Koobor. They demanded that Koobor return the stolen water but he refused. This angered Koobor's people no end[2]. Two clever medicine men climbed the tree and harshly beat Koobor and threw him to the ground shattering his little body.

As the people watched, they witnessed the shattered body of Koobor change into a Koala and climb into a nearby tree and sit in the top branches, where today he does not need water to keep him alive. Koobor then made a law that, although the Aborigines may kill him for food, his skin may not be removed or his bones broken until after he is cooked. Should anyone disobey, the spirit of the dead Koala will cause such a severe drought[3] that everyone except the Koalas will die of thirst.

Michael J. Connolly, *Dreamtime Kullilla-Art*

1. *gommier (arbre)* **2.** a lot **3.** /draʊt/ *sécheresse*

B *Between two Worlds*

Neil Symon, an Aboriginal storyteller, has come for a week of storytelling in the narrator's school. Milly Symon, the narrator, had always been told by her mother not to say they were Aborigines. She told everybody at school that her father was Italian.

"Um, Neil Symon says he lives near Seal Rocks[1]."

"So?" Mum said tersely[2]. She was tired. They were both sitting in front of the TV but Milly's thoughts were not on Young Talent Time. Her head was full of Neil's stories.

"So…" Milly's stomach had the old familiar burning sensation, "so you might know him, Mum. That's all. I thought he looked a bit, well, a bit familiar. And I thought he might know Grandma, you know, with his name being Symon and all…"

Mum turned to her, her eyes blazing[3]. "I said I don't know him! I wish you'd stop harping on about it[4]. I told you, Milly, to forget about all that. Forget about those places; that's the past, Milly. It's dead. We live here now. We're new people."

"We're the same," Milly said stubbornly. "I reckon I am anyway."

Her mother jumped to her feet, "What is this, Milly? Do you want to spoil[5] everything for us? Is that it? I told you to forget the past. Now I don't want to hear another word about Neil Symon or Seal Rocks or anything else."

Mum walked away from her in angry clipping footsteps across the room.

Milly felt tears of anger in her eyes. What was Mum so frightened of? Who were the *they* who would spoil everything for them? And how? It must be Mum's boyfriend, Bob, and his friends. Mum was frightened of Bob knowing it. But Bob loves Mum, that's easy to see, and if he really cares, then…

Milly lay in the dark that night staring out through the slice of window that the blind[6] did not cover. The old question tormented her. "Who am I?" she asked herself again and again. "Who is it that I'm not allowed to be?" She tossed[7] in her bed, hot and uncomfortable. She'd upset[8] Mum now and she was angry with herself.

"Well I'm not going to let it get me. I'll forget it. Like Mum says, I'll forget the past. Why should I worry? I won't think about it anymore. And I won't go to anymore of Neil's stories. I won't think about him or them anymore. I won't remember Grandma Pearl and Bill and…" She breathed deeply, closing her eyes, willing Neil's voice away. It was peaceful and quiet for a moment.

And then, *I am land and the land goes on and on…* It seemed to be inside the room, inside her head.

She sat up suddenly, angrily, and said aloud, "Alright, Neil Symon, you win! I'm Milly Symon from up Taree Way and I bet I'm from your family. Tomorrow I'm going to ask you. I am! I'm asking you about Grandma Pearl and Bill from Seal Rocks and of all the others too. And tomorrow I'm going to tell the kids at school that I'm Milly Symon from up Taree Way." She felt glad when she said this, but when she lay back, she thought of Mum's angry blazing eyes. Please, Mum, don't be angry with me. Don't get that hard, cold, closed-up look you get every time we talk about this. But I've got to know.

Libby Hathorn, *Dream Time, Up Taree Way,*
in: *New Stories by Sixteen Award-Winning Authors,* 1991

1. isolated coastal town 310km North of Sydney **2.** *sèchement* **3.** *pleins de colère*
4. *revenir toujours là-dessus* **5.** *gâcher* **6.** *store* **7.** *se tournait et se retournait* **8.** *bouleversé*

Évaluation

JE M'ENTRAÎNE

1 J'identifie le sujet

Lisez attentivement les sujets proposés ci-dessous et déterminez la tâche à accomplir. Plusieurs réponses sont parfois possibles (si besoin, reportez-vous à la page 236).

1. Do you approve or disapprove of what the narrator finally decides to do? Why or why not?
2. You have just come back from Australia. Write an account of your trip.
3. The four characters meet again after the war. Imagine the scene.
4. You are on holiday in Australia. Write a letter to a friend.
5. What does the word "hero" mean to you? Illustrate your answer with specific examples.
6. No war has ever been justified. Do you agree with this statement? Explain.
7. There are heroes who never make the headlines in the newspapers. Give examples and say why they can be admired.

2 Je mobilise le lexique

a. Observez cette carte mentale. Quel est le mot central ? À quel(s) sujet(s) peut-il renvoyer ?

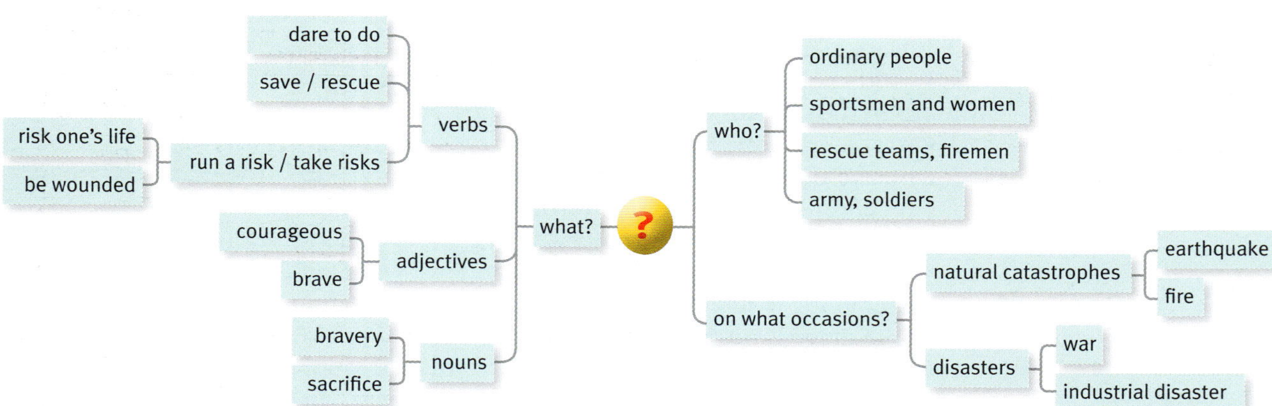

b. Mobilisez la grammaire et les mots de liaison nécessaires.
– Pour rédiger le(s) sujet(s) précédemment identifié(s) en **a.**, quels temps et formes verbales allez-vous utiliser : le présent simple • le présent en BE + -ING • le prétérit • le *present perfect* ? Justifiez votre réponse.
– Quels mots de liaison vous paraissent appropriés dans ce(s) sujet(s) : *on the one hand... on the other hand* • *whereas* • *although* • *and yet* • *however* • *even if* • *even though* • *for instance* • *besides* ?

3 Je prépare une introduction (et une conclusion)

Parmi les phrases suivantes, lesquelles vous semblent acceptables dans une introduction ?
Justifiez votre réponse.
– *I think it is right to say that there are heroes who never make the headlines...*
– *No, I don't agree with this idea...*
– *Every day people die or are injured while trying to save others and yet we do not hear about them.*
– *I must admit that we usually remember the heroes who make the news, nevertheless we should bear in mind all the ordinary people, people like you and me, who show enormous courage.*

4 Je me relis

Un élève a rédigé un paragraphe sur l'histoire de l'Australie. Il comporte dix erreurs (grammaticales ou d'orthographe) fréquemment relevées. Corrigez-les.

An English, the Captain Cook, discovered Australia in 1770. The first immigrants were of british origin. Australia was settle by convicts which were rejected by the British society. For get rid of their prisoners the British sent them to Australia, who was a colony. The others immigrants were the Chinese. They came after the gold was discovered in the 1850s.

5 Je m'auto-corrige

Corrigez vos réponses à ces exercices à l'aide de la fiche que vous trouverez sur le site compagnon et comptabilisez vos points.

JE FAIS LE BILAN

Analysez vos résultats à l'aide de cette grille d'évaluation où sont définis différents paliers de compétence en production écrite.

Je peux…	Paliers
Essais : exprimer mon opinion sur des thèmes généraux ainsi que décrire mes goûts et préférences.	B1
Récit : écrire un court récit, une description.	B1
Richesse du vocabulaire : montrer une bonne maîtrise du vocabulaire élémentaire, même si des erreurs sérieuses se produisent encore quand il s'agit d'exprimer une pensée plus complexe.	B1
Correction grammaticale : communiquer avec une correction suffisante dans des contextes familiers, même si parfois je suis encore influencé(e) par ma langue maternelle. Des erreurs peuvent se produire, mais le sens général reste clair.	B1
Orthographe : écrire avec une orthographe et une ponctuation assez justes pour être lu(e) facilement la plupart du temps.	B1
Correspondance : écrire une lettre personnelle pour donner des nouvelles ou exprimer ma pensée sur un sujet abstrait ou culturel, tel un film ou de la musique. Je peux écrire des lettres personnelles décrivant en détail expériences, sentiments et événements.	B1 / B2

ÉVALUATION

Votre professeur va vous distribuer une fiche d'évaluation de la production écrite sur une des unités travaillées en cours :

Unit 13 Everlasting Youth — Unit 14 Guns or Roses? — Unit 15 The Land of Oz

Une fois l'évaluation terminée, votre professeur pourra déterminer à quel palier vous vous situez par rapport à la grille du Cadre Européen Commun de Référence pour les Langues.

Unit 16

ART PROJECT

THE POWER OF LOVE

YOUR TASK AT THE END OF THIS UNIT

Your school is organizing an exhibition entitled *The Power of Love*. Choose a work of art representing your vision of love. Present it and defend your choice. You can also create your own masterpiece. → p. 235

TUNE IN!

Romeo + Juliet, a film by Baz Luhrmann (1996)

1 Observe and react

a. What catches your eyes first? Focus on the expression on the characters' faces and say what feelings they reveal.
b. What are Romeo and Juliet wearing? Guess on what occasion they could be wearing such clothes. What do the costumes symbolize?
c. Give a title to the scene.

PREPARE YOUR TASK →

2 Write an article

a. Go on the Internet and find out the names of famous lovers in Shakespeare's plays.
b. Write an article for your school blog or magazine for Valentine's Day. Present the story of Romeo and Juliet and explain why it still touches people today (120 words).

Help!

Costumes	Plot	Falling in love
knight's suit of **a**rmour: *armure de chevalier* wing: *aile* **a**ngel /eɪndʒəl/ b**a**ll dress: *robe de bal* disgu**i**sed / dressed up as	feud /fjuːd/: *querelle violente et longue* f**a**mily r**i**valry /raɪvəlri/ h**a**tred /heɪtrɪd/: *haine*	love at first sight bes**o**tted with: *fou de* l**o**ve-struck: *fou d'amour* fall (fell, fallen) woo /wuː/: *courtiser*

I. "MY FIRST, MY LAST, MY EVERYTHING…"

1 Love song

a. Read the lyrics once and say what you have understood.
b. Say why you like the song or not. Are there other love songs you like better?
c. Learn the song by heart and recite it in front of the class.

Whenever I'm alone with you
You make me feel like I am home again
Whenever I'm alone with you
You make me feel like I am whole again
Whenever I'm alone with you
You make me feel like I am young again
Whenever I'm alone with you
You make me feel like I am fun again

However far away I will always love you
However long I stay I will always love you
Whatever words I say I will always love you
I will always love you

Whenever I'm alone with you
You make me feel like I am free again
Whenever I'm alone with you
You make me feel like I am clean again

However far away I will always love you
However long I stay I will always love you
Whatever words I say I will always love you
I will always love you

The Cure, *Lovesong*, in: *Disintegration*, 1993

Shakespeare in Love, a film by John Madden (1998)

Pride and Prejudice, a film by Joe Wright (2005)

REPARE OUR TASK

2 Watch a film

Group work

a. Decide on a film you are going to watch with your group. Go to your town media library and hire a film from the following list: *Gone with the Wind* (1941) • *Casablanca* (1943) • *Laura* (1944) • *West Side Story* (1961) • *Love Story* (1970) • *Grease* (1978) • *A Room with a View* (1986) • *Pretty Woman* (1990) • *Four Weddings and a Funeral* (1994) • *Legends of the Fall* (1995) • *Notting Hill* (1999) • *Shakespeare in Love* (1999) • *The Girl with a Pearl Earring* (2003) • *Just a Kiss* (2004) • *Pride and Prejudice* (2005) • *Match Point* (2005) • *Bright Star* (2006) • *Inception* (2010).

b. Watch the film in English.

Class work

Prepare an oral account and report to the class. Choose a short extract, show it to the class and try to convince your classmates to see the film.

2. TILL DEATH DO US PART...

1 Get ready

a. Read the poem once and close your book.
b. What words do you remember? What has just happened? What is the poem about?

Stop all the clocks, cut off the telephone,
Prevent the dog from barking with a juicy bone,
Silence the pianos and with muffled[1] drum
Bring out the coffin[2], let the mourners come.

Let aeroplanes circle moaning[3] overhead
Scribbling on the sky the message He Is Dead,
Put crepe bows[4] round the white necks of the public doves[5],
Let the traffic policemen wear black cotton gloves.

He was my North, my South, my East and West,
My working week and my Sunday rest,
My noon, my midnight, my talk, my song;
I thought that love would last for ever: I was wrong.

The stars are not wanted now: Put out every one;
Pack up the moon and dismantle the sun;
Pour away the ocean and sweep up the wood.
For nothing now can ever come to any good.

W.H. Auden, *Stop all the Clocks*, 1936

1. *assourdi* **2.** *cercueil* **3.** *geignant* **4.** /bəʊz/*nœuds papillons* **5.** *colombes*

2 Listen to the poem

CD WB

Then study it with the help of your Workbook.

3 Recap

Use the notes you have taken to present your analysis of the poem to the class. Explain why you like it or not.

Help!

Poetry	Feelings
stanza: *strophe* line: *vers* rhyme rhythm iambic pentameter (five feet in the line): *pentamètre iambique* metaphor imagery	loss: *perte* grief /griːf/ = sorrow: *chagrin* broken-hearted: *au cœur brisé* desperate /ˈdespərɪt/: *désespéré* devastated: *effondré* mourn /mɔːn/ sb = grieve /griːv/ for sb: *pleurer qqn* collapse: *s'effondrer*

John William Waterhouse, *The Lady of Shalott*, 1888 (153cm x 200cm)

PREPARE YOUR TASK

4 Become an expert

You are the assistant curator *(conservateur)* of the museum. Choose one of these tasks for your WebQuest.

Group A: Write a short paragraph that will be displayed next to the painting to inform visitors.
Group B: *The Lady of Shalott* is exhibited in the Pre-Raphaelite room of the museum. Write the board presenting the movement at the entrance of the room and include information like dates, origins of the movement, three major painters, one or two paintings for each and key themes.

a. Answer these questions before you start:
– What elements do you find most striking in the painting?
– What feelings does the lady's face convey?
– What do the colours red, white and black symbolize?

b. Use the websites listed below to learn more.
– Where does the Lady live?
– What / who is "Camelot"? A person? A place? Justify.
– What is the Lady's occupation?
– How can she see the world outside? Why?
– What happens one day and what does this event result in?
– Who is Lancelot?
– What do the candles in the painting symbolize?
– Who wrote the poem illustrated by John William Waterhouse?

WEB BOX

– www.ibiblio.org/wm/paint/auth/
– www.castles.me.uk/legends-of-camelot.htm
– www.sir-lancelot.co.uk
– www.tate.org.uk/servlet/ViewWork?workid=15984

Help!

Subject
canvas: *toile, tableau*
tapestry: *tapisserie*
bow /baʊ/: *proue*
sleeve /sliːv/: *manche*
embroidered: *brodé*

Feelings
despair: *désespoir*
miserable: *malheureux*
desperate /despərɪt/: *abattu*
gloomy: *sombre*
hopeless
grief-stricken: *accablé de douleur*
down-hearted: *désespéré*
convey = express

3. Sense and Sensibility

1 A quick look

Observe the painting below for thirty seconds, close your book and try to remember as many details as you can.

William Hogarth, *Marriage-A-La-Mode*, 1743 (69.9cm x 90.8cm)

2 Learn more CD WB

a. Listen to the audio guide on the painting to understand the scene in more detail and turn to your Workbook for help.

b. Comment on the couple's behaviour. What can you infer about their feelings? What kind of marriage is represented here?

c. Choose the best title and justify with elements from the painting: The Marriage Contract • The Inspection • The Toilette • The Murder of the Earl • Suicide of the Countess.

d. What are the artist's goals?

Help!

Characters and feelings	Setting	Activities
distress: *angoisse, souffrance* pawn /pɔːn/ (in a game): *pion* bride: *mariée* groom: *marié* of aristocratic descent: *d'origine noble*	family tree engagement ring handkerchief: *mouchoir* quill: *plume (pour écrire)* wig: *perruque*	seal a contract: *sceller un contrat* whisper into sb's ear: *chuchoter à l'oreille de qqn* sit with one's back to look out of a window twirl: *tortiller*

3 Observe and react

a. What about the scenery (type of landscape, season)?

b. Observe the couple: What shows their social status? What is the man holding? Why?

c. Who is standing? Who is sitting? Why? Who are they looking at? What can we infer about their relationship?

Thomas Gainsborough, *Mr and Mrs Andrews*, 1750 (69.8cm x 119.4cm)

4 In the National Gallery CD

Listen to someone visiting the National Gallery in London and commenting on the painting.

a. What does the speaker find most striking? Pick out adjectives.

b. List the visitor's remarks about the husband and the wife's roles in the couple.
What is said about marriage in the eighteenth century?

c. Sum up the visitor's impressions and compare them with yours.

5 Marriage

a. What vision of marriage is given in these two paintings? Is it neutral, optimistic or pessimistic?

b. Do you think such marriages still exist today? Explain.

PREPARE YOUR TASK

6 A visit to the museum

You are planning a visit of the National Gallery in London with your school.
You have to introduce Hogarth or Gainsborough to your class (dates, country, main themes, other works).
Prepare a three-minute presentation. Show some of their works.

Help!

People

aristocracy
landowner
country gentleman
dressed up
stern: *sévère, sérieux*
stiff: *raide, guindé*

Accessories

rifle /raɪfl/: *carabine de chasse*
bench: *banc*

Scenery

field: *champ*
wheat: *blé*
harvest: *moisson*
fence: *clôture*
landscape: *paysage*

4. LOVE'S LABOUR'S LOST

Edward Hopper, *Room in New York*, 1932 (74cm x 91cm)

1 Observe

a. Where does the scene take place? What time of day is it? Who are the main characters (sex, age, social status, clothes, attitude)?

b. Where does the viewer seem to be? Is the couple aware of being watched?

c. Recap: Turn to your Workbook and fill in the blanks. WB

d. To what extent does this line from Shakespeare apply to the painting: "The course of true love never did run smooth"? (*A Midsummer's Night's Dream*, Act 1, scene 1)

PREPARE YOUR TASK

2 Which is which?

You want to publish an illustrated anthology of poetry. Read the two poems below and decide which could Hopper's painting illustrate best. Why? Confront your views.

I wanted one life
you wanted another
we couldn't have our cake
so we ate each other

Roger McGough, *Cake*, 1971

By the time you swear you're his,
Shivering and sighing,
And he vows his passion is
Infinite, undying –
Lady, make a note of this:
One of you is lying

Dorothy Parker, *Unfortunate Coincidence*, 1926

3 Love is the only inspiration WB

a. Read D.H. Lawrence's poem and the four lines from Shakespeare's *Sonnet 116*.
Turn to your Workbook for help.

b. Recap: Oppose the two poets' visions of love.

Love is not love
Which alters when it alteration finds [...]
Love alters not with his brief hours and weeks,
But bears it out[1] even to the edge of doom[2].

From *Sonnet 116*, William Shakespeare (1564-1616)

1. *supporte tout* 2. *bord de l'abîme*

We are all liars, because
the truth of yesterday becomes a lie tomorrow,
whereas letters are fixed,
and we live by the letter of truth.
The love I feel for my friend, this year,
is different from the love I felt last year.
If it were not so, it would be a lie.
Yet we reiterate love! love! love!
as if it were a coin[1] with a fixed value
instead of a flower that dies, and opens a different bud[2].

D.H. Lawrence (1885-1930), *Lies About Love*

1. *pièce de monnaie* 2. *bouton*

4 Timeline WB

Complete the timeline in your Workbook with the key information about the works of art studied in the unit (title and date, artist's name and dates).

YOUR TASK

Your school is organizing an exhibition entitled *The Power of Love*. Choose a work of art representing your vision of love. Present it and defend your choice. You can also create your own masterpiece.

A FEW TIPS

– You may choose the artistic expression you prefer or you know best, but you can also browse the Internet or talk to your school librarian and get familiar with other artistic forms.

– Use what you have discovered in the unit to present the work you have chosen.

– Prepare a presentation with a few slides. For a poem, choose large type (at least 18) and don't present the whole poem on one slide.

– If you choose a song, don't forget to mention the role of the melody and the rhythm, as well as the quality of the lyrics.

– If you choose a play or a film, insist on the director's choices and the actors' performance.

Robert Indiana, *Love*, 1960 (New York)

Rédiger un texte

■ **Avant de commencer à rédiger,** respectez les règles suivantes.

1. Identifiez le sujet : soulignez les mots clés. Que vous demande-t-on d'écrire : une lettre, un dialogue, un essai argumentatif, un récit ? En combien de mots ? Quel niveau de langue devez-vous employer : langue formelle, familière ?

2. Mobilisez vos connaissances : lexique, structures, mots de liaison, grammaire.

3. Organisez vos idées : les étapes du récit, les grandes parties de l'argumentation, les points de vue de chaque personnage dans un dialogue...

■ **Après avoir rédigé, relisez-vous** attentivement, en faisant attention à l'orthographe et à la ponctuation.

Gilbert Stuart, *Portrait of a Young Woman*, c. 1802-1804 (73cm x 61cm)

1 Déterminer la nature de la tâche à accomplir

Pour chacun de ces sujets, identifiez ce qui vous est demandé : faire un récit • décrire • expliquer un phénomène, un courant ou une tendance • donner votre opinion • comparer • parler de votre expérience personnelle. Associez chaque sujet au type de tâche demandée (plusieurs réponses sont parfois possibles).

1. If you had a serious problem would you rather ask your parents or your friends for support? Why?
2. Do you think a politician's family life should be of public concern?
3. Have you ever been involved in a situation which finally turned into a nightmare? Describe it and say where and when it happened, how it started, what the result was and how you reacted.
4. Some parents prefer their children to be taught at home. In your opinion, what are their motivations? Give your point of view.
5. Have you ever fallen in love with a particular object? What was it? What happened? Narrate your experience.
6. How important are your friends in your life?
7. Do you think the telephone is the best way to communicate between people?
8. Write a sequel to the story.
9. A young man tells his parents he has decided to leave school. Write their conversation.

a. Analyser les causes et les conséquences
b. Écrire un dialogue
c. Répondre à une question en fonction de son expérience, de son vécu
d. Raconter
e. Commenter
f. Imaginer, inventer
g. Analyser le pour et le contre, argumenter, discuter
h. Expliquer
i. Prendre position, donner son opinion

2 Écrire une lettre

Vous avez un(e) correspondant(e) dans un lycée américain, vous voulez suivre les cours avec lui ou elle pendant quelques semaines. Vous écrivez au proviseur pour lui demander l'autorisation.

1. Parmi les formules d'introduction suivantes lesquelles pourriez-vous utiliser :
Dear Sir • *Dear Mary* • *Dear Madam* • *Dear Mr Monroe* • *Hi John* • *Dear Mrs Robinson.*

2. Parmi ces formules de fin lesquelles conviendraient pour votre lettre : *Yours sincerely* • *Yours faithfully* • *Take care* • *Yours truly* • *Lots of love* • *Kindest regards* • *All the best.*

3. Classez toutes ces formules en deux colonnes : style formel, style informel.

4. Où sur la page allez-vous placer votre adresse et la date ?

5. Comment allez-vous signer ?

3 Écrire un dialogue

Lisez le dialogue suivant.

> My father entered the room. Then he said hello and stopped in the middle of his sentence. I turned around. He was staring at me.
> "What?" I said.
> "I know," my father said.
> "Know what?" I said.
> "I know you've been smoking," he said. "I smelt it in the car."
> "I was just trying it," I said.
> "Don't lie to me," he said. "How long have you been smoking?"
> "I—, I—"
> "That's enough now. Quit smoking immediately."

1. Quel est le niveau de langue utilisé ici ? Justifiez votre réponse à l'aide d'exemples.

2. Quelles différences avec le français remarquez-vous dans la ponctuation ?

3. Traduisez en français : *"my father said."* • *"I said."* Que remarquez-vous ?

4. Améliorez ce passage :
– Variez les verbes introducteurs. Choisissez dans la liste suivante : *add* • *admit* • *ask* • *answer* • *exclaim* • *explain* • *declare* • *hesitate* • *insist* • *reply* • *suggest* • *tell* • *wonder.*
– Enrichissez vos phrases à l'aide d'adverbes. Dans le dialogue ci-dessus lesquels pourriez-vous utiliser : *curiously* • *angrily* • *kindly* • *calmly* • *nervously* • *quietly* • *loudly* • *shyly* • *suspiciously* • *impatiently* ?
– Ajoutez des *gap fillers* (→ p. 249) : *well* • *you know* • *actually...*

4 Écrire un récit

1 Observez.

a. Lisez le paragraphe suivant et identifiez la situation.

> At eleven o'clock they all went to bed, and by half past eleven all the lights were out. Some time afterwards, Mr Brocklehurst was awakened by a curious noise in the corridor. He was sure he had heard something outside his room. It sounded like the clank of metal, and seemed to be coming nearer every minute. He got up at once, struck a match, and looked at the time. It was exactly one o'clock. The strange noise continued, and he could distinctly hear the sound of footsteps. He put on his slippers, and opened the door slowly. Right in front of him he saw an old man of terrible aspect. The strange figure tried to speak, then fled down the corridor and vanished into the night.

b. Quel temps est utilisé ici pour relater les événements successifs ?
c. Quelle forme verbale est utilisée pour parler d'une action vue dans son déroulement ?
d. Quelle forme verbale renvoie à un moment antérieur à celui du récit ?
e. Relevez les marqueurs de temps employés.

2 Rédigez.

Matthew Everingham a été envoyé en Australie pour purger une peine de prison. Il est arrivé à Sydney en 1788. Écrivez le récit de ce jeune Britannique à partir des images suivantes.

5 Rédiger un essai

1 Mobilisez votre lexique.

a. Lisez ce sujet, puis, parmi les mots proposés, choisissez ceux que vous utiliserez dans votre essai.

> "Travel broadens the mind," as the saying goes.
> Do you think that the more you travel the more open-minded you become?

foreign countries • go abroad • customs • quarrel • habits • natives • way of life • people • trip • integrate into • disappoint • different from • enriching • opportunities • change one's point of view • curiosity • discover • go sightseeing • harmful • interested in • local • take a break from • work • mentality • switch off • tropical beach • addicted to • sunbathing • vacation • friendship • colourful • impress • stories • visit • get acquainted with • understand • get a tan • be confronted with • bring people together

b. Classez ces mots en deux colonnes : arguments pour | objections que l'on peut y apporter

2 Trouvez un ordre logique.

Voici un essai dont les phrases ont été mises dans le désordre. Rétablissez l'ordre logique. Indiquez les indices qui vous ont mis sur la voie.

> Most teenagers try to find summer jobs. Explain why.
> You may mention your personal experience (150 words).

a. Lastly, I would say that having a summer job broadens our minds and helps us grow up and become more mature.
b. More and more teenagers try to find a summer job. What explains this growing trend?
c. Others can also have enough money to afford holidays with their friends.
d. For instance, I was a waiter in a café for a month and I realized it was a tough job.
e. Secondly, a work experience is more and more highly valued nowadays. Teenagers are given responsibilities and are confronted with the real world, which can be enriching.
f. First / First of all / To begin with, some teenagers have a summer job for economic reasons. Their goal is mainly to earn money and thus to acquire more financial independence. With the money they make, they can pay for their books, their clothes or their driving licence.
g. After four weeks I really looked forward to going back to school. Having a job had a positive influence on my schoolwork and my studies.
h. Besides, having a full-time job makes them realize how lucky they are to study.

3 Organisez un plan.

L'essai ci-dessous a été mis dans le désordre. Rétablissez l'ordre logique. Séparez l'introduction du corps du devoir. Distinguez les différents paragraphes et la conclusion. Donnez un titre à chaque partie.

How can you account for young people's attraction to designer clothes? Do you approve of it?

a. Personally, I refuse to spend money on expensive clothes. I refuse to be brainwashed by advertisers. Besides, I don't attach a lot of importance to clothes. I'd rather spend my money on DVDs or videogames.
b. Furthermore, they want to look "in", to follow the trend. Peer pressure is certainly an important factor. Being fashionable gives them a sense of identity, a sense of belonging to a group.
c. Finally, we shouldn't judge people on their appearance, as the saying goes: Don't judge a book by its cover.
d. Above all, young people want to identify with the stars they see in magazines, on TV or on billboards. Their goal is to look glamorous.
e. Some certainly want to show off, since designer clothes are used as status symbols and reveal you are well off.
f. Many teenagers in the developing world are attracted to designer clothes and accessories. They spend a lot of money to buy famous worldwide brands.

4 Utilisez des mots de liaison.

Complétez l'essai suivant à l'aide des mots de liaison choisis dans cette liste :
but • however • indeed • in my opinion • secondly • that's why • therefore • yet • first

What do you think of the Internet as a way to make friends?

Nowadays computers have invaded our world and there is no denying that the need to communicate has become essential. Many teenagers in the developed world own a computer and spend hours chatting with their friends. 1 we may wonder if it is the best way to make friends.
2, chatting on the Internet is easy, quick and quite cheap. 3 you can chat for hours while staying at home. 4 so many young people are addicted to the Internet.
5, it is fun to meet people in cyberspace and communicate with other people who have the same interests or passions as you throughout the world.
6 are these real friends? Do people really communicate? Can chatting on line replace a real face-to-face conversation?
7, meeting and seeing friends in the flesh is a real pleasure. I'd rather go out with them, chat with them after school, do sports or watch a film together. It seems to me that talking on a computer is too artificial.
8, we may conclude that talking on the Internet can help us keep in touch, make contacts with new people. 9, real friendship cannot be lived from a distance.

Apprendre du vocabulaire

Pour apprendre du vocabulaire, il existe plusieurs stratégies. En voici quelques-unes.

1 Créer des cartes mentales ou *mind-mapping*

Les mots peuvent être regroupés en diagrammes pour mieux les mémoriser. Voici quelques schémas possibles, en forme d'arborescence ou de bulles sur le thème du voyage *(Unit 7, Far and away)*.

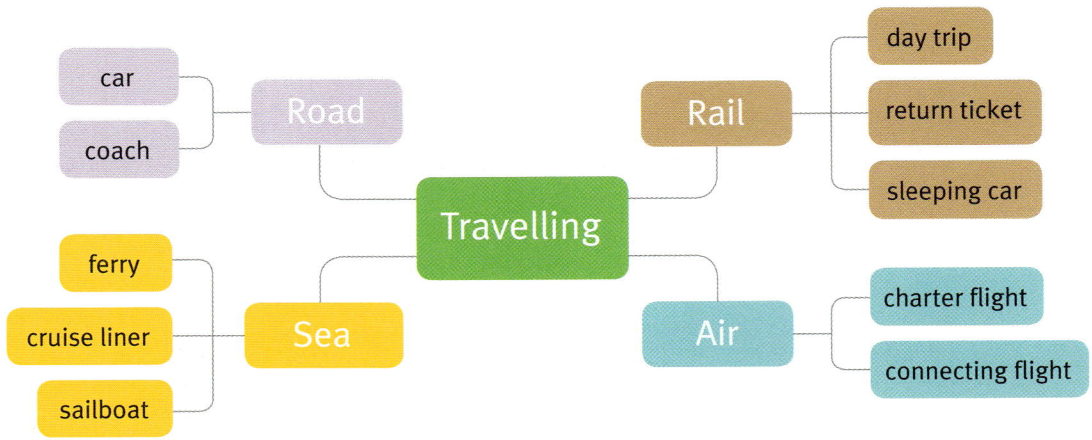

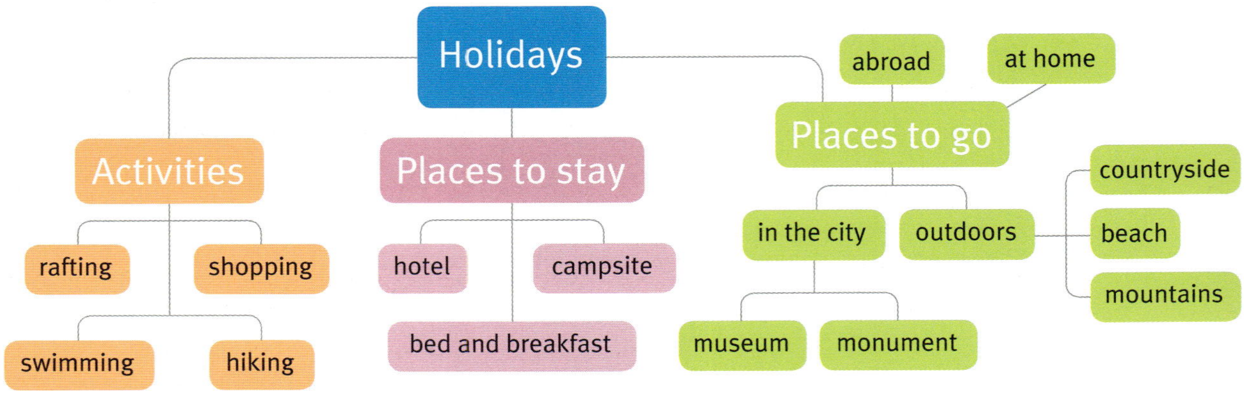

a. Quand vous avez une liste, cherchez-lui d'abord un titre. Quel mot écririez-vous au centre de celle-ci ?

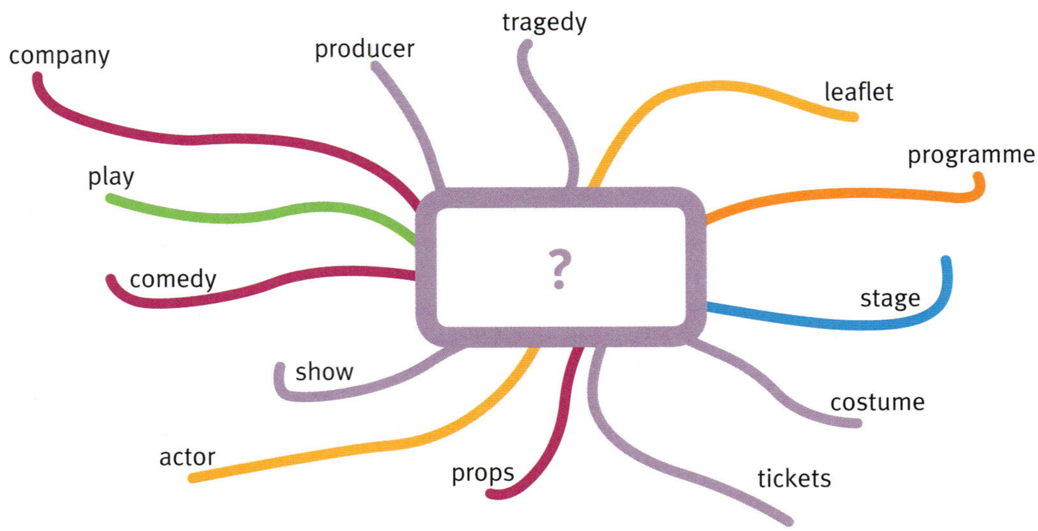

b. Observez le vocabulaire donné dans ce *Help* et la carte mentale ci-dessous.

Help!

Vampirism	Atmosphere
werewolf /ˈweəʳwʊlf/ (pl. -wolves): *loup-garou*	eerie: *sinistre*
bat: *chauve-souris*	scary
garlic: *ail*	unsettling: *dérangeant*
cross: *croix*	disquieting /dɪsˈkwaɪətɪŋ/: *troublant*
coffin: *cercueil*	mysterious
stake /steɪk/: *pieu*	gloomy: *lugubre*
feed on	weird /wɪəʳd/: *étrange*
suck blood /blʌd/	bloodcurdling
vanish	hair-raising
	give sb the creeps: *donner la chair de poule à qqn*

c. Sur papier libre, recopiez la carte ci-dessus et classez les mots du *Help* dans les catégories correspondantes.

d. Quels mots pouvez-vous ajouter à la carte sous les catégories suivantes ?
time of day • *building* • *suspense* • *sounds* • *colours and lights*

2 Chercher les antonymes

Exemples : *near* ≠ *far* (adjectifs) • *ally* /əˈlaɪ/ ≠ *enemy* (noms) • *praise* ≠ *blame* (verbes)

a. Trouvez les antonymes liés au thème de la guerre dans la liste ci-dessous *(Unit 14, Guns or Roses?)*. Utilisez un dictionnaire si nécessaire.
alive • *admit* • *bravery* • *bold* • *captivity* • *cowardice* • *dangerous* • *dead* • *defeat* • *deny* • *despair* • *fail* • *follower* • *freedom* • *hope* • *leader* • *safe* • *succeed* • *timid* • *victory*

b. Quels sont les opposés de ces mots appartenant au thème de la nourriture *(Unit 1, You are what you eat)* ? Utilisez un dictionnaire si besoin.
appetizing • *bitter* • *cheap* • *exotic* • *full meal* • *healthy* • *homemade* • *lean* • *lose weight* • *natural*

3 Étoffer une liste de mots avec des synonymes ou des mots de sens voisin

Exemples : *lazy* / *idle* (adjectifs) • *pain* / *ache* (noms) • *deceive* / *betray* (verbes)

a. Dans la liste ci-dessous, regrouper les synonymes ou mots de sens voisin par trois. Ils appartiennent aux champs sémantiques du tourisme et des vacances *(Unit 7, Far and away)*. Utilisez un dictionnaire si nécessaire.
boiling • *chaotic* • *comfortable* • *cold* • *cool* • *cosy* • *dirty* • *disordered* • *exciting* • *filthy* • *freezing* • *hiking* • *hot* • *luxurious* • *messy* • *pleasing* • *squalid* • *trekking* • *thrilling* • *walking* • *warm*

b. Classez les mots de chaque liste du moins fort au plus fort.

4 Mémoriser des expressions en tenant compte des registres de langue

Attention, vous devez adapter votre façon de vous adresser à votre interlocuteur (registre de langue) et aux tâches proposées. Si vous écrivez à des amis sur un blog, vous n'utiliserez pas les mêmes mots que pour envoyer une lettre à un employeur par exemple.

Voici une liste d'expressions liées au monde du travail *(Unit 11, Whatever works)*. Classez-les en deux colonnes selon le niveau de langue employé : *standard English* (courant) ou *colloquial* (familier). Utilisez un dictionnaire.
Get moving! • *What a snooty guy!* • *Please stop harassing me.* • *Don't overwork yourself.* • *Get off my back!* • *Easy does it.* • *Let's cancel the interview.* • *You should hurry up.* • *Drop the chat!* • *Say no more.* • *He is so full of himself.* • *Zip it.*

Apprendre à traduire

1 Effectuer les premiers repérages

Avant de commencer à traduire, suivez ces étapes essentielles.

1. Lisez le passage à traduire plusieurs fois. Assurez-vous que vous l'avez bien compris et résumez-le en français en une ou deux phrases (qui ?, où ?, quand ?, chronologie des événements ?).

2. Déterminez le style : familier, littéraire, journalistique ?

2 Deviner le sens des mots inconnus

1. Un signe ou une lettre en français peuvent correspondre à une autre lettre en anglais.

Français	Anglais	Exemples
^	...s... en milieu de mot	hôpital = *hospital* • coût = *cost*
é	s	étude = *study* • état = *state*
g	w	gaspiller = *waste* • garantie = *warrant*

2. Les préfixes et les suffixes permettent de deviner le sens général du mot. Voici quelques exemples de préfixes et de suffixes courants (vous en trouverez une liste plus complète p. 270).

Préfixes	Sens	Exemples
un- / mis- / dis-	contraire	*undo* • *misbehaviour* • *disrespectful*
im- / in- / ill- / ir-	contraire	*impolite* • *ineffective* • *illegal* • *irresponsible*
fore-	avant	*forecast* • *foreground*
out-	dépasser	*outnumber* • *outcast*

Suffixes	Sens	Exemples
-ly	manière	*shyly*
-less	sans, dépourvu de	*defenceless*
-hood	condition, état, âge	*childhood*
-ness	état, caractéristique	*loneliness*

3 Passer au français : les procédés de traduction

Anglais	Français	Procédés de traduction
Hundreds of them surrounded the bus,	Des centaines d'entre eux entourèrent le bus	Traduction littérale
and others held vicious German shepherds,	et d'autres tenaient en laisse des bergers allemands féroces,	Étoffement (emploi de plusieurs mots au lieu d'un seul)
growling and ready to attack these unarmed people.	qui grondaient et étaient prêts à attaquer ces gens non armés.	Transposition (changement de catégorie grammaticale)
The mob was just waiting	La foule hostile attendait simplement	Équivalence (appel à une expression propre à la langue) : *just* → simplement
to get their hands on the riders.	le moment favorable pour mettre la main sur les passagers du bus.	Équivalence

4 À vous !

1. La traduction du passage ci-dessous (*Whatever works*, p. 160) est fournie par un traducteur automatique. Améliorez ou corrigez cette traduction.

"I simply do not understand what takes you so long to speak after you pick up the phone," she stated.
I nodded like a six-year-old who'd just been reprimanded for throwing spaghetti on the ceiling, even though she couldn't see me. I concentrated on not calling her "ma'am", a mistake I'd made a week earlier that had almost gotten me fired.

« Je ne comprends pas simplement ce qui vous prend si longtemps pour parler après que vous prenez le téléphone », a-t-elle exposé.

J'ai incliné la tête comme une personne de six ans qui avait juste été réprimandée de jeter des spaghettis sur le plafond, bien qu'elle ne puisse pas me voir. Je me suis concentré en le non appel de sa « madame », une erreur que j'avais faite une semaine plus tôt qui m'avait presque fait renvoyer.

2. Utilisez le tableau des procédés de traduction de la page précédente.

a. Lisez ce passage.

Almost half the British population – some twenty-five million people – are thought to use social networking sites. There are already proposals under a European Union directive – dating back to after the 7 July 2005 bombs – for emails and Internet usage to be monitored and added to a planned database to track terror plots.

b. Traduisez-le en tenant compte des indications données.

Almost half the British population – some twenty-five million people –
are thought to use social networking sites.
There are already proposals under a European Union directive –
dating back to after the 7 July 2005 bombs –
for emails and Internet usage to be monitored and added to a planned database
to track terror plots.

- « – » (après *population* et après *people*) : Penser à d'autres signes de ponctuation possibles.
- *people* : Ne pas traduire par « gens ».
- *are thought to* : Mot à mot impossible. Penser à « on » et transformer la phrase.
- *under* : Ne pas traduire par « sous ». Trouver l'équivalent.
- *dating back to after* : Éviter de traduire *dating back to* par « datant du ». Étoffer *after*.
- *bombs* : Ne pas traduire mot à mot.
- *for* … *to be monitored and added* : Relier ces deux verbes à *for*.
- *terror* : Transposer : nom → adjectif.

c. Relisez votre traduction pour éliminer les fautes d'orthographe, vérifier la ponctuation et la correction de la langue.

Commenter une image fixe

1 Les différentes zones de l'image

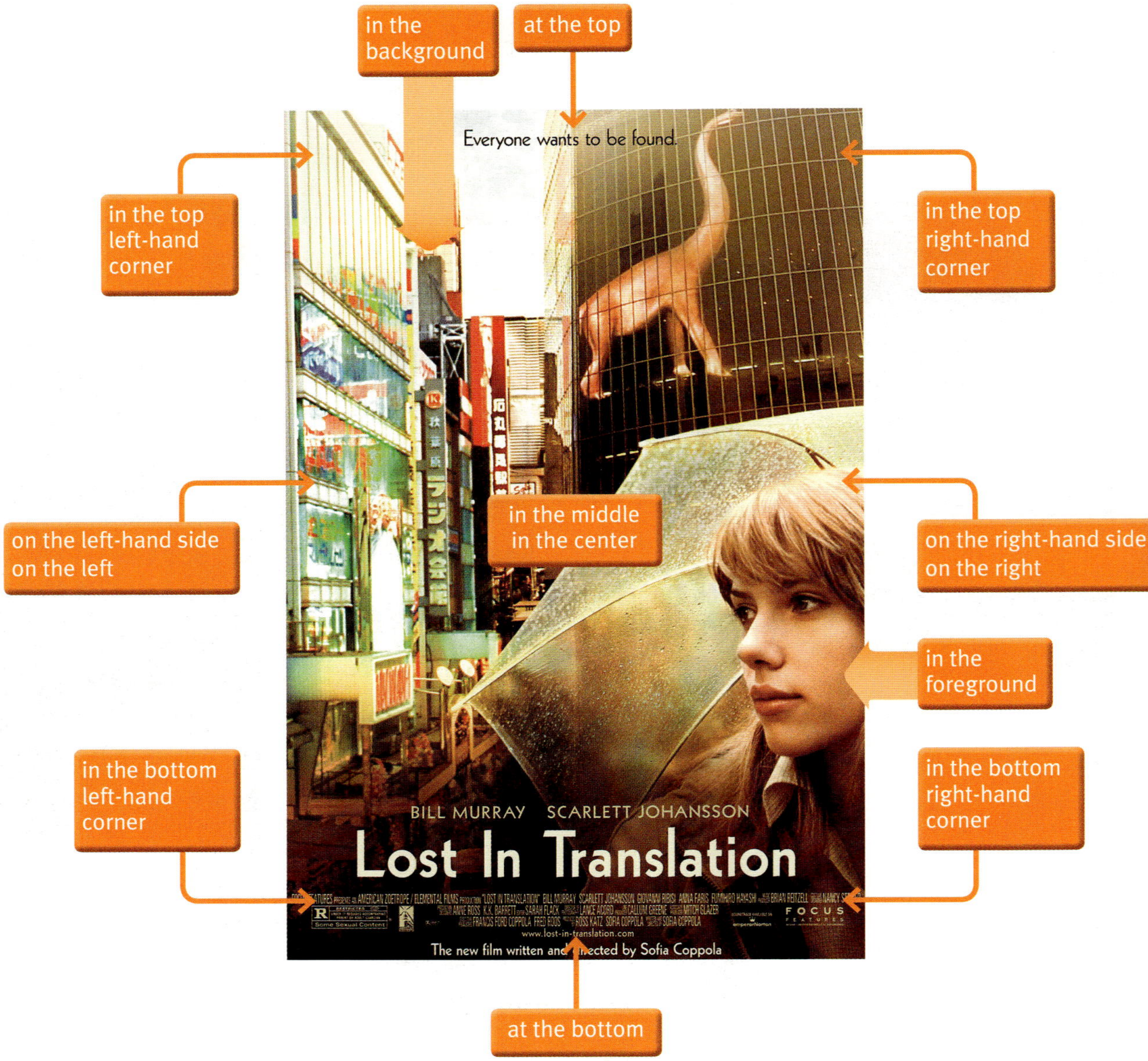

2 Les mots et expressions utiles

drawing
painting
cartoon
comic strip
poster
photograph
advertisement / advert / ad
still from a film

character
setting
balloon
caption
light and shade
layout
catchphrase
slogan

in: *dans*
on: *sur*
under / below: *sous*
above: *au-dessus*
between: *entre*
among: *parmi*
in front of: *devant*
behind: *derrière*
outside ≠ inside

- I can see...
- There is / are...
- The woman is V-ING...
- What strikes / surprises me is...
- It looks like...
- It conveys the impression that...
- It reminds me of...
- It symbolizes / stands for...
- It stands out against...
- It is meant to make us aware of...

Commenter une image animée

1 Les plans et les angles

Long shot

Close-up

Full shot

Medium shot

High-angle shot

Low-angle shot

Associez chacun des principaux plans et angles ci-dessus à la définition correspondante.
– The camera shows the characters standing.
– The camera shows a distant object or landscape.
– The character is seen from below and the viewer feels dominated.
– The camera focuses on the character's head and shoulders.
– The shot makes the character look smaller and the viewer dominates the scene.
– The viewer can see details on a face or an object, generally to convey (= express) emotion.

2 Les mots essentiels

black and white movie
disaster film
comedy
thriller
musical
detective film
war / adventure film
cartoon
blockbuster
documentary
commercial
trailer: *bande-annonce*

shoot (shot, shot): *tourner*

3 Les bruits et les sons

soundtrack: *bande-son*
sound effect: *bruitage*
film score: *musique*
voice-over: *voix off*
male / female voice

lively / cheerful
dramatic
spooky: *qui fait froid dans le dos*
romantic
sugary: *sirupeux*
deafening: *assourdissant*
dull / muffled (sound): *étouffé*

Améliorer sa prononciation

1 L'accent de mot

Dans les transcriptions en signes phonétiques, on utilise le signe /ˈ/, placé avant la syllabe accentuée, pour indiquer l'**accent principal** (*garden* /ˈgɑːdn/, *hotel* /həʊˈtel/), et éventuellement le signe /ˌ/ pour indiquer l'**accent secondaire** (*hospitality* /ˌhɒspɪˈtælɪti/).

2 L'accentuation des mots à suffixes

1 Mots à suffixe neutre (qui ne modifie pas l'accentuation)

a. Suffixes grammaticaux (= terminaisons grammaticales)

- ***-s*** ou ***-es*** (*actress* → *actresses*)
- ***-ed***, ***-ing*** (*interest* → *interested* / *interesting*)
- ***-er***, ***-est*** ajoutés à un adjectif (*happy* → *happier* / *happiest*)

b. Suffixes lexicaux (= servant à former un mot de la même famille). Notamment :

MP3 42

-er /əʳ/	*program*	→ *programmer*	programmeur
-ful /fʊl/, /fəl/	*beauty*	→ *beautiful*	beau
-hood /hʊd/	*child*	→ *childhood*	enfance
-less /lɪs/, /ləs/	*care*	→ *careless*	insouciant
-ly /li/	*narrow*	→ *narrowly*	étroitement
-ness /nɪs/, /nəs/	*careless*	→ *carelessness*	insouciance
-or /əʳ/	*govern*	→ *governor*	gouverneur
-ward(s) /wəʳdz/	*east*	→ *eastward(s)*	vers l'est

Remarque : ces suffixes ne sont **jamais accentués**, et par conséquent ils ont souvent une forme **réduite** (*-less* = /lɪs/ ou /ləs/, etc.).

Je m'entraîne

a. Lisez à haute voix chaque mot en respectant la syllabe accentuée, puis lisez le mot dérivé en respectant les règles d'accentuation énoncées ci-dessus.

– *hope* • *hopeful* • *hopeless* • *hopelessness*
– *neighbour* • *neighbourhood*
– *back* • *backwards*
– *teach* • *teacher*
– *dictate* • *dictator*
– *hesitate* • *hesitatingly*
– *happy* • *happily*

MP3 43

b. Vérifiez avec votre enregistrement.

2 Mots à suffixe contraignant (qui impose une place pour l'accent)

L'accent porte sur la syllabe qui précède le suffixe.

MP3 44

-ic, ***-ics***. Exceptions principales : *Arabic*, *Catholic*, *politic(s)*		*electric*, *robotics*
-ical		*electrical*
-ity, ***-ety***	*electric*	*electricity*, *anxiety* /æŋˈzaɪəti/
-ion (sauf *television*)	*irritate*	*irritation*
-ian, ***-iot***, ***-ial***, ***-ious***	*industry*, *mystery*	*pedestrian*, *idiot*, *industrial*, *mysterious*
-eous	*courage* /ˈkʌrɪdʒ/	*courageous* /kəˈreɪdʒəs/
-ible, ***-igible***		*comprehensible*, *intelligible*

Lorsque **plusieurs** suffixes contraignants s'ajoutent l'un à l'autre, **c'est le dernier qui l'emporte** : *music* → *musician* ; *electric*, *electricity* (= *electr-* + *-ic* + *-ity*).

Je m'entraîne

a. **Lisez à haute voix chaque mot en respectant la syllabe accentuée.**
– *ironic* • *scientific* • *romantic* • *dramatic* • *terrific*
– *incredible* • *invisible* • *terrible* • *responsible* • *possible*
– *gorgeous* • *outrageous* • *hideous*
– *precious* • *suspicious* • *mysterious* • *delicious* • *religious*
– *caption* • *opinion* • *attention* • *creation* • *generation*
– *dignity* • *charity* • *opportunity* • *nationality* • *stupidity*

MP3 45

b. **Vérifiez avec votre enregistrement.**

3 Les formes réduites

Ceci concerne de nombreux mots grammaticaux. Ainsi, le modal *can* a deux prononciations : /kæn/ **(forme pleine)** ou /kən/ **(forme réduite)**. Pour certains mots grammaticaux, la forme réduite correspond, dans la langue écrite, à une forme **contractée** : *He is* /ɪz/ *late* → *He's* /z/ *late*.

Forme écrite	Forme pleine	Forme réduite
am, *'m*	/æm/	/əm/
are, *'re*	/ɑːʳ/	/əːʳ/
were	/wɜːʳ/	/wəʳ/
have	/hæv/	/həv/
does	/dʌz/	/dəz/
them	/ðem/	/ðəm/
and	/ænd/	/(ə)n(d)/
of	GB /ɒv/, US /ɑːv/	/əv/

Les formes réduites sont par définition **inaccentuées**.
On n'utilise les formes pleines qu'en position finale *(Yes, I can* /kæn/.*)* ou pour un accent d'insistance *("Since you can't swim..." "But I* ***can*** /kæn/ *swim!")*.

4 L'enchaînement des mots dans la langue parlée

Les mots sont enchaînés les uns aux autres, en particulier dans les suites « consonne + voyelle » entre deux mots : *It was‿a stupid‿answer*.

Je m'entraîne

a. **Lisez ces phrases à haute voix en respectant les liaisons consonne-voyelle ainsi que les formes réduites.**
– *Come on! It's not so difficult after all. You can achieve your goal.*
– *You should have waited for the bus.*
– *I was reading at home. I could have come easily.*
– *"I'm not sure he has finished the work." "I'm sure he has."*
– *Switch it on.*
– *"Where are your uncle and your aunt?" "They are living in Scotland at the moment."*
– *This book is more interesting than I thought.*
– *Many teenagers spend a lot of time in front of their computers.*

MP3 46

b. **Vérifiez avec votre enregistrement.**

Enrichir sa prise de parole

Get started

- To begin with, I'd like to point out that...
- As a matter of fact...
- Well, in fact...
- First of all, I would like to say that...
- It cannot be denied that...
- All right, to start with...

How to check somebody has understood you

- Did you get my point?
- I'm sorry, what did you say?
- Do you know what I mean?
- Does that make sense?

When something is quite not clear

- I'm sorry, I didn't hear / catch what you said. (informal)
- Would you mind repeating what you said?
- Could you repeat, please?
- Pardon?
- May I interrupt you?
- Excuse me, what did you say?

How to introduce your opinion

- To my mind...
- As far as I am concerned, I think that...
- I believe...
- I have the feeling that...
- I can't help thinking that...
- To me...
- It seems to me that...
- In my opinion...
- To tell you the truth, I think that...
- As far as I know...
- I have the feeling that...

How to half agree

- Yes, I suppose so, however...
- That's worth thinking about...
- Yes, sure, but...
- Do you really think so?
- Yes, up to a certain point.
- I've got mixed feelings about that.
- Well, in a way, but...
- I only agree up to a point really...
- Well, it depends.
- Yes, in a way...

How to agree strongly

- That's absolutely true!
- That's a good point.
- How true!
- Exactly!
- Sure!
- I couldn't agree more.
- That's exactly what I think.
- That's just how I see it myself.
- That's right!

How to disagree politely

- Do you really think so?
- Well, I'm not so sure about that.
- Well, I don't think so.
- Yes, but...
- Well, the way I see it...
- Don't you think that...?
- Well, I think it depends (on)...
- Um, I'm not sure you're right.
- Well, if you ask me...
- It may be true, but...

How to disagree strongly

- You can't be serious about that!
- I don't see it that way.
- No, you're wrong!
- You must be joking / kidding! (informal)
- What a load of rubbish! (informal)
- I totally disagree with you.
- I'm afraid I can't agree with that.
- You can't actually mean that.
- Just the opposite!
- Rubbish! / Nonsense! (informal)

How to express a contradiction

- Unlike you, I think that…
- Even though…
- Although (+ verb)…
- However…
- Contrary to you…
- On the contrary…
- Despite (+ noun)…
- In spite of (+ noun)…

Moving on or changing subjects

- All right, go ahead…
- Let me finish…
- By the way…
- Before I forget…
- I nearly forgot…

How to give yourself time to think *(gap fillers)*

- Well…
- I mean…
- Actually, what I mean is…
- Well, how could I say that…
- I'll tell you what… (informal)
- Well, you see / you know…
- As a matter of fact…
- I'll tell you what! (informal)
- Um…
- So…
- It's obvious that…
- I'm trying to say that…
- Anyway…
- Hang on… (informal)
- Mind you… (informal)
- You see… / You know…

How to show different aspects of a question

- Generally…
- At first sight…
- On the one hand…, on the other hand…
- On second thoughts…

How to give an example

- For example…
- Take… for instance
- For instance…
- That is to say…

How to add something

- What's more…
- On top of that…
- By the way…
- I'd like to add that…
- Besides…
- In addition…
- I'd also like to say that…
- I'd like to make another point.

How to conclude

- In conclusion…
- All in all…
- Lastly…
- In short…
- To sum up…
- Finally…
- And so, … (informal)

Précis grammatical

Sommaire

1 Adjectifs

Deux règles importantes

- Les adjectifs anglais sont **invariables** :

*The T-shirts he bought are **blue**.*
Les tee-shirts qu'il a achetés sont bleus.

- Les adjectifs **épithètes** (= rattachés directement au nom) se placent **avant** le nom :

*He bought two **blue T-shirts**.*
Il a acheté deux tee-shirts bleus.

Adjectifs employés comme noms

En français, on peut employer les adjectifs comme noms :
« Nous avons vu trois Anglais », « Elle a choisi la verte ». En anglais, ce n'est généralement pas possible. L'adjectif est obligatoirement **associé à un nom** ou **au pronom *one*** :
*We saw three **English people**.*
*She chose the **green one**.*

- Cependant, on emploie un adjectif comme nom pour désigner l'ensemble d'une catégorie de personnes :

***The young** are the main target of this ad.*
Les jeunes sont la cible principale de cette pub.

Notez que l'adjectif est précédé de ***the***, qu'il reste invariable, et que le groupe *the* + adjectif a un **sens pluriel**.

Formation d'adjectifs à partir de verbes

Ne confondez pas les terminaisons ***-ing*** et ***-ed*** :
amuse → ***amusing*** : amusant
→ ***amused*** : amusé

La terminaison *-ing* équivaut à la terminaison française « -ant ».

interesting : intéressant	*interested* : intéressé
tiring : fatigant	*tired* : fatigué

VOIR 7 Comparatifs et superlatifs

2 Adverbes

Alors que les adjectifs modifient un nom *(an **interesting** story)*, les adverbes modifient d'autres catégories de mots : verbe *(He advanced **slowly**)*, adjectif *(It's a **very** difficult question)*, etc.

Formation

Un grand nombre d'adverbes se forment à partir d'adjectifs, auxquels on ajoute le suffixe ***-ly*** :
easy → *easily*, *sad* → *sadly*.

Certains mots en *-ly*, cependant, sont des adjectifs : *a **friendly** man* (un homme amical).

D'autres sont soit adjectifs soit adverbes :
*a **fast** car* (une voiture rapide), *he ran **fast*** (il a couru vite).

Place des adverbes de fréquence

Sometimes, rarely / seldom, often, always, never, ever se placent **devant le verbe** et, quand il y a un auxiliaire (*BE*, *HAVE*, *CAN*, etc.), **après l'auxiliaire** :
*She **sometimes goes** to work by bus.*
Elle va parfois au travail en bus.
*He **is often** late.*
Il est souvent en retard.
*They**'ve never** been to America.*
Ils ne sont jamais allés en Amérique.

Il ne faut pas séparer le verbe de son complément d'objet par un adverbe (comparez au français) :
Elle parle **bien** l'anglais. → *She speaks English **well**.*

3 Article indéfini *a / an*

Forme

- On utilise ***a*** /ə/ devant un son « consonne » : ***a*** *cat*. Attention à certains mots qui, **dans leur forme écrite**, commencent par une voyelle, mais **dans leur prononciation** commencent par une consonne :

a university (consonne transcrite /j/ : /ˌjuːnɪˈvɜːsɪti/)
a European country : /ˌjʊərəˈpiːən/
a one-parent family (consonne transcrite /w/ : /wʌn/).
Attention aussi au *h* initial, qui est une consonne **prononcée** (*a happy ending*), sauf dans :
– *honest*, *hono(u)r*, *hour* et *heir* (héritier)
– et leurs composés : ***an*** *honest transaction*, ***an*** *hour*, ***an*** *hourly train service*.

- On utilise ***an*** /ən/ devant un son « voyelle » *(**an** animal)*.

Emplois particuliers de *a / an* en anglais

- Pour indiquer le métier de quelqu'un (***a / an*** + nom de métier) :

*He's **an electrician**.*
Il est électricien.

- Pour indiquer un rapport prix / poids, distance / temps, etc. :

*€2.50 **a** kilo.*
2,50 € le kilo.
*Sixty miles **an** hour.*
Cent kilomètres à l'heure.
*Twice **a** week.*
Deux fois par semaine.

4 Auxiliaires et verbes

■ Liste des **auxiliaires** : *BE*, *HAVE*, *DO* et les **modaux** (essentiellement *CAN*, *MAY*, *MUST*, *SHALL* et *WILL*).

- Leur emploi est obligatoire pour former les constructions **interrogative, négative** et **emphatique** :

Can *Laura **swim**?*
Est-ce que Laura sait nager ?
*He **is** not **looking** at them.*
Il ne les regarde pas.
*They didn't win the cup but they **did play** the final.*
Ils n'ont pas gagné la coupe mais ce qui est certain c'est qu'ils ont joué en finale.

- Les auxiliaires servent également à former les ***question-tags*** et les **reprises par auxiliaire** :

*Ted isn't going to leave, **is he**?*
Ted ne va pas partir, hein ?
*He says he's done the dishes but I think **he hasn't**.*
Il dit qu'il a fait la vaisselle mais je pense qu'il ne l'a pas faite.

■ Parmi les auxiliaires, *DO* (c'est-à-dire ***do / does / did***) joue un rôle particulier : il sert à construire les formes interrogative, négative et emphatique du présent simple et du prétérit simple.
Exemple : *He **lived** in Boston.*
→ ***Did** he **live** in Boston?*
→ *He **didn't live** in Boston.*
→ *He **did live** in Boston.*

5 « Avoir » en français, *be* en anglais

Elle **a** faim. / Elle **a** soif.
*She**'s** hungry. / She**'s** thirsty.*
J'**ai** froid. / J'**ai** chaud.
*I**'m** cold. / I**'m** hot.*
Tu **as** de la chance.
*You**'re** lucky.*
« Quel âge **a**-t-elle ? » « Elle **a** 17 ans. »
*'How old **is** she?' 'She**'s** 17.'*
Il **a** peur.
*He**'s** scared.*
Le mur **a** trois mètres de haut.
*The wall **is** three metres high.*

6 « Beaucoup » et « peu » *(a lot of / many / much, few / little)*

■ **Suivis d'un nom (« beaucoup de... », « peu de... »)**

	Indénombrable (singulier)	Dénombrable au pluriel
beaucoup de	Il y a / Il n'y a pas beaucoup de pain. / Est-ce qu'il y a... ? *There's **a lot of / lots of bread**.* *There isn't **much bread**.* *Is there **much bread**?*	Il y a / Il n'y a pas beaucoup de bananes. / Est-ce qu'il y a... ? *There are **a lot of / lots of bananas**.* *There aren't **many bananas**.* *Are there **many bananas**?*
peu de	Il y a peu de pain. *There's **little bread**.*	Il y a peu de bananes. *There are **few bananas**.*
un peu de, quelques	Il reste un peu de pain. *There's **a little bread** left.*	Il reste quelques bananes. *There are **a few bananas** left.*

• ***Plenty of*** peut correspondre à « beaucoup de », mais seulement dans le sens de « largement assez » :
*We've got **plenty of time** left.* Il nous reste beaucoup de temps / largement le temps.

■ **Après un verbe (« Elle travaille beaucoup / peu. »)**

*Does she **work a lot / much**?* Est-ce qu'elle travaille beaucoup ?

*Yes, she **works a lot**.* Elle travaille beaucoup.

*No, she doesn't **work a lot / much**.* Elle ne travaille pas beaucoup. / Elle travaille peu.

(***Much*** est employé dans les phrases négatives ou interrogatives, ou dans un style formel. ***A lot*** est employé dans tous les types de phrases.)

*I **slept** very **little** last night.* J'ai très peu dormi la nuit dernière.

7 Comparatifs et superlatifs

■ **Adjectifs courts** : une syllabe, ou deux syllabes avec terminaison en ***-y*** ou ***-er***.
Adjectifs longs : autres adjectifs.

	Adjectifs courts	Adjectifs longs
Comparatif de supériorité (= plus... que...)	*Australia is **larg<u>er</u> than** /ðən/ India.* L'Australie est plus vaste que l'Inde.	*India is **<u>more</u> populated than** Australia.* L'Inde est plus peuplée que l'Australie.
Comparatif d'infériorité (= moins... que...)	*Australia is **not as** /əz/ **populated as** /əz/ India.* *Australia is **less populated than** India.*	
« de plus en plus... »	*It's **eas<u>ier</u> and eas<u>ier</u>**.* C'est de plus en plus facile.	*It's **<u>more</u> and <u>more</u> difficult**.* C'est de plus en plus difficile.
« de moins en moins... »	*It's **less and less easy / difficult**.* C'est de moins en moins facile / difficile.	
Comparatif d'égalité (= aussi... que...)	*Nora's flat is **as large / as comfortable as** Lily's.* L'appartement de Nora est aussi grand / aussi confortable que celui de Lily.	
Superlatif de supériorité (= le plus...)	*Russia is **the larg<u>est</u> country in** the world.* La Russie est le plus grand pays du monde (par sa surface).	*China is **the <u>most</u> populated country in** the world.* La Chine est le pays le plus peuplé du monde.

■ Le complément du superlatif est introduit par *in*, sauf s'il désigne :
– un ensemble d'éléments *(the largest country **of** all)*
– ou une période de temps *(the hottest day **of** the month)*.

■ **Modifications orthographiques** avec les terminaisons ***-er*** / ***-est*** :

• *happy* → *happier, happiest* : un *y* qui suit une consonne devient *i*.

• *big* → *bigger, biggest* : une consonne **finale** qui suit une voyelle est redoublée.

■ **Comparatifs et superlatifs de supériorité irréguliers**

good bon ***well*** bien	***better*** meilleur / mieux	***the best*** le / la / les meilleur(e)(s) / mieux
bad mauvais	***worse*** /wɜːʳs/ pire	***the worst*** /wɜːʳst/ le / la / les pire(s)
far loin	***farther*** ou ***further*** plus loin	***the farthest*** ou ***the furthest*** le / la / les plus éloigné(e)(s)

8 Condition / hypothèse *(if...)*

Hypothèse **possible** (sur un fait présent ou futur)	*If he **is** at home [now / tomorrow],* ***I'll** go [= I will go] and visit him.*	S'il est chez lui, je vais aller le voir. (Je ne sais pas s'il est / sera chez lui.)
Hypothèse **irréelle** portant sur un fait **présent**	*If he **was** at home,* ***I'd** go [= I would go] and visit him.*	S'il était chez lui, j'irais le voir. (... mais il n'est pas chez lui)
Hypothèse **non probable** portant sur un fait **futur**	*If I **won** the lottery,* ***I'd** buy [= I would buy] a boat.*	Si je gagnais au Loto, j'achèterais un bateau. (... mais il est peu probable que je gagne)
Hypothèse **irréelle** portant sur un fait **passé**	*If he **had been** at home, **I'd have gone** [= I would have gone] and visited him.*	S'il avait été chez lui, je serais allé le voir. (... mais il n'était pas chez lui)

9 Conditionnel (équivalents du conditionnel français)

■ En général, l'équivalent du conditionnel français est ***would*** **+ V** aussi bien :

- pour le conditionnel « temps » (= futur par rapport à un moment passé).

Je leur ai dit que je les **appellerais** plus tard.
*I told them **I'd call** them later.*

- que pour le conditionnel « mode » (= sens futur associé à une condition irréelle ou non probable, VOIR **8**).

Si je connaissais leur numéro, je les **appellerais**.
*If I knew their number, **I'd call** them.*

■ Cependant, on ne peut pas employer *would* **+** V dans les subordonnées qui interdisent l'emploi de *will* à sens futur (VOIR **10**), et en particulier dans les subordonnées de temps. À la place, il faut employer le **prétérit simple :**

J'ai dit que je leur enverrais un SMS dès que **j'arriverais** à Londres.
*I said I'd text them as soon as I **got** to London.*

■ Le conditionnel des verbes modaux du français (« pouvoir », « devoir », « falloir ») se traduit généralement par le **prétérit d'un modal :**

Tu **pourrais** me passer le sel ?
***Could** you pass me the salt?*

Il **faudrait** qu'elle fasse / Elle **devrait** faire attention.
*She **should** be careful.*

10 *'d* (après un pronom ou un nom)

Il s'agit de la contraction de ***had*** ou de ***would*** :
*She**'d** finished her work. (= had)* Elle avait fini son travail.
*She**'d** help him if she could. (= would)* Elle l'aiderait si elle pouvait.
*You**'d better** hurry. (= had better)* Tu ferais bien de te dépêcher.
*He**'d rather** wait until tomorrow. (= would rather)* Il préfère attendre demain.

11 Démonstratifs *(this / these et that / those)*

Emplois comme déterminants

• ***This*** /ðɪs/ (+ nom au **singulier**) et ***these*** /ði:z/ (+ nom au **pluriel**) s'emploient pour désigner ce qui est proche de l'énonciateur dans l'espace ou le temps, ou ressenti comme proche.

This country *enjoys a mild climate.*
Ce pays [= le pays où nous sommes en ce moment] jouit d'un climat doux.

These strawberries *are really good!*
Ces fraises [= les fraises que je suis en train de manger] sont vraiment bonnes.

• ***That*** /ðæt/ (+ nom au **singulier**) et ***those*** /ðəʊz/ (+ nom au **pluriel**) s'emploient pour désigner ce qui est éloigné de l'énonciateur (ou ressenti comme éloigné), a déjà été mentionné, ou fait l'objet d'un rejet.

What was ***that country*** *you mentioned?*
Quel est ce pays que vous avez mentionné ?

Stop ***that noise!***
Arrête ce bruit !

Emplois comme pronoms

Ils s'emploient comme pronoms :

• en général pour des « non animés ».

What's ***this****?*
Qu'est-ce que c'est, ça ? [que je tiens dans ma main]

What's ***that****?*
Qu'est-ce que c'est, ça ? [que tu tiens / sur la table, etc.]

• mais dans certains cas aussi pour des personnes.

This *is my brother Tom.*
Je vous présente mon frère Tom.

Emploi comme adverbe

It's not ***that*** *difficult!*
Ce n'est pas si difficile que ça !

12 « Depuis »

« Depuis » + indication d'une durée : *for* (et emploi du *present perfect / past perfect*, VOIR 26 et 30)

Ils se connaissent depuis **dix ans.**
They have known each other ***for ten years.***

Ils se connaissaient depuis **dix ans.**
They had known each other ***for ten years.***

« Depuis » + indication du point de départ d'un événement : *since* (et emploi du *present perfect / past perfect*, VOIR 26 et 30)

Ils se connaissent depuis **l'an dernier.**
They have known each other ***since last year.***

Ils se connaissaient depuis **leur enfance.**
They had known each other ***since their childhood.***

• « Depuis » employé seul a pour équivalent soit *ever since* soit *since then* (placés différemment dans la phrase).

Il a trouvé un travail à Londres en 2001, et **depuis** il y habite.
He found a job in London in 2001 and has lived there ***ever since.***

Ils se sont rencontrés l'an dernier et **depuis** il sont très amis.
They met last year and ***since then*** *they've been close friends.*

« Depuis que »

Ils sont amis **depuis qu'**ils se sont rencontrés en Irlande.
They have been friends ***since*** *they met in Ireland.*

> **Faites attention à trois choses :**
>
> • ***since***, qui indique un **point de départ** ;
>
> • emploi du ***present perfect*** dans la proposition principale, puisque l'événement dure encore au moment présent ;
>
> • emploi du **prétérit** après *since*, puisqu'on indique un point-repère dans le passé.

« Depuis quand... ? » / « Depuis combien de temps... ? »

Depuis quand / Depuis combien de temps vous le connaissez ?
How long *have you known him?*
(Réponse : *[I've known him]* ***for*** *ten years /* ***for*** *a week*, etc.)

VOIR 18 « Il y a », 30 *Present perfect* simple, 26 *Past perfect* (ou *pluperfect*)

13 « Devoir »

■ **« Je dois… » = « Il faut que je… » : *I must, I have to***

• ***Must***, qui est un **modal** (VOIR 22), exprime le point de vue de l'énonciateur, dans un style plutôt formel.

Tu dois m'obéir ! *You **must** obey me!*

• ***Have to*** exprime une obligation vue de façon neutre (notamment une contrainte extérieure).

Il doit se lever tous les matins à six heures.
*He **has to** get up every morning at six.*

Obligation située dans le **futur**	*I will have to* (« je devrai », « il faudra que je »)	*Next year, he**'ll have to** get up every morning at six.* L'an prochain, il devra se lever tous les matins à six heures.
Obligation située dans le **passé**	*I had to* (« j'ai dû », « il a fallu que je »)	*Yesterday I **had to** get up at six.* Hier, j'ai dû me lever à six heures.

À la forme négative, *must* et *have to* ont deux sens très différents :
*You **mustn't** /ˈmʌsnt/ speak to him!* Tu ne dois pas lui parler ! (= obligation de ne pas / interdiction de)
*You **don't have to** speak to him!* Tu n'es pas obligé de lui parler ! (= non obligation de)

■ **« Je devrais… » = « Il faudrait que je… » (conseil, etc.) : *I should***

Il devrait faire un peu plus d'exercice.
*He **should take** more exercise.*
Tu ne devrais pas utiliser ton téléphone en conduisant.
*You **shouldn't use** your phone while driving.*

■ **« J'aurais dû… » : *I should have* + participe passé**

Tu n'aurais pas dû dire ça.
*You **shouldn't have said** that.*

■ **« Je dois… » = « Il est probable que je… »**

Elle doit être très fatiguée.
*She **must be** very tired.*
Il a dû manquer son train.
*He **must have missed** his train.*

Pour la probabilité d'un fait **négatif** (« Il ne doit pas… »), on utilise *can't* en anglais britannique :
Il ne doit pas être content de ça !
*He **can't be** pleased about that!*

Attention aux équivalents de « il a dû » : distinguez le sens d'**obligation** de celui de **probabilité**.
En raison de la crise, il **a dû** vendre sa maison. *Owing to the crisis, he **had to sell** his house.*
Il **a dû** oublier de leur téléphoner. *He **must have forgotten** to call them.*

■ **« Je dois… » = « Il est prévu que je… »**

Ils doivent passer deux semaines en Grèce cet été.
*They **are to spend** two weeks in Greece this summer.*
(Notez qu'il ne s'agit pas ici d'un sens d'obligation – l'emploi de *must* est donc impossible.)

■ **« Il devait… » = « le destin a voulu que… »**

Il devait mourir à l'âge de 90 ans.
*He **was to die** at the age of 90.*

14 « Dire (que) » : *say* ou *tell* ?

■ **Principe général** : *say* est utilisé pour rapporter **des paroles** (des mots), ou dans le sens de prononcer, et ***tell*** est utilisé pour rapporter le **contenu** de paroles.

*He **said** <u>yes</u>. / He **said** <u>a few words</u>.*
Il a dit oui. / Il a dit quelques mots.
*He **told** <u>a lie</u>. / He **told** me <u>the news</u>.*
Il a dit un mensonge. / Il m'a appris la nouvelle.

■ Pour introduire le **complément de personne** : *say sth **to sb*** ou *tell **sb** sth.*

*He **said** 'Thanks a lot!' **to me**.*
Il m'a dit « Merci beaucoup ! »
*He **told me** that he was pleased.*
Il m'a dit qu'il était content.

■ **Discours direct / indirect (sans / avec complément de personne)**

He said, 'I'm pleased.' → *He **said** that he was pleased.*
→ *He **told me** that he was pleased.* (*Tell*, contrairement à *say*, a besoin d'un complément de personne.)

■ **Pour rapporter un ordre / un conseil, etc.**

Elle m'a dit de rester ici / de ne pas bouger.
*She **told me** <u>to stay here</u> / <u>not to move</u>.*

■ **Au passif, ne confondez pas :**

*He **was told to** stay there.*
On lui a dit de rester là.
*He **was said to** be very rich.*
On disait qu'il était très riche.

15 Discours direct / indirect : rapporter des paroles ou des pensées

Discours direct	Discours indirect
He said, 'I intend to ask them.'	*He said that he **intended** to ask them.*
He said, 'I have solved the problem.'	*He said that he **had** solved the problem.*
He said, 'They will be very surprised.'	*He said that they **would** be very surprised.*
He said, 'I can't answer that question.'	*He said that he **couldn't** answer that question.*

Caractéristiques du discours indirect

- Il n'utilise pas les guillemets.
- Il peut être introduit par la **conjonction *that*** (prononcée /ðət/) ou la **conjonction « zéro ».**
- Certains **pronoms** doivent être modifiés (dans les exemples, *I* devient *he*).
- Il faut respecter les règles dites de **concordance des temps** ; ces règles s'appliquent dans les récits au passé, quand le verbe qui introduit le discours indirect est au **prétérit** *(He said / He thought that...) :*

– le **présent** du discours direct devient un **prétérit** (voir tous les exemples du tableau) ;
– le **prétérit** du discours direct devient généralement un ***past perfect.***

*She said, 'I **called** him on June 8th.'*
→ *She said that she **had called** him on June 8th.*

- Les **adverbes de lieu et de temps** peuvent être modifiés.

When he discovered the island, he said, 'I want to live here.'
→ *When he discovered the island, he said that he wanted to live **there**.*
She said, 'I won't start until tomorrow.'
→ *She said she wouldn't start until **the day after / the following day**.*

Autres changements de ce type :
– *yesterday* → *the day before*
– *last week / month / year* → *the week / month / year before*
– *ago* → *before*

Le cas particulier des questions

- Les questions rapportées au style indirect sont à la **forme affirmative** : il n'y a pas d'inversion sujet-auxiliaire, ni d'auxiliaire *do / does / did*, ni de point d'interrogation.

He asked me, 'When does Tim intend to leave?'
→ *He asked when **Tim intended** to leave.*

- Pour rapporter au style indirect une *Yes / No question*, on utilise ***if*** (*whether* dans un style recherché) :

She asked me, 'Does Jenny know your parents?'
→ *She asked me **if** Jenny knew my parents.*

16 « Faire faire » (*make* / *have*, etc. + verbe)

Assez souvent, l'équivalent anglais du français « faire + verbe » est un verbe simple :
Faites suivre le courrier, s'il-vous-plaît.
*Please **forward** the mail.*
Il **a fait cuire** le repas de midi.
*He **cooked** the lunch.*

Dans les autres cas, « faire » peut avoir pour équivalent *make*, *have* ou *get*, dans des constructions différentes.

- ***Make* + nom / pronom + base verbale** exprime une idée de cause ou de forte contrainte :

*He **made everybody laugh**.*
Il a fait rire tout le monde. (Notez l'ordre des mots en anglais.)
*They **made him give up** the project.*
Ils lui ont fait abandonner le projet.

- ***Have* + nom / pronom + base verbale** exprime une contrainte plus neutre :

*Do you think I can **have him fix** the TV?*
Vous pensez que je peux lui faire réparer la télé ?

- ***Have / get* + nom / pronom + participe passé :** on s'intéresse au résultat plus qu'à la personne qui accomplit l'action :

*I'll **have** / I'll **get the coat dry-cleaned**.*
Je vais faire nettoyer le manteau.

17 Futur (situer un événement dans le futur)

■ Comme en français (exemple : « Les soldes **commencent** demain »), et à peu près dans les mêmes cas, on utilise souvent le **présent** pour parler du futur *(The sales **start** tomorrow)*. Mais attention : en anglais il faut choisir entre le **présent simple** et le **présent en** ***BE + -ING.***

• On emploie le **présent simple** pour un événement qui fait partie d'un **programme** (planning, horaire, calendrier, etc.) :

Leur train part demain matin à 6 h 15.
*Their train **leaves** tomorrow morning at 6:15.*

• On emploie le **présent en** ***BE + -ING*** pour exprimer une intention (décision déjà prise) :

Demain, je déjeune avec Sonia.
*Tomorrow I**'m having** lunch with Sonia.*

■ L'équivalent anglais du **futur simple** français est en général le modal ***will :***

Il **comprendra** votre point de vue.
*He**'ll understand** your point of view.*

■ L'équivalent anglais de **« aller + infinitif »** est souvent ***be going to :***

Il **va se demander** pourquoi tu n'es pas venu.
*He**'s going to wonder** why you didn't come.*

• Mais attention, on emploie ***will*** (et non *be going to*) pour exprimer une **décision prise au moment où l'on parle :**

D'accord, je **vais** les **appeler.**
*OK, I**'ll call** them.*

Dans certaines propositions subordonnées (notamment les subordonnées de temps), on ne peut pas utiliser *will* pour exprimer le futur, on utilise le **présent simple :**

Je t'enverrai un SMS dès que **j'arriverai** à Londres.
*I'll text you as soon as I **get** to London.*

Plus vous **crierez,** moins il comprendra.
*The louder you **shout,** the less he'll understand.*

Les subordonnées qui interdisent l'emploi du *will* de futur sont celles qui sous-entendent une condition :

I get to London → *I text you*
You shout louder → *He understands less*

18 « Il y a... »

■ **« Il y a... » (+ indication de temps)**

Il est arrivé il y a deux jours.
*He **arrived** two days **ago**.*

Donc : verbe au **prétérit** (événement situé tout entier dans le passé) + nombre d'heures / jours, etc. + ***ago***.

■ **« Il y a... que... »**

• Pas de problème si « il y a... que... » peut être remplacé par « il y a... » :

Il y a deux jours qu'il est arrivé. = Il est arrivé il y a deux jours. *He **arrived two days ago**.*

• Mais attention si le remplacement est impossible :

Il y a une demi-heure / Ça fait une demi-heure que j'attends.
*I**'ve been waiting for** half an hour.* (= J'attends depuis une demi-heure.) VOIR 12 « Depuis »

• Attention aussi quand le verbe français peut exprimer aussi bien un état qu'un changement d'état :

Il est mort il y a un an. (Deux traductions possibles, mais ne pas mélanger les constructions.)

*He**'s been dead for** a year.* (état qui dure encore au moment présent)

*He **died** a year **ago**.* (changement d'état entièrement situé dans le passé)

■ **« Il y avait... (que...) »**

Il y avait deux ans qu'elle avait acheté cette moto.
*She **had bought** that bike two years **before**.*

Il y avait un an que je les connaissais.
*I **had known** them **for** one year.*

■ **« Il y a... » (indication d'un lieu, d'une situation, etc.)**

Il y a une erreur / deux erreurs dans ces calculs.
***There is** one mistake /**There are** two mistakes in these calculations.*

Donc, accord avec le sujet « réel » : *mistake(s)* dans l'exemple.

Est-ce qu'il y avait une solution ?
***Was there** a solution?*

Pour l'interrogation, notez la place de ***there***.

Il y aura / Il doit y avoir une solution.
***There will be** / **There must be** a solution.*

BE se conjugue avec des auxiliaires – et dans ce cas ne remplacez pas ***there*** par *it* !

19 Infinitif en *to* (= *to* + V) ou gérondif (= V-*ING*) ?

■ Après les verbes exprimant une volonté et / ou une cause, on emploie l'**infinitif en *to*** :

*I **want** to stay here / him to stay here.*
Je veux rester ici. / qu'il reste ici.

*The crisis **caused** prices to rise.*
La crise a fait monte les prix.

*The boss finally **agreed** to raise the wages.*
Le patron a finalement accepté d'augmenter les salaires.

Notez ceci : quand le sujet du verbe à l'infinitif est un pronom personnel, il est à la forme complément (*me / him / her*, etc.).

■ Après les verbes exprimant une opinion, une appréciation, un sentiment, on emploie le **gérondif (V-*ING*)**.

*I really **enjoyed** talking to such a great actor.*
Ça m'a vraiment plu, de parler à un si grand acteur.

*He **misses** seeing his kids every day.*
Ça lui manque, de ne pas voir ses enfants tous les jours.

*He **resents** not being invited to the wedding.*
Il accepte mal de ne pas être invité au mariage.

■ Certains verbes sont suivis soit de ***to* + V** soit de **V-*ING*** selon le sens dans lequel ils sont employés :

*I must **remember** to post the letter.*
Il faut que je pense à poster la lettre. (C'est à faire.)

*I **remember** posting the letter.*
Je me rappelle avoir posté la lettre. (C'est fait.)

20 « Laisser » : *let* ou *leave* ?

■ **« Laisser » + nom ou pronom = *leave***

Laisse les clés sur cette étagère quand tu partiras.
***Leave** the keys on this shelf when you leave.*

Laisse ce chien tranquille. ***Leave** that dog alone.*

■ **« Laisser » (+ nom ou pronom) + verbe = *let* + nom / pronom + infinitif sans *to***

Ils ne l'ont pas laissé entrer dans la maison.
*They didn't **let** him enter the house.*

En français, le verbe « laisser » peut être suivi immédiatement de l'infinitif : « Il a laissé parler tout le monde. »

En anglais, il faut respecter l'ordre ***let* + nom / pronom + V :**

He let everybody speak.

21 « Le / la / les » : *the* ou Ø en anglais ?

■ Dans de nombreux cas, « le / la / les » (articles définis) ont pour équivalent ***the*** en anglais.

Tu sais où est le dictionnaire / où sont les DVD ?
Do you know where the dictionary is / where the DVDs are?

• L'article ***the*** se prononce :

– /ðə/ devant un son « consonne » : *the dog* /dɒg/, *the USA* /ˌjuːesˈeɪ/, *the one-way street* /ˌwʌnweɪˈstriːt/
– /ði/ devant un son « voyelle » : *the animal* /ˈænɪməl/, *the hour* /ˈaʊəʳ/.

(VOIR 3 sur les particularités de la relation son-écriture pour consonnes et voyelles)

■ Cependant, l'équivalent de « le / la / les » est l'article Ø (= « zéro » / absence d'article) dans les cas suivants :

• quand on parle de quelque chose **« en général »**, devant un nom **indénombrable au singulier**, ou devant un nom **dénombrable au pluriel**.

Le riz est la céréale principale cultivée en Asie.
***Rice** is the main cereal grown in Asia.*

Est-ce que vous aimez les films d'horreur ?
*Do you like **horror** films?*

• devant les **noms de pays, continents** ou **régions** : *Italy* (l'Italie), *Asia* (l'Asie), *Oregon* (l'Oregon). Exceptions pour les noms de pays au pluriel : *the USA* (les États-Unis), *the Netherlands* (les Pays-Bas).

• devant les noms de titre suivis d'un nom propre : *President Obama*, *Pope Benedict XVI* (lire *Pope Benedict the sixteenth*), etc.

22 Modaux (auxiliaires modaux) : généralités

■ **Les cinq modaux principaux sont :**

Présent	can /kæn/ /kən/	may /meɪ/	must /mʌst/ /məs(t)/	shall /ʃæl/ /ʃəl/	will /wɪl/, 'll /l/
Prétérit	could /kʊd/ /kəd/	might /maɪt/		should /ʃʊd/ /ʃəd/	would /wʊd/ /wəd/, 'd

La forme négative de *can*, ***cannot***, s'écrit en un seul mot. Sa forme contractée, ***can't***, se prononce /kɑːnt/ en anglais britannique et /kaent/ en anglais américain.

■ **Formes modales simples et composées** : exemples avec le modal *MAY*

Modal + **base verbale**	*He may / might work.*
Modal + *BE* + V-*ING*	*He may / might **be** work**ing**.*
Modal + *have* + **participe passé**	*He may / might **have** work**ed**.*
Modal + *have been* + V-*ING*	*He may / might **have been** work**ing**.*

■ **Caractéristiques importantes des modaux**

– Ce sont des auxiliaires : leur interrogation et leur négation se forment directement (sans *do / does / did*).
– Ils ne prennent pas de *-s* à la troisième personne du singulier.
– Ils ne sont jamais précédés ni suivis de *to*. Ils n'ont pas d'infinitif, ni de forme en *-ING*, ni de participe passé.
– Dans un groupe verbal, il ne peut y avoir qu'un seul modal, qui est nécessairement placé en tête.
*He **should** have been told the truth.*
On aurait dû lui dire la vérité.
VOIR 13 « Devoir »

23 *Most (of) / the most*

■ ***Most* = « la plupart (de / des) »**
***Most children** dislike vegetables.*
La plupart des enfants n'aiment pas les légumes.
***Most of his friends** live in the neighbourhood.*
La plupart de ses amis habitent dans le quartier.

Most ou ***most of the*** ?
***Most children** dislike vegetables.*
(On considère la catégorie *children* = les enfants.)
***Most of the children I know** dislike vegetables.*
(On établit un sous-ensemble dans la catégorie *children*.)

■ ***Most* = marque du superlatif** (VOIR 7 « Comparatifs et superlatifs »)
*Which song did you like **(the) most**?*
Quelle est la chanson que tu as aimée le plus ?

■ ***Most* = « très » (style formel)**
I was most surprised to see him.
J'ai été extrêmement surprise de le voir.

24 « On » (équivalents anglais)

■ **« On » = « nous » (en français parlé) → *we***
Tu te rappelles ? On s'est bien amusés.
*Do you remember? **We** had a lot of fun.*

■ **« On » = « n'importe qui » (vous ou moi, par exemple) → *you***
On ne fait jamais assez attention.
***You** can never be careful enough.*
Au Danemark, on voit beaucoup d'éoliennes.
*In Denmark **you** see a lot of wind turbines.*

■ **« On » = « une ou plusieurs personnes inconnue(s), ou que je n'éprouve pas le besoin de nommer » → construction passive**
Il y a un mois qu'on a autorisé la vente de ce médicament. *The sale of that medicine **was authorized** a month ago.*
Je n'aime pas qu'on me mente. *I don't like **being lied to**.*
On dit qu'il a l'intention de démissionner.
*He **is said to** intend to resign.*

25 Passif (la voix passive)

Formes

Construction active	Construction passive (*BE* + participe passé)
The Beatles ***wrote*** *this song.* Les Beatles ont écrit cette chanson.	*This song* ***was written*** *by the Beatles.* Cette chanson a été écrite par les Beatles.

- Si le complément du verbe se construit avec une **préposition**, cette dernière se place **après le verbe** :

Cette question a déjà été traitée.
This question ***has*** *already* ***been dealt*** ***with***.

- Avec certains verbes à deux compléments comme *give, ask, show, tell, offer* et *send*, deux constructions passives sont possibles.

They emailed me the link. → ***I was emailed*** *the link.*
On m'a envoyé le lien par email.
Cette construction est plus courante que la construction avec *to (The link was emailed to me)*.

Emplois

On utilise le passif, en particulier, quand on ne peut pas ou qu'on ne veut pas dire qui accomplit l'action. Dans ce cas, le français utilise généralement **« on »** (VOIR **24**) :

On nous a menti.
We ***have been lied to.***

On m'a dit que vous étiez parti en Amérique !
I was told *that you'd gone to America!*

26 *Past perfect* (ou *pluperfect*)

Forme

Auxiliaire ***had*** (forme contractée : ***'d***) pour toutes les personnes + participe passé.
I /You /He /She... ***had found*** *the solution.*

Sens

- **Valeur de résultat**

I ***had deleted*** *his number, so I couldn't phone him.*
J'avais effacé son numéro, donc je ne pouvais pas l'appeler.

Différence avec le *present perfect* (VOIR **30**) : il s'agit d'un résultat **par rapport à un moment du passé**, et non par rapport au moment présent.

- **Valeur de durée**

He ***had lived*** *in London for several years / since 2008.*
Il **habitait** à Londres depuis plusieurs années / depuis 2008.

L'événement dure jusqu'à un moment du passé (alors qu'avec le *present perfect* il dure jusqu'au moment présent). En français, le temps utilisé est ici l'**imparfait**.

- **Valeur imaginaire**

L'élément « prétérit » contenu dans l'auxiliaire *had* peut aussi avoir non pas une valeur de temps mais une valeur « imaginaire » (VOIR **34**).

I wish I ***had asked*** *them.*
Je regrette de ne pas leur avoir demandé.

27 « Pendant (que) »

« Pendant » : *for* ou *during* ?

He lived in London ***for two years during the war.***
Il a vécu à Londres pendant deux ans durant la guerre.

- ***During*** sert à indiquer **une période**, et répond simplement à la question *When...?*
- ***For*** sert à indiquer **une durée**, et répond à la question *How long...? (How long did he live in London?)*

« Pendant que » = *while*

Je ferai les courses pendant que tu feras le repassage.
I'll do the shopping ***while you do the ironing***.

28 Pluriel des noms

Les noms indénombrables sont **invariables**. Leur caractère « singulier » ou « pluriel » se voit uniquement dans les **accords** :
*This **information*** (indénombrable **singulier**) *is confidential.*
Ces renseignements sont confidentiels.
*These **clothes*** (indénombrable **pluriel**) *are new.*
Ces vêtements sont neufs.

■ **Pluriel des noms réguliers**

On ajoute la terminaison **-s** (*one cat* → *two cats*). Modifications orthographiques et prononciation : VOIR **39** « -s, 's »

■ **Principaux pluriels irréguliers**

child /tʃaɪld/ (enfant)	→ *children* /ˈtʃɪldrən/
man /mæn/ (homme)	→ *men* /men/
woman /ˈwʊmən/ (femme)	→ *women* /ˈwɪmɪn/
foot /fʊt/ (pied)	→ *feet* /fiːt/
tooth /tuːθ/ (dent)	→ *teeth* /tiːθ/
mouse /maʊs/ (souris)	→ *mice* /maɪs/
goose /gʊːs/ (oie)	→ *geese* /giːs/

■ **Principaux noms dénombrables invariables** (*one sheep* → *two sheep*)

sheep • *series* • *aircraft* (avion) • *spacecraft* • *means* (moyen)

■ Certains noms qui se terminent par **-f** ou **-fe** ont un pluriel en **-ves** :
half /hɑːf/ → ***halves***, *wife* → ***wives*** (mais *roof* → *roofs*).
Parmi les plus courants :
life • *shelf* (étagère) • *knife* • *leaf* (feuille) • *wolf* (loup).

■ Avec les **noms collectifs** comme ***people***, ***police*** ou ***personnel***, l'accord se fait au **pluriel.**
*Five **people** / **medical personnel are** reported missing.*
Cinq personnes / membres du personnel médical sont porté(e)s disparu(e)s.
*The police **were** eventually called.*
On a finalement appelé la police.

Pour donner un singulier au mot *people* utilisé dans le sens de « gens », on a recours au mot *person* : *There was only one person present.*

29 « Pour », subordonnées de but

Il faut distinguer :

■ **« Pour » + nom ou pronom = *for***

Il y a une lettre pour Jane.
*There's a letter **for** /fəʳ/ Jane.*

■ **« Pour » = « dans le but de » (introduit une proposition de but)**

• ***So (that)*** ou (dans un style recherché) ***in order that***
Je vais te donner une carte pour que tu ne te perdes pas.
*I'll give you a map **so (that)** you won't get lost.*

• ***To*** ou (plus explicite) ***in order to / so as to***
*He got up early **to** / **in order to** / **so as to** catch the 7:15 train.*
Il s'est levé de bonne heure pour avoir / afin d'avoir le train de 7 h 15.

• Dans les propositions de but en *to / in order to*, ***for*** peut être utilisé pour introduire le sujet de la proposition (et non pour exprimer l'idée de but) :
*She gave him a map **for him to find** his way more easily.*
Elle lui a donné une carte pour qu'il trouve son chemin plus facilement.
*I emailed you the article **for you to read**.*
Je t'ai envoyé l'article par email pour que tu le lises.
(Notez l'omission du complément : ... *~~for you to read it~~*.)

30 *Present perfect* simple

Forme

Forme affirmative	Forme interrogative	Forme négative
*I **have finished**.* *You **have finished**.* *He / She / It **has finished**.* *We / You / They **have finished**.*	***Have** I **finished**?* ***Have** you **finished**?* ***Has** he / she / it **finished**?* ***Have** we / you / they **finished**?*	*I **have not / haven't finished**.* *You **have not / haven't finished**.* *He / She / It **has not / hasn't finished**.* *We / You / They **have not finished**.*

- Pour les verbes réguliers, le participe passé se forme comme le prétérit : on ajoute la terminaison ***-ed*** à la base verbale.
- Pour les verbes irréguliers, voir p. 268-269, colonne 3.

Valeur de résultat

On s'intéresse au résultat présent d'un événement passé.

*I**'ve deleted** his phone number.*
J'ai effacé son numéro de téléphone.

- Ce qui importe ici pour l'énonciateur, c'est le **résultat** : « Je n'ai plus son numéro de téléphone ». Par contre, on utilise le **prétérit** quand on s'intéresse en premier lieu à l'événement passé, ou à ses circonstances.

*'When **did** you **delete** it?' '[I **deleted** it] last week.'*
« Quand est-ce que tu l'as effacé ? » « La semaine dernière. »

Pour le même événement passé, on peut donc choisir, **en fonction du point de vue qu'on adopte**, soit le *present perfect* soit le prétérit.

- Avec le *present perfect*, on emploie souvent des adverbes ou compléments de temps comme *already*, *ever / never*, *not... yet*, *over the past few weeks / months*, qui font implicitement référence au moment présent :

*I've **already** seen that film.*
J'ai déjà vu ce film.

*They've scored six goals **so far**.*
Ils ont marqué six buts jusqu'à maintenant.

- Par contre, certains adverbes, ainsi que les indications de date, d'heure, etc., sont **incompatibles avec le *present perfect***, et exigent l'emploi du **prétérit** :

*He **scored** six goals **yesterday / on May 5th / two weeks ago**.*

Passé récent

Associé à l'adverbe ***just***, le *present perfect* exprime un passé récent.

***I've just emailed** him.*
Je viens de lui envoyer un email.

En anglais US, on emploie le **prétérit** pour exprimer un passé récent :

*I **just emailed** him.*

Valeur de durée

On emploie le *present perfect* pour une action ou un état qui a commencé dans le passé et qui **dure encore au moment présent** :

*He**'s had** this problem <u>for three weeks</u>.*
Il **a** ce problème depuis trois semaines. Il y a / Ça fait trois semaines qu'il a ce problème.

*He**'s had** this problem <u>since last year</u>.*
Il **a** ce problème depuis l'an dernier.

VOIR **12** « Depuis » ; **18** « Il y a... »

For peut aussi indiquer la durée d'un événement qui est **entièrement coupé du présent**, et donc est exprimé avec un **prétérit**. Comparez :

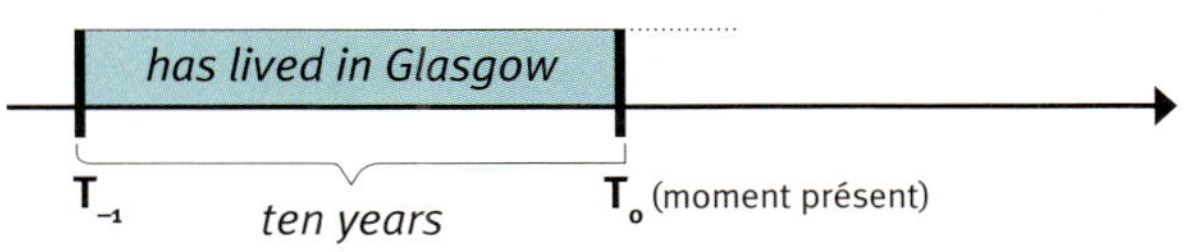

*He **has lived** in Glasgow **for ten years**.*
Il habite Glasgow **depuis** dix ans. (Il y habite encore.)

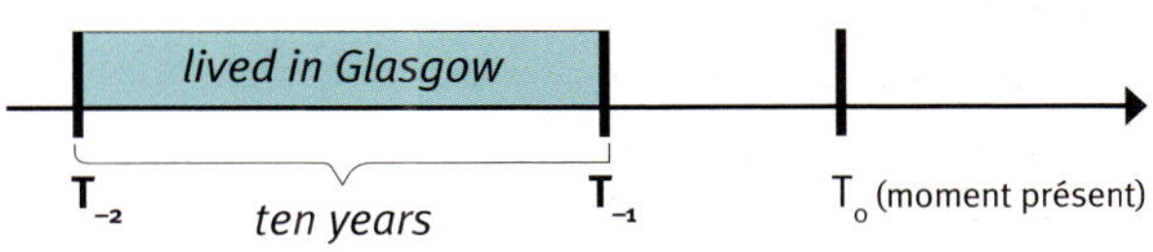

*He **lived** in Glasgow **for ten years**.*
Il a habité Glasgow **pendant** dix ans. (Il n'y habite plus.)

L'emploi du prétérit est normal dans le second cas : l'événement est séparé du présent.

31 *Present perfect* en *BE + -ING*

■ Valeur de résultat

	Forme	Valeur
***Present perfect* simple**	*Tim **has painted** the door. Look, it looks new!* Tim a peint la porte. Regarde, elle a l'air neuve !	Exprime simplement un résultat : la porte est peinte.
Present perfect* en *BE + -ING	A: *The floor is stained with paint! What's happened?* A: Il y a des taches de peinture sur le sol. Qu'est-ce qui s'est passé ? B: *Ken **has been** painting the door.* B: Ken a peint la porte.	On a constaté un résultat (« Il y a des taches de peinture sur le sol »), et la forme verbale en *BE + -ING* exprime un « coup de projecteur » sur l'action qui a provoqué le résultat (sur l'action « Ken a peint la porte »).

Notez qu'en français on a la même forme verbale dans les deux cas (« a peint la porte »).

■ Valeur de durée

Avec les verbes *know*, *look* (= sembler), *understand*, etc., difficilement compatibles avec *BE + -ING* (VOIR **32**), on utilise obligatoirement le *present perfect* **simple** :

*He**'s known** them for six months.*
Il les connaît depuis six mois.

Avec les autres verbes, on utilise généralement le *present perfect* en ***BE + -ING*** :

*He**'s been working** in that bank for six months.*
Il travaille dans cette banque depuis six mois.

32 Présent simple et présent en *BE + -ING*

■ Forme du présent simple : terminaison *-s* à la 3e personne du singulier.

Modifications orthographiques et prononciation de ***-s*** : VOIR **39** « -s (terminaison), 's ».

■ Emplois du présent simple

Le présent simple est utilisé pour parler d'un fait, ou d'une série de faits, considérés au moment présent et **vus dans leur totalité.**

• **Caractéristique du sujet :**

*Cindy **does** a lot of sport.*
Cindy fait beaucoup de sport.

*Sonia **loves** black chocolate.*
Sonia adore le chocolat noir.

• **Comportement habituel :**

*Alan **gets up** every morning at 6:15.*
Alan se lève tous les matins à 6 h 15.

• Action brève située au moment présent, et **considérée dans sa totalité :**

*Now I **press** this button, and the yellow light **starts** blinking.*
Maintenant j'appuie sur ce bouton, et le voyant jaune se met à clignoter.

■ Emplois du présent en *BE + -ING*

Alors que le présent simple voit l'événement **dans son ensemble,** le présent en *BE + -ING* réalise un « coup de projecteur » **sur un moment de l'événement** (ou sur plusieurs moments). Ce « coup de projecteur » peut prendre plusieurs formes.

• Il se situe au **moment où on parle**, et pendant la durée de l'action :

*Look, he**'s waiting** for you.*
Regarde, il t'attend.

• Il permet de **dire en quoi**, précisément, **une action consiste** :

*When you vote for that candidate, you **are voting** against your own interests.*
Quand vous votez pour ce candidat, vous votez contre vos propres intérêts.

• Il porte sur un événement **futur** (expression d'une **intention**) :

*Linda and Bob **are getting married** in June.*
Linda et Bob se marient en juin.

> **Certains verbes sont difficilement compatibles avec *BE + -ING* :** ce sont des verbes comme *know* (savoir, connaître) ou *look* (employé dans le sens de « sembler ») ; ces verbes expriment un sentiment ou un état mental vus nécessairement « en bloc » : *I know her* (Je la connais) ou *It looks difficult* (Ça a l'air difficile).

33 Prétérit et *present perfect* : VOIR 30 « *Present perfect* simple »

34 Prétérit imaginaire (ou prétérit « modal »)

■ Ce prétérit n'exprime pas un passé. Il renvoie à un fait qui est soit « contraire à la réalité », soit peu probable.

*If you **had** Internet access I could email it to you.* Si tu avais l'Internet je pourrais te l'envoyer par e-mail. (Sous-entendu : tu n'as pas l'Internet.)

*If I **won** the lottery...* Si je gagnais au loto... (Notez le supplément de doute par rapport à *If I **win** the lottery...* = « Si je gagne au loto... ».)

C'est cette valeur « imaginaire » qu'on a très souvent avec le prétérit des modaux :

*If he **could** swim...* S'il savait nager... (mais il ne sait pas.)

*You **should** phone him.* Tu devrais lui téléphoner. (mais je ne sais pas si tu vas le faire.)

Pour BE, il existe une forme pour exprimer ce prétérit imaginaire : ***were*** utilisé à toutes les personnes. *If I were Canadian...* (« Si j'étais canadien... »).
Dans la langue courante, on dit *If I was Canadian...*

■ On trouve ce prétérit non seulement après *if*, mais aussi après :

- le verbe ***wish*** (« souhaiter que... », « regretter que... ne... pas »)

*I wish I **had** Internet access!* Je regrette de ne pas avoir l'Internet (cf. *If only I had Internet access!*)

*I wish I **could** talk to him.* Je regrette de ne pas pouvoir lui parler.

*I wish he **would** stop complaining.* Je voudrais qu'il arrête de se plaindre.

*I wish I **had asked** him to come.* Je regrette de ne pas lui avoir demandé de venir. (Il s'agit ici d'un *past perfect* dont l'élément prétérit a une valeur « imaginaire » VOIR 26.)

- ***It's time...***

*It's time you **learnt** to cook!* Il est temps que tu apprennes à faire la cuisine !

35 Prétérit simple et prétérit en BE + -ING

La différence est la même qu'entre le présent simple est le présent en BE + -ING. Le cas le plus fréquent est celui des récits, dans lesquels le prétérit simple raconte la progression de l'action, tandis que le prétérit en BE + -ING est utilisé pour des événements qui servent de « toile de fond » à l'action. Comparez (et notez en français l'utilisation du passé composé dans un cas, de l'imparfait dans l'autre) :

*When I entered the office, he **phoned** the boss.*
Quand je suis entré dans le bureau, il a téléphoné au patron.

*When I entered the office, he **was phoning** the boss.*
Quand je suis entré dans le bureau, il téléphonait au patron.

36 Pronoms personnels et possessifs

Pronoms sujets	Pronoms compléments	Déterminants possessifs	Pronoms possessifs	Pronoms réfléchis (voir 37)
I	*me*	*my* (mon / ma / mes)	*mine* (le(s) mien(s) / la mienne / les miennes)	*myself* (accentuation sur *self*)
you	*you*	*your* /jɔː^{r}/	*yours* /jɔː^{r}z/	*yourself*
he	*him*	*his*	*his*	*himself*
she	*her*	*her*	*hers*	*herself*
it	*it*	*its*	*its own*	*itself*
we	*us*	*our* /aʊə^{r}/	*ours* /aʊə^{r}z/	*ourselves*
you	*you*	*your*	*yours*	*yourselves*
they	*them*	*their*	*theirs*	*themselves*

Les possessifs (*my, your*, etc. ; *mine, yours*, etc.) s'accordent uniquement avec le « possesseur ».

***He** introduced me to **his** sister / **his** brother.* Il m'a présenté à sa sœur / son frère.

***She** introduced me to **her** sister / **her** brother.* Elle m'a présenté à sa sœur / son frère.

37 Pronoms réfléchis et réciproques (cf. verbes pronominaux français)

■ Le français utilise la même forme pour le sens **réfléchi** (« Ils **se sont vus** sur la photo. » = chacun a vu lui-même) et pour le sens **réciproque** (« Ils **se sont vus** [= rencontrés] hier. »).

■ En anglais :
– pour le **sens réfléchi,** on utilise un **pronom réfléchi** (*myself, yourself*, etc. VOIR **36**) :
*They **saw themselves** in the photo.*
– pour le **sens réciproque,** on utilise l'un des deux **pronoms réciproques *each other* / *one another* :**
*They **saw each other** / They **saw one another** yesterday.*

Pour le choix entre les deux formes, la règle habituellement donnée est « *each other* pour un groupe de deux éléments » *(The two men saw each other)*, « *one another* dans les autres cas », mais dans la pratique il arrive très souvent que cette règle ne soit pas appliquée.

■ Les verbes comme *get up, shave, dress, wash, meet* et *quarrel* se construisent sans pronom réfléchi ou réciproque (car le sens réfléchi ou réciproque est évident) :
*He **shaves** every morning before breakfast.*
Il **se rase** tous les matins avant le petit déjeuner.
*They never **quarrel**.*
Ils ne **se disputent** jamais.

38 Relatifs : propositions relatives, pronoms relatifs

■ Les propositions relatives sont introduites par des **pronoms relatifs,** qui sont :
– les pronoms relatifs en *wh-* (***who*** /huː/, ***which, whose*** /huːz/ et ***whom***) ;
– ***that*** (prononcé /ðət/) ;
– le relatif « zéro » *(Ø)*, c'est-à-dire un vide, comme dans *The man you saw is my brother*, (L'homme que tu as vu est mon frère).

Le choix entre ces pronoms est déterminé par :
• le type d'**antécédent** (c'est-à-dire de nom que le pronom relatif remplace) ;
• la **fonction** du pronom relatif (sujet du verbe, complément du verbe, ou complément d'un nom).
Il est souvent possible de choisir entre plusieurs relatifs. Le tableau ci-dessous indique le choix le plus courant.

■ **Règles à appliquer absolument :**
• ***who / whom*** uniquement pour les personnes et ***which*** uniquement pour les choses ;
• ***Ø*** n'est **jamais utilisé en fonction sujet.** Il ne peut pas remplacer *who / which / that* dans des phrases comme *The man who told you that is a liar* (L'homme qui t'a dit ça est un menteur) ou comme *The scooter which / that is for sale is Karen's.* (Le scooter qui est en vente est celui de Karen).

■ **Le pronom complément *whom*** appartient à une langue plutôt formelle.
His brother, whom you have never met, works in Geneva.
Son frère, que tu n'as jamais rencontré, vit à Genève.

	Antécédent humain	Antécédent non humain
Sujet	*The man **who** told you that...* L'homme qui t'a dit ça...	*The scooter **which / that** is for sale...* Le scooter qui est en vente...
Complément direct	*The man Ø you saw...* L'homme que tu as vu...	*The scooter Ø you saw...* Le scooter que tu as vu...
Complément indirect	*The man Ø you're looking **for**...* L'homme que tu cherches...	*The music Ø you're listening **to**...* La musique que tu écoutes...
Complément de nom	*The man **whose** car...* L'homme dont la voiture...	*The car **whose** driver...* La voiture dont le conducteur...

Faites attention lorsque le verbe se construit avec une **préposition** (ci-dessus : prépositions *for* et *to*). Avec le **relatif Ø**, la préposition est obligatoirement **placée après le verbe** (et éventuellement après son complément direct). La règle est semblable avec le **passif** (VOIR **25**) et les **constructions interrogatives** (VOIR **4**).

39 -s (terminaison), 's

■ **La terminaison *-s*** peut être soit la **marque du pluriel** d'un nom *(two dogs)*, soit la **marque de la 3e personne du présent** d'un verbe *(Ted works)*.

• **Modifications orthographiques :**

– Quand le nom ou le verbe se termine par *-s, -x, -z, -ch, -sh* ou *-o*, on ajoute ***-es***.

pass → ***passes***, *box* → ***boxes***, *watch* → ***watches***, *wash* → ***washes***, *go* → ***goes***

– Quand le nom ou le verbe se termine par un ***-y*** précédé d'une consonne, ce *-y* devient ***-i***, et on ajoute ***-es***.

spy → ***spies***, *marry* → ***marries*** (mais dans *play*, le *y* est précédé d'une voyelle, donc *play* → *plays*)

• **Prononciation de *-(e)s***

– la terminaison ***-es*** se prononce /ɪz/ lorsqu'elle **suit une consonne** : *passes* /ˈpɑːsɪz/, *boxes* /ˈbɒksɪz/, *judges* /ˈdʒʌdʒɪz/, etc.

– dans tous les autres cas, la terminaison écrite ***-s*** / ***-es*** se prononce :

• soit /z/ (*plays* /pleɪz/, *knows* /nəʊz/, *goes* /gəʊz/, *lies* /laɪz/),

• soit /s/ (*looks* /lʊks/, *sits* /sɪts/).

– Deux cas particuliers : ***does*** se prononce /dʌz/, et ***says*** se prononce /sez/.

■ **La terminaison *'s*** peut être :

– la forme contractée de ***is*** : *He**'s** English.*

– la forme contractée de ***has*** : *He**'s** finished his work.*

– la forme contractée de ***does*** (langue familière) : *What's that mean? (= What does that mean?)*

– la marque du génitif (ou « cas possessif ») : *It's Tom**'s** computer.*

La prononciation de *'s* est la même que celle de *-(e)s*.

These singers /ˈsɪŋəʳz/ *are famous.*

This is the singer's /ˈsɪŋəʳz/ *guitar.*

What was the judge's /ˈdʒʌdʒɪz/ *decision?*

The judges /ˈdʒʌdʒɪz/ *are impartial.*

40 *They, their, theirs, there's*

Les prononciations de ces mots sont voisines ou identiques. Apprenez à les distinguer et à reconnaître la prononciation de chacun d'entre eux.

They're /ðeəʳ/ *ready.*

Ils sont prêts. / Elles sont prêtes.

Their /ðeəʳ/ *car's ready.*

Leur voiture est prête.

*The phone's not mine, it's **theirs*** /ðeəʳz/.

Le téléphone n'est pas à moi, il est à eux.

There's /ð(e)əʳz/ *a telephone in the room.*

Il y a un téléphone dans la pièce.

41 « Tout », « tous », « chacun » : *all, every, each*, etc.

all = tout(e), tous, toutes	*He ate **all** the meat / **all** the bananas.* Il a mangé toute la viande / toutes les bananes.
the whole = la totalité (de)	*He ate **the whole** dish.* Il a mangé tout le plat.
every = chaque	***Every** moment is precious.* Chaque moment est précieux. / Tous les moments sont précieux. (Notez l'emploi du **singulier** à la suite de *every*.)
each = chaque, chacun(e)	***Each** guest received a special gift.* Chacun des invités a reçu un cadeau spécial.
both = les deux (sous-entendu : pas seulement un / une)	***Both twins** came on that occasion.* Les deux jumeaux sont venus en cette occasion.

VERBES IRRÉGULIERS COURANTS

CD

	Base verbale	Prétérit	Participe passé	Traduction
B	be	was / were	been	*être*
	bear /eə/	bore /ɔː/	borne /ɔː/	*porter*
	beat /iː/	beat /iː/	beaten /iː/	*battre*
	become /ɪ/ /ʌ/	became /ɪ/ /eɪ/	become /ɪ/ /ʌ/	*devenir*
	begin /ɪ/ /ɪ/	began /ɪ/ /æ/	begun /ɪ/ /ʌ/	*commencer*
	bend /e/	bent /e/	bent /e/	*courber*
	bet /e/	bet /e/	bet /e/	*parier*
	bite /aɪ/	bit /ɪ/	bitten /iː/	*mordre*
	bleed /iː/	bled /e/	bled /e/	*saigner*
	blow /əʊ/	blew /uː/	blown /əʊ/	*souffler*
	break /eɪ/	broke /əʊ/	broken /əʊ/	*casser*
	breed /iː/	bred /e/	bred /e/	*élever*
	bring /ɪ/	brought /ɔː/	brought /ɔː/	*apporter*
	build /ɪ/	built /ɪ/	built /ɪ/	*bâtir*
	burn /ɜː/	burnt /ɜː/, burned /ɜː/	burnt /ɜː/, burned /ɜː/	*brûler*
	burst /ɜː/	burst /ɜː/	burst /ɜː/	*éclater*
	buy /aɪ/	bought /ɔː/	bought /ɔː/	*acheter*
C	cast /ɑː/	cast /ɑː/	cast /ɑː/	*lancer*
	catch /æ/	caught /ɔː/	caught /ɔː/	*attraper*
	choose /uː/	chose /əʊ/	chosen /əʊ/	*choisir*
	come /ʌ/	came /eɪ/	come /ʌ/	*venir*
	cost /ɒ/	cost /ɒ/	cost /ɒ/	*coûter*
	cut /ʌ/	cut /ʌ/	cut /ʌ/	*couper*
D	deal /iː/	dealt /e/	dealt /e/	*distribuer*
	do /uː/	did /ɪ/	done /ɒ/	*faire*
	draw /ɔː/	drew /uː/	drawn /ɔː/	*tirer*
	dream /iː/	dreamt /e/, dreamed /iː/	dreamt /e/, dreamed /e/	*rêver*
	drink /ɪ/	drank /æ/	drunk /ʌ/	*boire*
	drive /aɪ/	drove /əʊ/	driven /ɪ/	*conduire*
E	eat /iː/	ate /e/	eaten /iː/	*manger*
F	fall /ɔː/	fell /e/	fallen /ɔː/ /ə/	*tomber*
	feed /iː/	fed /e/	fed /e/	*nourrir*
	feel /iː/	felt /e/	felt /e/	*(res)sentir*
	fight /aɪ/	fought /ɔː/	fought /ɔː/	*combattre*
	find /aɪ/	found /aʊ/	found /aʊ/	*trouver*
	fly /aɪ/	flew /uː/	flown /əʊ/	*voler (dans les airs)*
	forbid /ə/ /ɪ/	forbad(e) /ə/ /eɪ/	forbidden /ə/ /ɪ/ /ə/	*interdire*
	forget /ə/ /e/	forgot /ə/ /ɒ/	forgotten /ə/ /ɒ/ /ə/	*oublier*
	forgive /ə/ /ɪ/	forgave /ə/ /eɪ/	forgiven /ə/ /ɪ/ /ə/	*pardonner*
	freeze /iː/	froze /əʊ/	frozen /əʊ/	*geler*
G	get /e/	got /ɒ/	got /ɒ/, gotten /ɒ/ (US)	*obtenir*
	give /ɪ/	gave /eɪ/	given /ɪ/	*donner*
	go /əʊ/	went /e/	gone /ɒ/	*aller*
	grow /əʊ/	grew /uː/	grown /əʊ/	*pousser (= croître)*
H	have /æ/	had /æ/	had /æ/	*avoir*
	hang /æ/	hung /ʌ/	hung /ʌ/	*pendre, suspendre*
	hear /ɪə/	heard /ɜː/	heard /ɜː/	*entendre*
	hide /aɪ/	hid /ɪ/	hidden /ɪ/	*cacher*
	hit /ɪ/	hit /ɪ/	hit /ɪ/	*frapper*
	hold /əʊ/	held /e/	held /e/	*tenir*
	hurt /ɜː/	hurt /ɜː/	hurt /ɜː/	*blesser*
K	keep /iː/	kept /e/	kept /e/	*garder*
	know /əʊ/	knew /uː/	known /əʊ/	*connaître*
L	lay /eɪ/	laid /eɪ/	laid /eɪ/	*poser à plat*
	lead /iː/	led /e/	led /e/	*mener*
	leap /iː/	leapt /e/	leapt /e/	*sauter*
	learn /ɜː/	learnt, learned /ɜː/	learnt, learned /ɜː/	*apprendre*

	Base verbale	Prétérit	Participe passé	Traduction
	leave /iː/	left /e/	left /e/	*quitter*
	lend /e/	lent /e/	lent /e/	*prêter*
	let /e/	let /e/	let /e/	*laisser*
	lie /aɪ/	lay /eɪ/	lain /eɪ/	*être couché*
	light /aɪ/	lit /ɪ/	lit /ɪ/	*éclairer*
	lose /uː/	lost /ɒ/	lost /ɒ/	*perdre*
M	make /eɪ/	made /eɪ/	made /eɪ/	*faire*
	mean /iː/	meant /e/	meant /e/	*signifier*
	meet /iː/	met /e/	met /e/	*rencontrer*
P	pay /eɪ/	paid /eɪ/	paid /eɪ/	*payer*
	put /ʊ/	put /ʊ/	put /ʊ/	*mettre*
R	read /iː/	read /e/	read /e/	*lire*
	ride /aɪ/	rode /əʊ/	ridden /ɪ/	*aller à cheval*
	ring /ɪ/	rang /æ/	rung /ʌ/	*sonner*
	rise /aɪ/	rose /əʊ/	risen /ɪ/	*s'élever*
	run /ʌ/	ran /æ/	run /ʌ/	*courir*
S	say /eɪ/	said /e/	said /e/	*dire*
	see /iː/	saw /ɔː/	seen /iː/	*voir*
	sell /e/	sold /əʊ/	sold /əʊ/	*vendre*
	send /e/	sent /e/	sent /e/	*envoyer*
	set /e/	set /e/	set /e/	*placer*
	shake /eɪ/	shook /ʊ/	shaken /eɪ/	*secouer*
	shoot /uː/	shot /ɒ/	shot /ɒ/	*faire feu, tirer*
	show /əʊ/	showed /əʊ/	shown /əʊ/	*montrer*
	shut /ʌ/	shut /ʌ/	shut /ʌ/	*fermer*
	sing /ɪ/	sang /æ/	sung /ʌ/	*chanter*
	sink /ɪ/	sank /æ/	sunk /ʌ/	*couler, sombrer*
	sit /ɪ/	sat /æ/	sat /æ/	*être assis*
	sleep /iː/	slept /e/	slept /e/	*dormir*
	smell /e/	smelt /e/	smelt /e/	*sentir*
	speak /iː/	spoke /əʊ/	spoken /əʊ/ /ə/	*parler*
	spell /e/	spelt /e/	spelt /e/	*épeler*
	spend /e/	spent /e/	spent /e/	*dépenser*
	spill /ɪ/	spilt /ɪ/	spilt /ɪ/	*répandre (par mégarde)*
	split /ɪ/	split /ɪ/	split /ɪ/	*fendre*
	spoil /ɔɪ/	spoilt /ɔɪ/	spoilt /ɔɪ/	*gâter*
	spread /e/	spread /e/	spread /e/	*répandre, étaler*
	spring /ɪ/	sprang /æ/	sprung /ʌ/	*bondir*
	stand /æ/	stood /ʊ/	stood /ʊ/	*être debout*
	steal /iː/	stole /əʊ/	stolen /əʊ/ /ə/	*voler (qqch)*
	stick /ɪ/	stuck /ʌ/	stuck /ʌ/	*coller*
	strike /aɪ/	struck /ʌ/	struck /ʌ/	*frapper*
	swear /eə/	swore /ɔː/	sworn /ɔː/	*jurer*
	sweep /iː/	swept /e/	swept /e/	*balayer*
	swim /ɪ/	swam /æ/	swum /ʌ/	*nager*
	swing /ɪ/	swung /ʌ/	swung /ʌ/	*(se) balancer*
T	take /eɪ/	took /ʊ/	taken /eɪ/ /ə/	*prendre*
	teach /iː/	taught /ɔː/	taught /ɔː/	*enseigner*
	tear /eə/	tore /ɔː/	torn /ɔː/	*déchirer*
	tell /e/	told /əʊ/	told /əʊ/	*dire*
	think /ɪ/	thought /ɔː/	thought /ɔː/	*penser*
	throw /əʊ/	threw /uː/	thrown /əʊ/	*lancer*
U	understand /æ/	understood /ʊ/	understood /ʊ/	*comprendre*
W	wake /eɪ/	woke /əʊ/	woken /əʊ/	*réveiller*
	wear /eə/	wore /ɔː/	worn /ɔː/	*porter (un vêtement)*
	win /ɪ/	won /ʌ/	won /ʌ/	*gagner*
	write /aɪ/	wrote /əʊ/	written /ɪ/	*écrire*
	weep	wept	wept	pleurer

PRINCIPAUX SUFFIXES ET PRÉFIXES

FORMATION DES NOMS			
		SENS	**EXEMPLES**
Préfixes	*mis- / mal-*	péjoratif, contraire	*misfortune • malpractice*
	non-	contraire	*nonsense*
	super-	au-dessus	*superpower*
Suffixes	*-er / -or / -ar / -ess / -ist*	agent, profession	*baker • actor • liar • actress • violinist*
	-ition	fonction, condition	*addition*
	-dom /dəm/	rang, condition, domaine	*freedom • wisdom*
	-hood /hʊd/	condition, état, âge	*neighbourhood*
	-ism /ɪzəm/	doctrine, pratique	*communism • tourism*
	-ness /nɪs/	état, caractéristique	*sadness*
	-ship	état, condition	*dictatorship*

FORMATION DES ADJECTIFS			
		SENS	**EXEMPLES**
Préfixes	*dis- / im- / in- / ill- / ir- / un-*	contraire	*disrespectful • immature • incorrect • illegitimate • irrational • unreal*
	over-	excès	*overcrowded*
Suffixes	*-able / -ible*	capable de, pouvant être	*washable • eligible*
	-al / -y / -ish / -ic	se rapportant à, comme	*political • noisy • greyish • pessimistic*
	-ful	plein de	*hopeful*
	-en	matière	*wooden*
	-ed / -ing / -ly	pourvu de, ayant la qualité de	*interested • admiring • manly*
	-less /lɪs/	sans, dépourvu de	*breathless*
	-some /səm/	qui provoque	*awesome*
	-ch / -sh / -ss / -ese / -an /ən/	nationalité	*French • Swedish • Swiss • Chinese • Indonesian*

FORMATION DES VERBES			
		SENS	**EXEMPLES**
Préfixes	*dis- / un-*	contraire	*disarm • undo*
	re- /riː/	répétition	*reread*
Suffixes	*-en*	transformation	*shorten*

FORMATION DES ADVERBES			
		SENS	**EXEMPLES**
Suffixes	*-ly*	manière	*angrily*

Table des illustrations

p. 8h © Keep Britain Tidy **p. 8m** © Mc Donald's / Leo Burnett, New Dehli, Inde **p. 8b** ph © Masterfile **p. 9h** ph © Sally Mundy / Trevillion Images **p. 9m** © Reporters sans Frontières **p. 9b** © From New York Times, 11/17/2008, pages 68-69; © 2008 New York Times **p. 10h** ph © Utah Office of Tourism **p. 10m** ph © Cate Gillon / Getty Images **p. 10b** © Roger Shimomura, Courtesy of the artist **p. 11h** ph © PoddlesRock / Corbis **p. 11m** ph © Simon Meaker / PA / Abaca Press **p. 11b** Coll. Christophe L. **p. 12h** Coll. Christophe L / © Ealing Studios **p. 12m** ph © Peter Mac Diarmid / Getty Images **p. 12b** ph © Penny Tweedie / PANOS-REA **p. 13** ph © Heritage images / Leemage **p. 15h** © Dave Granlund **p. 15b** © Universal Press Syndicate **p. 16-17** BCA / Rue des Archives **p. 18** Canada Medal Count by Tab, 2008 politicalcartoons.com **p. 19** © Keep Britain Tidy. **p. 20** Reproduced by courtesy of the Norman Rockwell Family Agency, Inc. **p. 22h** Chip Simons / Getty Images **p. 22b** © 2010 Délifrance / Saatchi & Saatchi, Düsseldorf **p. 23** Eduardo Contreras / SDUT / ZUMA Press / MAXPPP **p. 24** © PETA USA **p. 25** From the *How To Be British Collection* © LGP, Brighton, UK www.lgpcards.com **p. 26g** The Advertising Archives © Kodak **p. 26d** Des Moines Art Center Permanent Collections; Purchased with funds from the Edmundson Art Foundation, Inc., 1958.2 © D.R. **p. 27** Peter Menzel / Cosmos **p. 29** Christine Basler / plainpicture **p. 30** © Mc Donald's / Leo Burnett, New Dehli, Inde **p. 31** The Advertising Archives © Heinz **p. 32** Mark Fairhurst / UPPA / Photoshot **p. 33** akg-images © Campbell's Soup : © 2007 Andy Warhol Foundation / ARS, NY / ADAGP Paris 2011, Licensed by Campbell's Soup Co. All rights reserved **p. 34** Ocean / Corbis **p. 35** Adbusters Media Foundation **p. 36** Rod Morata / Getty Images / Y & R Tel Aviv **p. 37** © Save the Children Australia / MC Saatchi Melbourne **p. 39** © Bund / McCann-Erickson BCA Frankfurt **p. 40** ImageZoo / Corbis **p. 41** © FARE, Londres **p. 42** © Government of the State of Santa Catarina, Brazil / Fórmula Comunicação, Florianópolis **p. 43** Rankin / trunkarchives.com / Photosenso **p. 44** Masterfile **p. 46** Dibyangshu Sarkar / AFP Photo **p. 47** Patrick de Wilde / Gamma Rapho **p. 48g** Prod DB © Ashutosh Gowariker Productions - UTV / DR **p. 48d** Prod DB © Ashutosh Gowariker Productions / DR **p. 49** Michael Rubenstein / Redux-REA **p. 50** Christopher Pillitz / Getty images **p. 51** AFP Photo **p. 53** Marie Dorigny / Signatures **p. 55** Johann Rousselot / Signatures **p. 56** © Greenpeace Romania **p. 58-59** Lisa Maree Williams / Getty Images / AFP Photo **p. 60g** © Bantam Classic Book Series / Random House, Inc. **p. 60m** © iap publishing **p. 60d** © Littlebrown **p. 61** Maggie Brodie / Trevillion Images **p. 62** Clayton Bastiani / Trevillion Images **p. 64** Marico Fayre / Trevillion Images **p. 65** Collection Christophe L. **p. 66** *Rebecca* de Alfred Hitchcock, 1940 / Collection Christophe L. **p. 67** Sally Mundy / Trevillion Images **p. 70** Collection Christophe L. **p. 72** From Time Magazine, 2/16/2009 © 2009 Time Inc. Used under License. **p. 74** © Associated Newspapers Ltd **p. 75h** **© 2011 The New York Times Company** **p. 75b** © Independent.co.uk **p. 76** www.CartoonStock.com **p. 77** Collection Christophe L. **p. 78h** Cartoon by Nicholson from The Australian www.nicholsoncartoons.com.au **p. 78b** © David Sipress / The New Yorker Collection / www.cartoonbank.com **p. 79** © Cam by politicalcartoons.com 2010 **p. 80** © Reporters sans Frontières **p. 82** www.CartoonStock.com **p. 83** © Alex Gregory / The New Yorker Collection / www.cartoonbank.com **p. 84** From Newsweek, 3/2/2009, p. 54 © 2009 Newsweek **p. 87** Jacob Silberberg / PANOS-REA **p. 88** Elliott Erwitt / Magnum Photos **p. 89h** The Estate of Jean-Michel Basquiat / © Adagp, Paris 2011 **p. 89b** © www.allposters.com **p. 90** BCA / Rue des Archives **p. 91g** Flip Schulke / Corbis **p. 91d** Getty-Images **p. 92** Bettmann / Corbis **p. 94** From New York Times, 11/17/2008, Pages 68-69 © 2008 New York Times **p. 96h** © Grondhal by politicalcartoons.com **p. 96b** © Steve Greenberg **p. 99** © Norman Rockwell Family Agency, Inc. **p. 100** © Alex Boeckl / www.fatamerican.tv **p. 102** Collection Christophe L. **p. 104** Ricardo Demurez / Trevillion Images **p. 106-107** Tom Merton / Getty Images **p. 108** Martin Paar / Magnum Photos **p. 109** © Utah Office of Tourism **p. 110** Jean du Boisberranger / hemis.fr **p. 111** Mikhial Metzel / AP Photo / Sipa Press **p. 112** Josette Starck **p. 113** akg-images © Adagp, Paris 2011 **p. 114** John Maier / The New York Times / REA **p. 116** © Seppo Leinonen **p. 117** © Lee waters **p. 118** © Shepard Fairey / ObeyGiant.com **p. 119** CalamityJane / Alamy / Photo12.com **p. 120** Cate Gillon / Getty Images **p. 122** © M.E.N. Syndication **p. 123** Roger Bamber / Alamy / Photo12.com **p. 124** © Simanca Osmani 2004 politicalcartoons.com **p. 125** Dessin du 17 mai 2008 © Delize **p. 127** © Chris Sargent / The Sunday Times / nisyndication.com **p. 128** www.CartoonStock.com **p. 129** Simon Holdcroft / Alamy / Photo12.com **p. 130** Transport for London / M&C Saatchi London **p. 131h** © 2009 Geek Culture **p. 131b** © Slane Cartoons Limited http://www.slane.co.nz/ **p. 132** Poster reprinted by permission of CIDBIA (Chinatown-International District Business Improvement Area) **p. 133** Wen-ti Tsen and David Fichter, *Unity / Community – Chinatown Community Mural,* 1986, acrylic on brick, 40 feet x 30 feet (12.19m x 9.14m), Boston, Massachusetts, U.S.A.-*Demolished 2002* Photo Wen-ti Tsen **p. 134** © Random House, Inc. **p. 135** Collection Christophe L. **p. 136** Collection Christophe L. **p. 137** *One night in Seattle during the mid-1960s, after meeting some college friends for dinner, Roger noticed an elderly woman carrying an umbrella over her shoulder. As he got into his car, she stopped in the middle of the street and yelled, "You Japs ought to go back to where you came from!" Roger got out of his car and asked her to repeat what she had said. She stepped toward him and threatened to hit him with her umbrella. As Roger turned to get back into his car, she threw her umbrella at him, screaming something about Pearl Harbor. Roger watched the woman from inside his car as she recovered her umbrella, swearing something unintelligible about the Japanese and the war"* © Roger Shimomura, Courtesy of Greg Kucera Gallery **p. 138** © Roger Shimomura, Courtesy of Flomenhaft Gallery **p. 139** © Roger Shimomura, Courtesy of the artist **p. 141** Justin Sullivan / Getty Images **p. 142h** Bill O'Leary / The Washington Post / Getty Images **p. 142m** Ethan Miller / Getty Images **p. 142b** Adam Stoltman / Corbis **p. 143** Corbis **p. 144** Jean-Paul AZAM / hemis.fr **p. 146-147** Imagezoo / Images.com / Getty Images **p. 148** © Turbine Inc / D.R. **p. 149h** Illustration from page 16 of *The Boy's King Arthur*: "And when they came to the sword that the hand held, King Arthur took it up." In *The Boy's King Arthur: Sir Thomas Malory's History of King Arthur and His Knights of the Round Table,* Edited for Boys by Sidney Lanier (New York, Charles Scribner's Sons, 1922) – PoodlesRock / Corbis **p. 149m** Illustration from page 306 of *The Boy's King Arthur*: the death of Arthur and Mordred – "Then the king ran towards Sir Mordred, crying, 'Traitor, now is thy death day come.'" In *The Boy's King Arthur: Sir Thomas Malory's History of King Arthur and His Knights of the Round Table,* Edited for Boys by Sidney Lanier (New York, Charles Scribner's Sons, 1922) - Licence Creative Commons PD US **p. 149b** *Arthur's Death,* Archer, James (1824-1904); oil on millboard ; 600 x 512 - Manchester Art Gallery / Bridgeman Giraudon **p. 151** Collection Christophe L. **p. 152** Aisa / Leemage **p. 156** Collection Christophe L. **p. 157** William Morris Gallery, Walthamstow, UK / Bridgeman-Giraudon **p. 158** NHPA / Sunset **p. 159** Simon Meaker / PA / Abaca Press **p. 160** Collection Christophe L. **p. 162** *Le monde de Sempé* (volume 1) © 2002, by Sempé et Editions Denoël **p. 163** Courtesy The New Yorker © 2008 Sempé **p. 164** Saswat Pattanyak **p. 167** www.CartoonStock.com **p. 168** "Six Chix" used with the permission of Ann Telnaes and the Cartoonist Group. All rights reserved. **p. 169** www.CartoonStock.com **p. 171** © Serve Marketing **p. 172** © Barbara Kruger / Mary Boone Gallery, New York. Courtesy Thomas Ammann Fine Art AG, Zurich **p. 173** Collection Christophe L. **p. 174** © Columbus Dispatch / Dist. by United Feature Syndicate, Inc. **p. 175** Amy Sancetta / AP Photo / Sipa Press **p. 176** Collection Christophe L. **p. 177** © 2007 Anchor / Random House, Inc. **p. 178** Adbusters Media Foundation **p. 179** Chris Jordan **p. 180** © Polyp cartoons www.polyp.org.uk **p. 181** Steve Kelley Editorial Cartoon used with the permission of Steve Kelley and Creators Syndicate. All rights reserved / The Cartoonist Group **p. 182** Ron Fehling / Masterfile **p. 183hg** Westend61 / Masterfile **p. 183hd** Andrew Kolb Masterfile **p. 183mhg** Masterfile **p. 183mhd** Apolonia / Masterfile **p. 183mb** Walt Mancini / Pasadena Star-News / SGVN **p. 183b** Brooke Fasani Auchincloss / Corbis **p. 184** Colin Beavan, No impact Man, 2009 © Farrar Straus and Giroux D.R. **p. 185** Image Courtesy of Pest Control Office **p. 186** © McPHOTO / age fotostock **p. 188-189** FIA / Rue des Archives **p. 190** Walker Art Gallery, National Museums Liverpool / Bridgeman-Giraudon **p. 191** www.CartoonStock.com **p. 192** © Ealing Studios / The Kobal Collection / The Picture Desk **p. 193** © Stanislas Plutenko, *Portrait of Dorian Gray,* 1996. 125 x 100cm **p. 194** akg-images **p. 195** © Roger Blachon in *Les 7 Pêchés Capitaux* - Ed Les Humoristes Associés, 1983 **p. 197** © Ealing Studios / Collection Christophe L. **p. 198** © National Archives photo no. 44-PA-135 **p. 199g** David Pollack / Corbis **p. 199d** Stacy Pearsall / www.F8PJ.com **p. 200** Peter Stackpole / Time & Life Pictures / Getty Images

p. 201 *That 2,000-Yard Stare*, Tom Lea, 1944, U.S. Army Center for Military History, Washington, D.C. - Photo courtesy of Tom Lea Institute, El Paso, Texas **p. 202** Peter Macdiarmid / Getty Images **p. 203** Don Wright / AFP Photo **p. 204g** *The History of War*, 1980, acrylic on Canvassette © Graph Tec - www.graph-tec.net **p. 204d** Eamonn McCormack / Getty Images **p. 207** © Harold Shull - www.haroldshull.com **p. 209h, m et b** Collection Christophe L. **p. 210** Collection privée / © D.R. **p. 211** © Shepard Fairey / ObeyGiant.com **p. 212** D.R. **p. 213b** Tips / Photononstop **p. 214** Penny Tweedie / PANOS-REA **p. 215h et b** Cartoon by Nicholson from The Australian www.nicholsoncartoons.com.au **p. 216** Horniman Museum, London, UK / Photo Heini Schneebeli / Bridgeman-Giraudon **p. 217b** Liwirringki Jukurrpa (Burrowing Skink) by Paddy J. Nelson (b.c.1919) & Ross, Jack J. (b.c.1925) - acrylic on canvas - Private Collection / Dreamtime Gallery, London / Bridgeman-Giraudon **p. 218** © 2002 Miramax Film Corp / Hyperion **p. 219** Rob Griffith / AP Photo / Sipa Press **p. 221** Catherine de Bernis **p. 223** Look / Photononstop **p. 224** Dreamtime Kullilla-Art http://www.dreamtime.auz.net **p. 228** Collection Christophe L. **p. 229h** Prod DB © Miramax / D.R. **p. 229b** Collection Christophe L **p. 230** Mary Evans / Rue des Archives **p. 231** Heritage images / Leemage **p. 232** National Gallery, London, UK / Bridgeman-Giraudon **p. 233** National Gallery, London, UK / Bridgeman-Giraudon **p. 234** Sheldon Museum of Art, Lincoln, Nebraska / Superstock / The Art Archive / The Picture Desk © D.R. **p. 235** Simon Kirwan / www.the-lightbox.com © Adagp, Paris 2011 **p. 236** Indianapolis Museum of Art, USA / Gift of Mr and Mrs William H. Ball / Bridgeman-Giraudon **p. 243** Brian Buckley Photo Inc. **p. 244** Collection Christophe L. **p. 245 hg et bg** Wall-E, Andrew Stanton, 2008 / Collection Christophe L. **p. 245mh et hd** Berverly Hills, 2009 / Collection Christophe L. **p. 245mb et bd** Spiderman 1, Sam Raimi, 2002 / Collection Christophe L.

Crédits textes

p. 20-21 Excerpted from FAST FOOD NATION by Eric Schlosser. © 2001 by Eric Schlosser. Reprinted by permission of Houghton Mifflin Harcourt Publishing Company. All rights reserved. **p. 22** © 1999 Anita Desai. Reproduced by permission of the author c/o Rogers, Coleridge & White Ltd., 20 Powis Mews, London W11 1JN. **p. 22** Colin Beavan, No impact Man, 2009 © Farrar Straus and Giroux D.R. **p. 28-29** Rick Beyer, True Tales of American Life, edited by Paul Auster (Faber & Faber 2001) **p. 32-33** Will Pavia, in The times, January 14, 2008 **p. 34** Laurie Hassle Anderson, Speak, 1999 © Farrar Straus and Giroux D.R. **p. 45** BBC News, January 22, 2007 © bbc.co.uk/news. **p. 46** Karishma Vaswani, Business correspondent, BBC News,Mumbai, August 14, 2007 © bbc.co.uk/news. **p. 47** from Q & A by Vikas Swarup, published by Black Swan. Reprinted by permission of The Random House Group Ltd. **p. 49** from The painter of Signs by RK Narayan, published by William Heinemann. Reprinted by permission of The Random House Group Ltd. **p. 50** "India Is Missing 10 Million Daughters", 9 January 2006 issue © New Scientist Magazine **p. 51** Sanchita Sharma, Hindustan Times, Kolkata, April 12, 2009 © Hindustan Times **p. 61** Rebecca, Daphne du Maurier, 1938 © Virago Press, janvier 2003. **p. 64** New Moon, Stephanie Meyer, Little, Brown and Company, 2006 D.R. **p. 70-71** Revelations in Black, Carl Jacobi edited by Alan Ryan. Arkham House D.R. **p. 73** Jeff Jacoby, The Boston Globe, October 2007 **p. 76** from Notes from a Big Country by Bill Bryson, published by Doubleday. Reprinted by permission of The Random House Group Ltd. **p. 80** Beverley Naidoo, The Other Side of Thruth, 2000 © Penguin UK D.R. **p. 85** By Jeremy Laurance, Health Editor Wednesday, 22 September 2010 **p. 85** Edwin Moses, Newsweek, March 2, 2009 **p. 86-87** Beverley Naidoo, The Other Side of Truth, 2000 © Penguin UK D.R. **p. 89** "Merry-Go-Round" from The Collected Poems of Langston Hugues by Langston Hughes, edited by Arnold Rampersad with David Roessel, Associate Editor, © 1994 by the Estate of Langston Hugues. Used by permission of Alfred A. Knopf, a division of Random House, inc. **p. 90** Sit-ins, cutting edge in a war on bias, Greensboro, N.C., 1960, Chronicles of America. D.R. **p. 92-93** From THE FREEDOM WRITERS DIARY by The Freedom Writers with Erin Gruwell, © 1999 by The Tolerance Education Foundation. Used by permission of Doubleday, a division of Random House, Inc.**p. 94-95** "will.i.am and other artists, Yes we can, 2008 Copyright 2010 Dipdive Inc." **p. 100-101** Fearless Jones by Walter Mosley, A phoenix paperback, 2004 **p. 102-103** Holes, Louis Sachar Copyright © Louis Sachar 1998 © Farrar Straus and Giroux D.R. **p. 110** from In The Heart of The Canyon, by Elisabeth Hyde, © 2009 by Elisabeth Hyde. Used by permission of alfred A. Knopf, a division of Random House, Inc. **p. 112** E.M. Forster, A Passage to India D.R. **p. 114** New York Times, Eric Weiner, March 9, 2008 **p. 119** Nineteen Eighty Four by George Orwell (© George Orwell, 1949) by permission of Bill Hamilton as the Literary Executor of the Estate of the Late Sonia Brownell Orwell and Secker & Warburg Ltd. **p. 121** British Home Office, February 2009 **p. 122** Jessica Shepherd, 4 August 2009 © Guardian News & Media Ltd 2009 **p. 124** The Sunday Times, March 9, 2008. Jonathan Leake, Science Editor **p. 125** Adapted from The Independent, Sunday, 10 February 2008 **p. 133** Seattle's International District. The Making of a Pan-Asian American Community, Doug Chin. D.R. **p. 134** From Shanghai Girls, A NOVEL by Lisa Lee, © 2009 by Lisa See. Used by permission of Random House, Inc. **p. 136** Excerpt from Snow Falling on Cedars, © 1994 by David Guterson, reproduced by permission of Houghton Mifflin Harcourt Publishing Company. This material may not be reproduced in any form or by any means without the prior written permission of the publisher. **p. 150** Scène extraite du film Monty Python and The Holy Grail, 1975 **p. 152-153** Une autre scène extraite du film Monty Python and The Holy Grail, 1975 **p. 159** Sting, Broken music, © Steerpike (Overseas) limited 2003. All rights reserved **p. 160** Lauren Weisberger, The Devil Wears Prada, 2003 © Harper Collins UK **p. 163** D.H. Lawrence, The Complete Poems **p. 164** Ed Pilkington, The Guardian, 05 June 2010 © Guardian News & Media Ltd 2010 **p. 170-171** Jean Sheldon **p. 173** from Confessions of a Shopaholic by Sophie Kinsella, published by Black Swan. Reprinted by permission of The Random House Group Ltd. **p. 175** Wal-Mart worker killed in Black Friday shopping stampede © Guardian News & Media Ltd 2008 **p. 176** INTO THE WILD ®& Copyright © 2009 by Paramount Pictures. All rights Reserved **p. 178** Sam Jones, 24 November 2007 © Guardian News & Media Ltd 2007 **p. 179** www.webecoist.com **p. 191** Alice Haine, www.mirror.co.uk, June 15, 2010 **p. 200** Ken Follet, Night over Water, 1991 D.R. **p. 201** From JOHNNY GOT HIS GUN. Copyright © by Dalton Trumbo, 1939, 1959, 1991. All rights reserved. Published by arrangement with Citadel Press an imprint of Kensington Publishing Corp. **p. 203** The Washington Post, Sunday, May 14, 2006 **p. 204** James Blunt, No Bravery, 2006 **p. 206** ©2009 Cappy Hall Rearick. **p. 213** from Down Under by Bill Bryson, published by Doubleday. Reprinted by permission of The Random House Group Ltd. **p. 214** Adapted from website. Australia today Mag D.R. **p. 214-215** Earth Times, July 8 2009 D.R. **p. 216** The National Geographic, February 2008, vol. 173, n°2, p. 276, The First Australians, écrit par Stanley Breeden / National Geographic Stock **p. 217** www.aboriginalart.com D.R. **p. 218-219** Rabbit-Proof Fence, Doris Pilkington, 1996 **p. 224** nouvelle de Michael J. Connolly, publié sur le site dreamtime.auz.net **p. 225** Excerpted from "Up Taree Way" by Libby Hathorn from DREAM TIME edited by Toss Gascoigne, Jo Goodan and Margot Tyrrell. © 1989 by Libby Hathorn. Collection © 1989 by the Children's Book Council of Australia. Reprinted by permission of Houghton Mifflin Harcourt Publishing Company. All rights reserved. **p. 229** The Cure, Lovesong, dans l'album: Disintegration, 1993 **p. 230** W.H. Auden, Collected Poems © 1976, 1991, The Estate of W.H. Auden **p. 224** "Cake" by Roger McGough from After the Merrymaking (© Roger McGough 1971) is printed by permission of United Agents (www.unitedagents.co.uk) on behalf of Roger McGough. **p. 234** Unfortunate coincidence, Dorothy Parker, 1926 **p. 235** Lies about love, D.H. Lawrence

Achevé d'imprimer par Rotolito à Seggiano di Pioltello - Italie
Depôt légal : 95333-0/02 - Août 2011